THE AGE OF MADNESS

Dr. Thomas S. Szasz is Professor of Psychiatry at the State University of New York Upstate Medical Center in Syracuse, New York. He is a member of the editorial board of *The Humanist, Journal of Humanistic Psychology, Journal of Drug Addiction,* and *Contemporary Psychoanalysis,* and of the board of consultants of *The Psychoanalytic Review;* a member of the American Psychoanalytic Association; a fellow of the American Psychiatric Association and the Royal Society of Health (London); a consultant to the Committee on Mental Hygiene of the New York State Bar Association; and a co-founder and Chairman of the Board of Directors of the American Association for the Abolition of Involuntary Mental Hospitalization. He is the author of more than two hundred articles and book reviews, and of eight books, including *The Myth of Mental Illness, Ideology and Insanity, The Manufacture of Madness,* and *The Second Sin.*

THE AGE OF MADNESS

The History of Involuntary Mental Hospitalization
Presented in Selected Texts

Edited with Preface, Introduction, and Epilogue by
THOMAS S. SZASZ, M.D.

Anchor Books
Anchor Press/Doubleday   Garden City, New York

The Anchor Press edition is the first publication of *The Age of Madness*. Anchor Press Edition: 1973

"Ward No. 6" by Anton Pavlovich Chekhov from *The Portable Russian Reader* edited and translated by Bernard Guilbert Guerney. Copyright 1947 by The Viking Press, Inc. Reprinted by permission of The Viking Press, Inc.

"Ward 7" by Valeriy Tarsis from the book *Ward 7* by Valeriy Tarsis. Translated by Katya Brown. Copyright © 1965 by Collins and Harvill Press, and E. P. Dutton & Co., Inc., publishers, and used with their permission.

"Faces in the Water" by Janet Frame. George Braziller, Inc., from *Faces in the Water* by Janet Frame; reprinted with the permission of the publisher. Copyright © 1961 by Janet Frame.

"The Unicorn in the Garden" by James Thurber. Copyright © 1940 by James Thurber. Copyright © 1968 by Helen Thurber. From *Fables for Our Time*, published by Harper & Row, New York. Originally printed in *The New Yorker*.

"The Insanity Bit" by Seymour Krim. From the book *Views of a Nearsighted Cannoneer* by Seymour Krim. Copyright © 1948, 1951, 1952, 1953, 1956, 1957, 1958, 1959, 1960, 1961, 1968 by Seymour Krim. Published by E. P. Dutton & Co., Inc., and used with their permission.

"City Psychiatric" by Frank Leonard. From *City Psychiatric* by Frank Leonard. Copyright © 1965 by Frank Leonard. Reprinted by permission of Ballantine Books, Inc. All rights reserved.

"Sanity Through Suffocation." Reprinted from *Medical World News*. Copyright © 1970, McGraw-Hill, Inc.

Selection from *The Plague* by Albert Camus. Copyright 1947. Reprinted with the permission of Alfred A. Knopf, Inc.

"The Moral Career of the Mental Patient" by Erving Goffman, *Psychiatry*, 1959, 22:123–142, is reprinted by special permission of the William Alanson White Psychiatric Foundation, Inc. Copyright © 1959 by the William Alanson White Psychiatric Foundation, Inc.

Library of Congress Catalog Card Number 72–89952
ISBN: 0-385-04638-3
Copyright © 1973 by Thomas S. Szasz
All Rights Reserved
Printed in the United States of America

TO
MARGARET BASSETT

ACKNOWLEDGMENTS

Once again I wish to thank my brother, George Szasz; my editor at Doubleday, Bill Whitehead; and my secretary, Margaret Bassett, for their devoted and invaluable help.

AUTHOR'S NOTE

This book is composed of selections from sources identified in the footnotes accompanying the text. Each selection is introduced by a brief explanatory note. While the titles of most of the selections are the same as the titles of the original sources from which they have been extracted, several selections appear under titles of my own choosing. In each case, however, the original title and source are supplied.

PREFACE

The incarceration in special institutions of persons said to be mentally ill—or madmen, as they used to be called—is a relatively recent phenomenon in the history of Western civilization. Originating in France in the seventeenth century, the practice soon spread across Europe and was later introduced into North and South America and Australia. For the last hundred years, hospital psychiatry, recognized as an integral part of medical practice, has played an increasingly important role in the social structure of Western nations.

Today, especially in the United States, the hospital—including the "mental hospital"—stands as the very symbol of the modern, enlightened community and state. So much is this the case that to question the desirability of mental hospitals seems as absurd to most people as to question the desirability of good health.

However, things are not always as they seem. As in Orwell's *Animal Farm*, where "all animals are equal, but some animals are more equal than others,"[1] so in the modern Western world, all hospitals are medical, but some hospitals are more medical than others. Some—mental hospitals, for example—are medical in name only; actually, they are prisons disguised as hospitals. If this is so—and the reader must decide this for himself or herself—is it not rea-

[1] George Orwell, *Animal Farm* (New York: Harcourt, Brace & Co., 1946), p. 123.

sonable to doubt the desirability of increasing our prisons and prison-populations, and of measuring our "enlightenment" and "humanism" by the number of our psychiatric institutions and inmates?

Mental hospitalization is not the first, nor probably the last, social intervention which is ostensibly helpful but actually harmful to its supposed beneficiaries. A century ago, impoverished pregnant women, crowded into the obstetrical wards of the public hospitals of Budapest and Vienna, died in great numbers because of streptococcal infection; at the same time, childbed fever was a rarity among the well-to-do women who delivered their babies at home. The great Hungarian physician, Ignaz Philipp Semmelweis, had the temerity to suggest that the hospital conditions and the doctors were responsible for the epidemics of puerperal fever. This idea was less than warmly received in contemporary obstetrical circles. Finally Semmelweis himself became a victim of institutional psychiatry: he was incarcerated and died in a private madhouse.[2]

In my judgment, the relationship between the institutional (or hospital) psychiatrist and his involuntary patient is more like the relationship between master and slave than between physician and adult medical patient. Like slavery, institutional psychiatry[3] is a complex social-economic phe-

---

[2] See William J. Sinclair, *Semmelweis, His Life and His Doctrine: A Chapter in the History of Medicine* (Manchester, England: University Press, 1909).

[3] Institutional psychiatry comprises all psychiatric interventions imposed on persons by others. These interventions are characterized by the complete loss of control by the client over his relationship with the expert. The most important economic characteristic of institutional psychiatry is that the institutional psychiatrist is a bureaucratic employee, paid for his services by a private or public organization (not by the individual who is his ostensible client). Its most important social characteristic is the use of force and fraud. The actual client of institutional psychiatry is some social interest or organization, for example, a state mental hygiene department. As against this, contractual psychiatry comprises all psychiatric interventions secured for themselves by persons prompted by their own personal difficulties or suffering. These interventions are characterized by the retention of complete con-

nomenon of long standing and great practical importance. For millennia, slavery flourished. While it did, the greatest minds sincerely believed that slavery was a boon not only for the master but also for the slave. Only recently did the people of the Western world feel ready to abolish this institution and replace it with labor relations based on contract. In comparison, hospital psychiatry is a young institution; indeed, it seems probable that it is still in the ascendancy, and that it will grow and flourish before mankind will feel morally moved and socially prepared to replace it, too, with patterns of social welfare based on mutual consent. I hope that this work will hasten that day.

To this end, I have assembled in this volume the evidence which the layman needs—and which perhaps even those in the mental health professions will find useful—to form a sound opinion about the nature of involuntary mental hospitalization and treatment. This evidence is presented not in my own words, but rather in a wide variety of documents written by a great many men and women—physicians, journalists, attendants, and patients; famous and unknown; Americans, Russians, Frenchmen, and others; living and dead. I invite the reader to look through these pages and see for himself the image of involuntary mental hospitalization and treatment that emerges.

---

trol by the client over his relationship with the expert. The most important economic characteristic of contractual psychiatry is that the contractual psychiatrist is a private entrepreneur, paid for his services by his client. Its most important social characteristic is the avoidance of force and fraud (with legal penalties for their use), and reliance instead on a clear contractual agreement between client and expert.

For detailed discussion and exposition of these two types of psychiatry, see especially Thomas S. Szasz, *The Manufacture of Madness: A Comparative Study of the Inquisition and the Mental Health Movement* (New York: Harper & Row, 1970); and *The Ethics of Psychoanalysis: The Theory and Method of Autonomous Psychotherapy* (New York: Basic Books, 1965).

CONTENTS

PREFACE   xi

INTRODUCTION   1

PART ONE: THE BIRTH OF PSYCHIATRIC POWER
 (1650–1865)   5

 1. Observations on Psychiatric Confinement, by
    Daniel Defoe, Sir John Fortesque-Aland, and
    John Conolly   7

 2. The Pennsylvania Hospital: Its Founding and
    Functions, by Thomas G. Morton   12

 3. The Utility of Public Asylums for Lunatics, by
    Philippe Pinel   18

 4. Deception and Terror as Cures for Madness, by
    Benjamin Rush   23

 5. A Lunatic's Protest, by John Perceval   29

 6. Madness and Blackness, from *The American
    Journal of Insanity* (1840)   43

 7. Democracy as Mental Disease, from *The American Journal of Insanity* (1851)   47

 8. "In Case You Refuse . . ." from the Records
    of the Dorothea Dix Hospital, Raleigh, N.C.   48

PART TWO: THE GROWTH OF PSYCHIATRIC POWER (1865–1920) — 51

1. Madness and Marriage, by E. P. W. Packard — 53
2. Expert Testimony in Judicial Proceedings, by John Ordronaux — 77
3. The Psychiatric Assassination of King Ludwig II of Bavaria, by Werner Richter — 82
4. The "Boodle Gang," by S. V. Clevenger — 84
5. Ward No. 6, by Anton Pavlovich Chekhov — 89
6. Madness and Morality, by Karl Kraus — 127
7. The Commitment of Bishop Morehouse, by Jack London — 142

PART THREE: THE FLOWERING OF PSYCHIATRIC POWER (1920–) — 151

1. From the Slaughterhouse to the Madhouse, by Ugo Cerletti — 153
2. The Discovery of Lobotomy, by Egas Moniz — 157
3. The Sick and the Mad, by Frigyes Karinthy — 161
4. Ward 7, by Valeriy Tarsis — 171
5. "Patient Labour" in the British Mental Hospital System, by J. A. R. Bickford — 193
6. Illegitimacy and Insanity, from *The Guardian* — 198
7. Faces in the Water, by Janet Frame — 203
8. Psychiatric Justice in Canada, by Harvey Currell, Peter Bruton, and Sidney Katz (from the Toronto *Daily Star* and the Toronto *Telegram*) — 217
9. Position Statement on the Medical Treatment of the Mentally Ill, by the American Psychi-

CONTENTS xvii

atric Association and the National Association for Mental Health   231

10. Out of Sight, Out of Mind, by Frank L. Wright, Jr.   242

11. The Moral Career of the Mental Patient, by Erving Goffman   251

12. Adjustment to the Total Institution, by Byron G. Wales   267

13. The Unicorn in the Garden, by James Thurber   278

14. The Insanity Bit, by Seymour Krim   280

15. Johnny Panic and the Bible of Dreams, by Sylvia Plath   300

16. City Psychiatric, by Frank Leonard   318

17. The Machine in Ward Eleven, by Charles Willeford   333

18. Sanity Through Suffocation, from *Medical World News*   356

EPILOGUE   360

INDEX   363

THE AGE OF MADNESS

INTRODUCTION

Every age and civilization has its characteristic ideology and institutions which both shape and reflect the essential meanings with which men endow their lives.

The millennium from the fall of Rome in the fifth century to the fall of Constantinople to the Turks in the fifteenth is often called the Age of Faith, because it was characterized by the progressive Christianization of Europe. The religiosity of this period reached its zenith during the Middle Ages. The authority and power of the rulers were then legitimized and sustained by the Christian world view. The universe and everything in it were God's property: in particular, the world was regarded as His pasture, man as His flock, and the ecclesiastic and secular rulers as His shepherds. The aim of the Church was to insure adherence to the Divine Law, keeping God in a "happy" and thus "loving" frame of mind toward his fallen creation, man. Hence, in the theological societies of the Age of Faith, the Church was the dominant institution; the pope was God's representative on earth; kings ruled by divine right; cathedrals and religious icons and festivities were the leading social symbols; Latin was the official language; and sin, redemption, and salvation, Hell and Heaven, were the images and rhetoric that filled the popular imagination. To be truly human meant to worship God (Jesus), to be virtuous meant to be an undeviatingly faithful Christian (saint), and to be evil meant to be a heretic (witch).

Although the Age of Faith is usually considered to end in the fifteenth century, giving way to the Renaissance and the Reformation, it could as well be regarded as ending about one hundred years later, with a slow transformation of the theological into the scientific world view. Historians thus often call the seventeenth and eighteenth centuries the Age of Reason, the nineteenth century the Age of Ideology, and the twentieth, the Age of Anxiety. I depart from this usage here, and apply the name "Age of Reason" comprehensively to the entire period from 1648 (the end of the Thirty Years' War) to the present. My justification for this usage—and for my proposal to rename this period the Age of Madness—lies in the fact that, whereas prior to the seventeenth century, the dominant ideology of the West had been Christian, since then it has been scientific.

Whether the Age of Reason has reached its zenith in our day, or is still waxing in power, its crest—and with it, perhaps, the end of mankind—yet to come, is not given for us to know. The defining characteristics of this age are, however, clearly discernible. The authority and power of the rulers are now legitimized and sustained by a democratic-secular world view. The State, considered the property of the majority of its citizens (or of Mass Man), is governed on their behalf by a political and managerial elite, and seeks to secure the greatest happiness of the greatest numbers. Hence, in the therapeutic societies of the Age of Reason, Science (Technology) is the dominant institution; the scientist-intellectual is the interpreter of the Laws of Nature; schools, hospitals, and technological artifacts are the leading social symbols; scientistic jargon is the official language; and sickness and health, treatment and cure, Death and Life, are the images and rhetoric that fill the popular imagination. To be truly human now means to worship Science (Technology, Progress), to be virtuous means to be healthy (happy), and to be evil means to be mentally sick (unhappy).

Although there have been important changes in social organizations and technological development during the Age of Reason, my emphasis in this volume is on a single idea and institution common to, and increasingly important in, all of the societies since the dawn of this age: namely, the idea of madness and the institution of the madhouse.

In an earlier work, *The Manufacture of Madness*,[1] I offered a detailed historical reconstruction of the creation and progressive articulation of the concept of madness or mental illness as a viable replacement for the now defunct concept of heresy, and showed that as science displaced theology, the Christian concept of man as a spiritual being was superseded by the positivistic concept of man as a biological machine. The criteria of good and evil, of socially harmonious and deviant belief and behavior, underwent corresponding changes. What had been true faith in God and acquiescence in His will, became true faith in Nature and the acceptance of her Laws; what had been the heretical repudiation of God and the power of faith that alone could insure man's salvation, became the insane rejection of Nature and the power of reason that alone can make man the supreme being. Thus was the Age of Faith transformed into the Age of Reason. The crucial similarity between these two historical epochs lies in the following: That whereas in the Age of Faith, to lose one's faith, or to repudiate its object, God, meant the loss of one's humanity and resulted in the expulsion from the social order of the offending individual as a heretic—so, in the Age of Reason, to lose one's reason, or to repudiate its object, Reality, means the loss of one's humanity, and results in the expulsion from the social order of the offending individual as a madman. Who, then, could scoff at, much less oppose, God in a Theological Society? Only a heretic! And who can scoff at, much less oppose (mental) health in a Therapeutic Society? Only a madman! No punishment could be unjust, no "therapy" can be unjustified, in society's efforts to combat these threats to its core values.

In the present work, which is intended both as an independent contribution and as a companion to *The*

[1] Thomas S. Szasz, *The Manufacture of Madness: A Comparative Study of the Inquisition and the Mental Health Movement* (New York: Harper & Row, 1970).

Manufacture of Madness, I offer an anthology of illustrative historical accounts—some old, the majority modern or contemporary—of the method of social control characteristic of the Age of Reason: namely, involuntary mental hospitalization.

My justification for organizing the selections in this volume around the theme of involuntary mental hospitalization is that I consider this quasi-medical imprisonment of the citizen as madman the most significant social-symbolic manifestation of the therapeutic societies characteristic of the Age of Reason. In short, I hold that as in the Age of Faith political power was the monopoly of Church and State, so in the Age of Reason, it is the monopoly of Science and State. The former celebrated its values by constructing cathedrals and religious shrines and by forcibly converting nonbelievers, while the latter does so by constructing hospitals and insane asylums and by forcibly treating madmen. In the Age of Faith, men confirmed the existence and glory of God by creating witches who worshiped the Devil, and confirmed the power of God by multiplying the number and magnifying the dangerousness of witches; in the Age of Reason, men confirm the existence and glory of Reason by creating madmen who worship Unreason, and confirm the power of Reason by multiplying the number and magnifying the dangerousness of madmen.

Hence, it should not surprise us that men regarded themselves as most faithful when they were surrounded by heretics; and that they regard themselves as most reasonable when surrounded by madmen. Ineluctably, this perspective generates the conditions that support and validate it: in the past, to feel themselves devout and faithful, men created and persecuted witches; now, to feel themselves reasonable and sane, they create and persecute madmen.

This, then, is why the Age of Faith was teeming with heretics; why the Age of Reason is teeming with madmen; and why I propose to rename the Age of Reason, in honor of its victims, the Age of Madness.

PART ONE

THE BIRTH OF PSYCHIATRIC POWER (1650—1865)

1

OBSERVATIONS ON PSYCHIATRIC CONFINEMENT, 1728–1830

Daniel Defoe, Sir John Fortesque-Aland, and John Conolly

Three Hundred Years of Psychiatry, 1535–1860, by Richard Hunter and Ida MacAlpine (London: Oxford University Press, 1963), is unquestionably the finest single source of original materials on the early history of psychiatry—that is, on the early history of involuntary mental hospitalization. From their voluminous collection I have selected three especially revealing excerpts each of which is further identified below.

I

One of the earliest English critics of "mad-houses" and "mad-doctors" was Daniel Defoe (1661–1731), the journalist and novelist. The following excerpt, from *Augusta Triumphans* (1728), is concerned with "the public control of madhouses."* It started a demand for reforms which led, in 1774, to the enactment by Parliament of the first "Act for Regulating Madhouses."

This leads me to exclaim against the vile Practice now so much in vogue among the better Sort, as they are called, but the worst sort in fact, namely, the sending their Wives to Mad-Houses at every Whim or Dislike, that they may

---

* Daniel Defoe, "Demand for Public Control of Madhouses (1728)," in Richard Hunter and Ida MacAlpine, op. cit., pp. 266–67.

be more secure and undisturb'd in their Debaucheries: Which wicked Custom is got to such a Head, that the number of private Mad-Houses in and about London, are considerably increased within these few Years. This is the height of Barbarity and Injustice in a Christian Country, it is a clandestine Inquisition, nay worse. How many Ladies and Gentlewomen are hurried away to these Houses, which ought to be suppress'd, or at least subject to daily Examination, as hereafter shall be proposed? How many, I say, of Beauty, Vertue, and Fortune, are suddenly torn from their dear innocent Babes, from the Arms of an unworthy Man, who they love (perhaps too well) and who in Return for that Love, nay probably an ample Fortune, and a lovely Off-spring besides; grows weary of the pure Streams of chaste Love, and thirsting for the Puddles of lawless Lust, buries his vertuous Wife alive, that he may have the greater Freedom with his Mistresses?

If they are not mad when they go into these cursed Houses, they are soon made so by the barbarous Usage they there suffer, and any Woman of spirit who has the least Love for her Husband, or Concern for her family, cannot sit down tamely under a Confinement and Separation the most unaccountable and unreasonable. Is it not enough to make any one mad to be suddenly clap'd up, stripp'd, whipp'd, ill fed, and worse us'd? To have no Reason assign'd for such Treatment, no Crime alledg'd, or accusers to confront? And what is worse, no Soul to appeal to but merciless Creatures, who answer but in Laughter, Surliness, Contradiction, and too often Stripes? All conveniences for Writing are denied, no Messenger to be had to carry a Letter to any Relation or Friend; and if this tyrannical Inquisition, join'd with the reasonable Reflections, a woman of any common Understanding must necessarily make, be not sufficient to drive any Soul stark staring mad, though before they were never so much in their right Senses, I have no more to say . . .

How many are yet to be sacrificed, unless a speedy Stop be put to this most accursed Practice I tremble to think; our Legislature cannot take this Cause too soon in hand:

This surely cannot be below their Notice, and twill be an easy matter at once to suppress all these pretended Mad-Houses. Indulge, gentle Reader, for once the doing of an old Man, and give him leave to lay down his little System without arraigning him of Arrogance or Ambition to be a Law-giver. In my humble Opinion all private Mad-Houses should be suppress'd at once, and it should be no less than Felony to confine any Person under pretence of Madness without due Authority. For the cure of those who are really Lunatick, licens'd Mad-Houses should be constituted in convenient Parts of the Town, which Houses should be subject to proper Visitation and Inspection, nor should any Person be sent to a Mad-House without due Reason, Inquiry and Authority.

II

The case of "The Queen versus Fellows, Dr. of Physik," tried in 1714, is—according to Hunter and MacAlpine—"possibly the earliest recorded conviction of a mad-doctor for illegally detaining and maltreating a sane person 'as a madman'"† It would be difficult, if not impossible, to find a similar decision in contemporary court records.

I Moved for Judgment against the Defendant to have corporal Punishment, because he was worth nothing. It was a Conviction on an information in K[ing's] B[ench] for assaulting and beating one Alderman, pretending he was Lunatick, and for imprisoning him as a Madman, *quousque* he procured him to sign and execute a Letter of Attorney directed to his Wife, by colour of which he had received and disposed of to the Value of 1000*l*. but it did not set out that it was disposed of to his own Use . . . the Defendant had Judgment given against him, it appearing by

† Sir John Fortesque-Aland (1670–1746), Justice of the Common Pleas, Solicitor General, *Report of Select Cases in all the Courts of Westminster-Hall*, 1748 (London, Lintot, pp. 166–67); in Richard Hunter and Ida MacAlpine, op. cit., p. 297.

the Evidence, that by this Cheat and Violence he had procured to himself about 1000*l.* that he had debauched his Wife, that pretending to cure him of Lunacy, he beat him, hand-cuffed him, gave him several strong Purges in the Night, and carried him at one or two o'Clock in the Morning bare-headed when it rained.

The Judgment was, To stand in the Pillory, to be sent to the House of Correction in Southwark, and to be whipped naked, and to be kept at Work there for the Space of a Year, to be fined 600*l.* and to find Sureties for his Behaviour during Life.

III

John Conolly (1794–1866) was a distinguished professor of medicine in the University of London and, from 1839 until his death, physician superintendent of the Middlesex County Lunatic Asylum at Harwell. In the passage here quoted‡ he warns of the ease with which a person may be confined as insane, and of the difficulty which a man so confined would experience in attempting to regain his freedom. Again, it would be difficult to find a comparable passage in the writings of contemporary mental hospital superintendents.

Let no one imagine that even now it is impossible or difficult to effect the seclusion of an eccentric man; or easy for him, when once confined, to regain his liberty. The timidity, or ignorance, or, it may be, a dishonest motive of relatives, leads to exaggerated representations; and the great profit accruing from a part of practice, almost separated from general medicine, cannot but now and then operate against proper caution in admitting such representations. When men's interests depend upon an opinion, it is too much to expect that opinion always to be cautiously formed, or even in all cases honestly given . . .

‡ John Conolly, *An Inquiry Concerning the Indications of Insanity, with Suggestions for the Better Protection and Care of the Insane* (London: John Taylor, 1830), in Richard Hunter and Ida MacAlpine, op. cit., p. 807.

Once confined, the very confinement is admitted as the strongest of all proofs that a man must be mad. When, after suffering so much wrong, he has an opportunity of speaking to the appointed visitors of the house,—supposing him to be confined where he can be visited, and supposing him not to give way to his feelings, but to control them,—his entreaties, his anxious representations, his prayers for liberty, what do they avail!

The keeper of the asylum is accustomed to all these things; he knows that the truly and dangerously insane can act in the same way; and from ignorance, in the absence of any bad intention, does away with all the effect of the patient's words. The visitors, knowing nothing of the shades of disordered mind, or not reflecting upon them, are told that they see 'the best of him'; that it is one of his 'good days'; that he is often 'dreadfully violent'; and they shrink from the responsibility of deciding where they know it is very possible they may be wrong. Besides this, there is the ready and indisputable Certificate, signed by a medical man,—physician, surgeon, or apothecary, stating that the man is mad and must be confined in a lunatic asylum. It matters not that the certificate is probably signed by those who know little about madness or the necessity of confinement; or by those who have not carefully examined the patient: a visitor fears to avow, in the face of such a document, what may be set down as mere want of penetration in a matter wherein nobody seems in doubt but himself; or he may even be tempted to affect to perceive those signs of madness which do not exist.

2

THE PENNSYLVANIA HOSPITAL: ITS FOUNDING AND FUNCTIONS*

Thomas G. Morton

The Pennsylvania Hospital was the first general hospital in Colonial America. As the following excerpt shows, this hospital was actually founded, in part, to protect the populace, under the guise of providing medical care, from certain classes of persons who annoyed or threatened them. Some of the persons destined for such "hospitalization," but, as the second excerpt shows by no means all of them, were considered and labeled as "distempered in mind" or "lunaticks." It is also of interest that, contrary to current view, "hospitalizing" people for mental illness in general hospitals is not something new, but, on the contrary, was the practice not only in the Pennsylvania Hospital, but also in the New York Hospital, the second hospital to be opened in the Colonies.

The history of the Pennsylvania Hospital abounds in interesting and revealing facts, such as that the first two mental patients to be admitted to it were women; that the physicians exercised despotic powers over at least some of the "patients"—in particular, over blacks, women, debtors, and mental patients; and that, from the beginning, the institution functioned as an extra-

* From *The History of the Pennsylvania Hospital, 1751–1895*, Revised Edition (Philadelphia: Times Printing House, 1897), pp. 3–4, 127, 134–35.

THE PENNSYLVANIA HOSPITAL

legal prison, not only for "mental patients" but, as the Döer Petition shows, for persons who were confined without any pretense of illness or treatment.

THE PENNSYLVANIA HOSPITAL

From a petition presented, the 23d of January, 1751, to the Assembly of the Province of Pennsylvania, by "sundry Inhabitants," it appears that, prior to the founding of the Pennsylvania Hospital, no permanent, public provision had been made in this Province for the care of persons "distemper'd in Mind and depriv'd of their rational Faculties," or for the relief of sick and injured inhabitants. The petitioners speak of the insane as:

> Some of them going at large, a Terror to their Neighbours, who are daily apprehensive of the Violences they may commit: And others are continually wasting their Substance, to the great Injury of themselves and Families, ill-disposed Persons wickedly taking Advantage of their unhappy Condition, and drawing them into unreasonable Bargains, etc. . . .

The Public provision made for the sick and distempered immigrants above referred to had, in all probability, been inspired, not so much by tender concern for their welfare, as by the desire to keep such persons out of the city, and by thus isolating them, to prevent the introduction of contagious disease. The provisions here referred to constituted the first attempts to protect the inhabitants by the establishment of quarantine at the port of Philadelphia. . . .

In the earlier days of the Hospital, even down to quite recent times, the mode of commitment of the insane was so easy and free from formality that a few words hastily scribbled upon a chance scrap of paper were sufficient to place a supposed insane patient in the Hospital and deprive him of personal liberty. If he did not remain passive, chains or some other form of mechanical restraint were used. A sufficient number of such scraps of paper have survived to show the astonishing informality of the lunacy proceedings. The friend (or it may in some instances have been the enemy) of an alleged lunatic, applied to the Managers, or to one of the physicians, for an order of admission. If, as now, the friends or custodians were able to pay board, bond was taken for its regular settlement and, in the earlier years of the Hospital, this obligation contained a provision covering the funeral expenses of the patient if he died while under treatment. If the patient was indigent he was admitted as a free case, after being seen by one of the physicians and upon his report to the Managers that the patient was a fit subject for detention. Once in the cells, or quarters for insane, the patient had no appeal from the opinion of the attending physician.

The following are the very brief records on the minutes of some of the early admissions and discharges.

> Dr. Moore's Negro man, a Lunatick, was received 3rd Mo. 26th, 1753. His master promised payment. . . . 1st. Mo. 23d, 1754. Admitted Negro Adam, a Lunatick and pay patient belonging to Mrs. Margaret Clymer, under the care of Dr. Thos. Bond. . . . 6th Mo. 26th, 1754. Admitted Negro George, a Lunatick belonging to Mr. Carrington of Barbadoes, a pay patient at 10$ a week, under ye particular care of Doctor Shippen who engages for his board.

At the foot of this paper the visiting physician writes what was then equivalent to a medical certificate of insanity:

> I think the above named James Holland is a proper subject for the Hospital.
>   Wm. Shippen

TO THE MANAGERS OF THE PENNSYLVANIA HOSPITAL

The Petition of Conrad I. Döer, the Father of Mary Elizabeth Döer, a Child about 13 years of Age, a Convalescent in your Hospital.

Give me leave Gentlemen to lay before you a true State of my Case,

To represent to you my deep Concern for my said Daughter and that I may endeavour to move your goodness to gratify the natural desire of a Father by restoring to him his darling Child which is now in a better Condition than when she was committed to your Charitable Care.

I embarked on board the Ship Hero with my late dear Wife and four Children. My said Wife and one Child died when we were in the Mouth of the River Maase and my unhappy Daughter was at the moment of her parting with her dear Mother seized with so violent a Grief as would not yield to any Comfort, her Mind was disturbed and she cried Day and Night, etc.

In this Condition we arrived in the Port of Philadelphia, when Ralph Foster the Commander of the Ship told me she must be brought to the Hospital and that her Cure and Maintenance should not cost me a Penny, In which particular I never mistrusted the Captain as the General notion we entertain of Hospitals in Germany is that they are founded by public or private Benevolence for the relief of the poor unhappy sick and that never anything is charged to their Account, Except in the Case of Rich Pensioners whose relations sometimes agree with the Governors of such Hospitals for a better accommodation than common.

I then settled with the Owners of the Ship, all the Freight money for my poor Family was paid to them So that the Contract between the Owners of the Ship and me is entirely ended. I was bound a Servant for the Term of 3 years to . . . . Patten Esq. but I agreed with my Master that I would Serve him one Year longer in Case he would suffer a little Child of mine 3 years old to live with his Family during the Term of my Servitude.

When I lately had an Account from Philadelphia that my Daughter in the Hospital was pretty well again, I addressed my kind Master to give me leave to fetch my Child up to his House and he gave me leave that she might stay six Months at his House and I agreed with a Neighbour of my Master to maintain her till I was free. So having provided every thing for the reception of my Daughter and flattering myself how soon I would have her near me and see her daily, I came to the Philadelphia Hospital and was told that the Managers would deliver up the Girl to the Owners of the Ship who had assumed to pay for her cure and Accommodation and that these Merchants would sell her for the Charges of the Hospital. As I expect that the Captain will have forgot his Word he gave me when I gave up my Daughter to the Hospital, or put me off with an Equivocation that it will not cost me Money but that it must cost me my Daughter who is as dear to me as my own life, As I expect no Mercy from the Merchants, who look upon poor Germans as upon other Merchandize and as the obtaining of Justice against them if they should attempt to sell my Child against my will is too expensive for a poor Stranger, All my hopes is in you Gentlemen who preside over the Contributions of a Wealthy and charitable people in this and the neighbouring Provinces.

And your petitioner humbly prayeth that you will be pleased to forgive the Cost of Curing and Maintaining my poor Child and not to commit me to an Argument with Merchants in which they might get the better of me when I being a poor Servant myself may be unable to support my natural Right to my Daughter.

And your Petitioner shall ever pray.

> Conrad I. Döer
> Philadelphia
> March 23, 1765

Although no action appears upon the minutes, it is reasonable to suppose from their previous acts of kindness towards patients, that the Managers did not refuse to grant this pathetic appeal of a father for his child.[1]

---

[1] What seemed "reasonable to suppose" to Dr. Morton in 1897, does not seem so to me. This heart-rending petition, and all it implies for the despicable tyranny exercised by the physicians at the Pennsylvania Hospital at that time, must have been more than Dr. Morton could accept; hence, his attempt to undo the record, first, by the totally unsupported reference to the physicians' "previous acts of kindness toward patients"; second, by ignoring that, had the physicians been well-disposed toward this child and her father, they could have released her long before being petitioned to do so; and third, and last, by the most unlikely assumption that, given the meticulous record-keeping of the period—after all, the Petition was preserved!—the physicians would have released the child without entering that fact also in the record. (Ed.)

3

THE UTILITY OF PUBLIC ASYLUMS FOR LUNATICS

Philippe Pinel

> Philippe Pinel (1745–1826) was physician to the Bicêtre from 1793 to 1795, and to the Salpêtrière from 1795 to 1826. He is the undisputed founder of "modern psychiatry," celebrated for having "struck the chains from the insane." Although he is widely recognized as a great humanitarian and an influential spokesman for the "moral treatment" of insanity, in actuality Pinel's "treatment" of the mental patient rested squarely on coercion: as the excerpts below illustrate, he advocated the use of both force and fraud in dealing with hospitalized madmen. The selection here reprinted is from his classic *A Treatise on Insanity* (1801),* the first and perhaps still the most famous textbook of psychiatry.

I

Few subjects in medicine are so intimately connected with the history and philosophy of the human mind as insanity. There are still fewer, where there are so many errors to rectify, and so many prejudices to remove. Derangement of the understanding is generally considered as an

---

* From *A Treatise on Insanity*, translated from the French, *Traité médico-philosophique sur l'aliénation mentale, ou la manie* (Paris: Richard et al., 1801), by D. D. Davis. Facsimile of the London 1806 edition (New York: Hafner Publishing Co., 1962), pp. 3–4, 14–16, 63–68, 87.

effect of an organic lesion of the brain, consequently as incurable; a supposition that is, in a great number of instances, contrary to anatomical fact. Public asylums for maniacs have been regarded as places of confinement for such of its members as are become dangerous to the peace of society. The managers of those institutions, who are frequently men of little knowledge and less humanity, have been permitted to exercise towards their innocent prisoners a most arbitrary system of cruelty and violence; while experience affords ample and daily proofs of the happier effects of a mild, conciliating treatment, rendered effective by steady and dispassionate firmness. Availing themselves of this consideration, many empirics have erected establishments for the reception of lunatics, and have practiced this very delicate branch of the healing heart with singular reputation. A great number of cures have undoubtedly been effected by those base born children of the profession; but, as might be expected, they have not in any degree contributed to the advancement of science by any valuable writings. . . .

II

To believe that the different species of insanity depend upon the particular nature of its causes, and that it becomes periodical, continued or melancholic, according as it may have originated from unfortunate love, domestic distress, fanaticism, superstition, or interesting revolutions in the state of public affairs, would be, to fall into a very great error. My experience authorizes me to affirm, that there is no necessary connection between the specific character of insanity, and the nature of its exciting cause. Among the cases of periodical mania, which I have seen and recorded in my journals, I find some which originated in a violent but unfortunate passion; others in an ungovernable ambition for fame, power or glory. Many succeeded to reverses of fortune; others were produced by devotional phrenzy; and others by an enthusiastic patriotism, unchastened by the sober and steady influence of solid judgement. The violence of maniacal paroxysms appears, likewise, to be independent of the nature of the exciting cause; or to depend, at least, much more upon the constitution of the individual, —upon the different degrees of his physical and moral sensibility. . . .

I cannot here avoid giving my most decided suffrage in favour of the moral qualities of maniacs. I have no where met, excepting in romances, with fonder husbands, more affectionate parents, more impassioned lovers, more pure and exalted patriots, than in the lunatic asylum, during their intervals of calmness and reason. A man of sensibility may go there every day of his life, and witness scenes of indescribable tenderness associated to a most estimable virtue. . . .

III

In the preceding cases of insanity, we trace the happy effects of intimidation, without severity; of oppression, without violence; and of triumph, without outrage. How different from the system of treatment, which is yet adopted in too many hospitals, where the domestics and keepers are permitted to use any violence that the most wanton caprice, or the most sanguinary cruelty may dictate. . . .

We are informed by Dr. Gregory, that a farmer, in the North of Scotland, a man of Herculean stature, acquired great fame in that district of the British empire, by his success in the cure of insanity. The great secret of his practice consisted in giving full employment to the remaining faculties of the lunatic. With that view, he compelled all his patients to work on his farm. He varied their occupations, divided their labour, and assigned to each, the post which he was best qualified to fill. Some were employed as beasts of draught or burden, and others as servants of various orders and provinces. Fear was the operative principle that gave motion and harmony to this rude system. Disobedience and revolt, whenever they appeared in any of its operations, were instantly and severely punished.

A system of management analogous to the above, was adopted in a monastic establishment in the South of France. One of the inspectors visited each chamber, at least, once every day. If he found any of the maniacs behaving extravagantly, stirring up quarrels or tumults, making any objections to his victuals, or refusing to go to bed at night, he was told in a manner, which of itself was calculated to terrify him, that unless he instantly conformed, he would have to receive in the morning ten severe lashes, as a punishment for his disobedience. The threat was invariably executed with the greatest punctuality; while good conduct, on the contrary, was not less equally and punctually rewarded. Those who were disposed to behave orderly, and to observe the rules of the institution, were admitted to dine at the governor's table. But, if any one abused this indulgence, he was immediately reminded of it, by a smart stroke over his fingers with a ferule, and informed, with an air of great gravity and coolness, that it became him to conduct himself with more propriety and reserve.

It is painful to close this sketch by a reference to an imperfection in the treatment of insanity, by one of the most successful practitioners of any age. I allude to the practice of the celebrated Dr. Willis. In the establishment under his direction in the vicinity of London, it would appear that every lunatic is under the control of a keeper, whose authority over him is unlimited, and whose treatment of him must be supposed, in many instances, to amount to unbridled and dangerous barbarity:—a delegated latitude of power totally inconsistent with the principles of a pure and rigid philanthropy.

To apply our principles of moral treatment, with undiscriminating uniformity, to maniacs of every character and condition in society, would be equally ridiculous and unadviseable. A Russian peasant, or a slave of Jamaica, ought evidently to be managed by other maxims than those which would exclusively apply to the case of a well bred irritable Frenchman, unused to coercion and impatient of tyranny. . . .

To render the effects of fear solid and durable, its influence ought to be associated with that of a profound regard. For that purpose, plots must be either avoided or so well managed as not to be discovered; and coercion must always appear to be the result of necessity, reluctantly resorted to and commensurate with the violence or petulance which it is intended to correct. Those principles are strictly attended to at Bicêtre. That great hospital is far from possessing such advantages of site, insulation, extent of liberty, and interior accommodations, as that of Dr. Fowler. But I can assert, from accurate personal knowledge, that the maxims of enlightened humanity prevail throughout every department of its management; that the domestics and keepers are not allowed, on any pretext whatever, to strike a madman; and that straight waistcoats, superior force, and seclusion for a limited time, are the only punishments inflicted. When kind treatment, or such preparations for punishment as are calculated to impress the imagination, produce not the intended effect, it frequently happens, that a dexterous stratagem promotes a speedy and an unexpected cure. . . .

Improper application for personal liberty, or any other favour, must be received with acquiescence, taken graciously into consideration, and withheld under some plausible pretext, or postponed to a more convenient opportunity. The utmost vigilance of the domestic police will be necessary to engage the exertions of every maniac, especially during his lucid intervals, in some employment, laborious or otherwise, calculated to employ his thoughts and attention.

4

DECEPTION AND TERROR AS CURES FOR MADNESS

Benjamin Rush

> Benjamin Rush (1746–1813) signed the Declaration of Independence, was Physician General of the Continental Army, and served as Professor of Physic and Dean of the Medical School at the University of Pennsylvania. He is the undisputed father of American psychiatry: his portrait adorns the official seal of the American Psychiatric Association. With Pinel, Rush pioneered in the medical conceptualization of madness, that is, he claimed that madness was a disease whose control was a medical responsibility. And like Pinel, Rush advocated the "moral treatment" of insanity, that is, he believed that the principal method of treatment used by the alienist ought to be coercion of the patient, by means of both force and fraud. The selections here reprinted, from *Medical Inquiries and Observations Upon the Diseases of the Mind*,* illustrate Rush's approach to the insane.

I

If our patient imagine he has a living animal in his body, and he cannot be reasoned out of a belief of it, medicines must be given to destroy it; and if an animal, such as he

---

* From *Medical Inquiries and Observations Upon the Diseases of the Mind* (1812). Facsimile of the Philadelphia 1812 Edition (New York: Hafner Publishing Co., 1962), pp. 109–10, 211, 264–68, 273–74.

supposes to be in his body, should be secretly conveyed into his close stool, the deception would be a justifiable one, if it served to cure him of his disease.

If our patient should believe himself to be transformed into an animal of another species by transmigration, or in any other way, our remedies should be accommodated to the grade of his madness, and the nature of the animal into which he supposes himself to be changed. Ridicule has sometimes been employed with success in such cases. Mr. Pinel mentions an instance of its sudden efficacy in curing a watch-maker in Paris, who believed that his head had been cut off, and that he carried the head of a man who had been guillotined, instead of his own.

A physician, formerly of this city, used to divert his friends, by relating the history of a cure which had been performed of a patient in this form of madness, who believed himself to be a plant. One of his companions, who favoured his delusion, persuaded him he could not thrive without being watered, and while he made the patient believe, for some time, he was pouring water from the spout of a tea-pot, discharged his urine upon his head. The remedy in this case was resentment and mortification.

Cures of patients, who suppose themselves to be glass, may easily be performed by pulling a chair, upon which they are about to sit, from under them, and afterwards showing them a large collection of pieces of glass as the fragments of their bodies. . . .

II

Terror acts powerfully upon the body, through the medium of the mind, and should be employed in the cure of madness. I once advised gentle exercise upon horseback, in the case of a lady in Virginia who was deranged. In one of her excursions from home, her horse ran away with her. He was stopped after a while by a gate. The lady dismounted, and when her attendants came up to her, they found her, to their great surprise and joy, perfectly restored to her reason, nor has she had since the least sign of a return of her disease. . . .

III

When the will becomes the involuntary vehicle of vicious actions, through the instrumentality of the passions, I have called it *moral derangement*. For a more particular account of this moral disease in the will, the reader is again referred to a printed lecture delivered by the author, in the University of Pennsylvania, in November 1810, upon the Study of Medical Jurisprudence, in which the morbid operations of the will are confined to two acts, viz. murder and theft. I have selected those two symptoms of this disease (for they are not vices) from its other morbid effects, in order to rescue persons affected with them from the arm of the law, and to render them the subjects of the kind and lenient hand of medicine. But there are several other ways, in which this disease in the will discovers itself, that are not cognizable by law. I shall describe but two of them. These are, *lying* and *drinking*.

There are many instances of persons of sound understandings, and some of uncommon talents, who are affected with this *lying* disease in the will. It differs from exculpative, fraudulent and malicious lying, in being influenced by none of the motives of any of them. Persons thus diseased cannot speak the truth upon any subject, nor tell the same story twice in the same way, nor describe any thing as it has appeared to other people. Their falsehoods are seldom calculated to injure anybody but themselves, being for the most part of an hyberbolical or boasting nature, but now and then they are of a mischievous nature, and injurious to the characters and property of others. That it is a corporeal disease, I infer from its sometimes appearing in mad people, who are remarkable for veracity in the healthy states of their minds, several instances of which I have known in the Pennsylvania Hospital. Persons affected with this disease are often amiable in their tempers and manners, and sometimes benevolent and charitable in their dispositions.

Lying, as a vice, is said to be incurable. The same thing may be said of it as a disease, when it appears in adult life. It is generally the result of a defective education. It is voluntary in childhood, and becomes involuntary, like certain muscular actions, from habit. Its only *remedy* is, bodily pain, inflicted by the rod, or confinement, or abstinence from food; for children are incapable of being permanently influenced by appeals to reason, natural affection, gratitude, or even a sense of shame.

The use of strong drink is at first the effect of free agency. From habit it takes place from necessity. That this is the case, I infer from persons who are inordinately devoted to the use of ardent spirits being irreclaimable, by all the considerations which domestic obligations, friendship, reputation, property, and sometimes even by those which religion and the love of life, can suggest to them. An instance of insensibility to the last, in an habitual drunkard, occurred some years ago in Philadelphia. When strongly urged, by one of his friends, to leave off drinking, he said, "Were a keg of rum in one corner of the room, and were a cannon constantly discharging balls between me and it, I could not refrain from passing before that cannon, in order to get at the rum."

The *remedies* for this disease have hitherto been religious and moral, and they have sometimes cured it. They would probably have been more successful, had they been combined with such as are of a physical nature. For an account of several of them, the reader is referred to the first volume of the author's Medical Inquiries and Observations. To that account of physical remedies I shall add one more, and that is, the establishment of a hospital in every city and town in the United States, for the exclusive reception of hard drinkers. They are as much objects of public humanity and charity, as mad people. They are indeed more hurtful to society, than most of the deranged patients of a common hospital would be, if they were set at liberty. Who can calculate the extensive influence of a drunken husband or wife upon the property and morals of their families, and of the waste of the former, and corruption of the latter, upon the order and happiness of society? Let it not be said, that confining such persons in a hospital would be an infringement upon personal liberty, incompatible with the freedom of our governments. We do not use this argument when we confine a thief in a jail, and yet, taking the aggregate evil of the greater number of drunkards than thieves into consideration, and the greater evils which the influence of their immoral example and conduct introduce into society than stealing, it must be obvious, that the safety and prosperity of a community will be more promoted by confining them, than a common thief. To prevent injustice or oppression, no person should be sent to the contemplated hospital, or *sober house*, without being examined and committed by a court, consisting of a physician, and two or three magistrates, or commissioners appointed for that purpose. If the patient possess property, it should be put into the hands of trustees, to take care of it. Within this house the patient should be debarred the use of ardent spirits, and drink only, for a while, such substitutes for them, as a physician should direct. Tobacco, one of the provocatives of intemperance in drinking, should likewise be gradually abstracted from them. Their food should be simple, but for a while moderately cordial. They should be employed in their former respective occupations, for their own, or for the public benefit, and all the religious, moral, and physical remedies, to which I have referred, should be employed at the same time, for the complete and radical cure of their disease. . . .

IV

This faculty of the mind [i.e., the Principle of Faith, or the Believing Faculty] is subject to disorder as well as to disease; that is, to an inability to believe things that are supported by all the evidence that usually enforces belief. Mr. Burke has described the conduct of persons affected with this disorder in the following words: "They believe nothing that they do not see, or hear, or measure by a twelve inch rule." An Indian once expressed the state of mind in which this torpor in the principle of faith takes place, by saying, when a truth was proposed to his belief, "that it would not believe for him." This incredulity is not confined to human testimony. It extends to the evidence of reason, and (it has been said) of the senses. The followers of Dr. Berkley either felt, or affected, the last grade of this disorder in the principle of faith. That it is often affected, I infer from persons who deny their belief in the utility of medicine, as practiced by regular bred physicians, believing implicitly in quacks; also from persons who refuse to admit human testimony in favour of the truths of the christian religion, believing in all the events of profane history; . . .

The remedy for this palsy of the believing faculty, should consist in proposing propositions of the most simple nature to the mind, and, after gaining the assent to them, to rise to propositions of a more difficult nature. The powers of oratory sometimes awaken the torpor of the principle of faith. This was evinced, in a remarkable manner, in the speech which King Agrippa made to St. Paul, after he had heard his eloquent oration in favour of christianity; "almost thou persuadest me to be a Christian." Perhaps great bodily pain would have the same, or a greater, effect in curing this disorder of the mind. It has often cured paralytic affections of the body, and of other faculties of the mind.

5

A LUNATIC'S PROTEST

John Perceval

John Thomas Perceval, the fifth son of Spencer Perceval, the Prime Minister of England, was born in 1803. When he was nine years old, his father was assassinated.

At the age of twenty-seven, Perceval suffered what we would now call a "schizophrenic episode." Much against his will, his family placed him in the asylum of Dr. Fox at Brisslington near Bristol, where he was confined from January 1831 until May 1832. He was then removed to the asylum of Mr. Charles Newington at Ticehurst in Sussex, where he remained until the beginning of 1834.

After securing his release, he married, had four daughters, and apparently lived the life of an upper-class English gentleman, without further recurrence of his "nervous troubles." He is remembered for his two-volume account of his experiences as a mental patient and especially for his criticisms of the treatment of lunatics. His book, *A Narrative of the Treatment Experienced by a Gentleman, during a State of Mental Derangement; Designed to Explain the Causes and Nature of Insanity, and to Expose the Injudicious Conduct toward Many Unfortunate Sufferers under that Calamity*, was published in London by Effingham Wilson in 1838 and 1840. This work was discovered for the modern student of psychiatry by Gregory Bateson who, by careful editing, reduced the two volumes to one.* It is the source of the following selection.

I

Why was I confined? because I was a lunatic. And what is a lunatic, but one whose reasoning cannot be depended upon; one of imperfect and deranged understanding, and of a diseased imagination? What, then, was the natural consequence of my being placed in the most extraordinary, difficult, and unreasonable circumstances, without explanation, but that I should, as I did, attribute that insult which was heaped upon me to the most absurd causes; to the nonperformance of the very acts, which in a sane mind I might have condemned; or to the performance of those which I might have applauded. With me, conscience was entirely confounded—judgment perverted. That which others called sin, I deemed virtue; that which men called folly, I called wisdom. What can be said, when I struck, kicked, wrestled, endangered my own security and that of others, as the acts most pleasing to them to witness, most dutiful for me to attempt?

The reader now, perhaps, wonders at treatment like this being possible; but if he does now resent it, in nine cases out of ten it is not without my having been obliged to reason with him as with a child; so rooted is the prejudice, *that lunacy cannot be subdued, except by harsh treatment*. If he asks why these things are so, I will tell him why: *because it is the interest of the lunatic doctors*. That is the end. And the cause lies in the servile folly of mankind, of which these lunatic doctors make their profit.

But such treatment is impolitic, not in the lunatic doctor, but in the conduct of such as, in good faith, desire a patient's cure; because, if discovered or suspected, it may work, as it did in me, a deadly hate towards those dealing with me, and a resolution to endure any thing, rather than

---

* Gregory Bateson, Editor, *Perceval's Narrative: A Patient's Account of His Psychosis, 1830–1832* (Stanford, California: Stanford University Press, 1961), pp. 100–325.

bow a haughty and stubborn spirit to their cunning, address, or cruelty. In return for their insolent severity, the mind mocks at their care and vigilance, their respect and their benevolence. The question, then, lies between the power of the patient to endure, and the power of the quack to break his spirit. The latter is shamefully uncontrolled by law, in consequence of the very generous, legitimate, and simple confidence placed by chancellors, magistrates and law-officers of the crown in the humane, and tender, and scrupulous doctor. . . .

II

Now with regard to my treatment, I have to make at first two general observations, which apply, I am afraid, too extensively to every system of management yet employed towards persons in my condition. First, the suspicion and the fact of my being incapable of reasoning correctly, or deranged in understanding, justified apparently every person who came near me, in dealing with me also in a manner contrary to reason and contrary to nature. These are strong words; but in the minutest instances I can, alas! prove them true. Secondly, my being likely to attack the rights of others gave these individuals license, in every respect, to trample upon mine. My being incapable of feeling, and of defending myself, was construed into a reason for giving full play to this license. Instead of my understanding being addressed and enlightened, and of my path being made as clear and plain as possible, in consideration of my confusion, I was committed, in really difficult and mysterious circumstances, calculated of themselves to confound my mind, even if in a sane state, to unknown and untried hands; and I was placed amongst strangers, without introduction, explanation, or exhortation. Instead of great scrupulousness being observed in depriving me of any liberty or privilege, and of the exercise of so much choice and judgment as might be conceded to me with safety;— on the just ground, that for the safety of society my most valuable rights were already taken away, on every occasion, in every dispute, in every argument, the assumed premise immediately acted upon was, that I was to yield, my desires were to be set aside, my few remaining privileges to be infringed upon, for the convenience of others. Yet I was in a state of mind not likely to acknowledge even the justice of my confinement, and in a state of defencelessness calculated to make me suspicious, and jealous of any further invasion of my natural and social rights: but this was a matter that never entered into their consideration.

Against this system of downright oppression, enforced with sycophantish adulation and affected pity by the doctor, adopted blindly by the credulity of relations, and submitted to by the patients with meek stupidity, or vainly resisted by natural but hopeless violence, I had to fight my way for two years, wringing from my friends a gradual but tardy assent to the most urgent expostulations: not from the physicians; their law is the same for all qualities and dispositions, and their maxim to clutch and hold fast. . . .

I was never told, such and such things we are going to do; we think it advisable to administer such and such medicine, in this or that manner; I was never asked, Do you want any thing? do you wish for, prefer any thing? have you any objection to this or to that? I was fastened down in bed; a meagre diet was ordered for me; this and medicine forced down my throat, or in the contrary direction; my will, my wishes, my repugnances, my habits, my delicacy, my inclinations, my necessities, were not once consulted, I may say, thought of. I did not find the respect paid usually even to a child. . . .

I was not . . . once addressed by argument, expostulation, or persuasion. The persons round me consulted, directed, chose, ordered, and force was the unica and ultima ratio applied to me. If I were insane, in my resolution to be silent, because I was sure that neither of the doctors, or of my friends, would understand my motives, or give credit to facts they had not themselves experienced; they were surely no less insane, who because of my silence, forgot the use of their own tongues, who, because of my neglect of the duties I owed to them, expunged from their consciences all deference to me; giving up so speedily and entirely all attempt at explanation; all hope of sifting the cause of my delusions; all hope of addressing my reason with success; all hope of winning me to speak. If I needed medicine and light diet, still, I say to myself, surely that was not all; surely air and exercise, and water, and occupation or amusement, and a little solid food, would have done me no harm. . . .

III

When I began first to write to my mother and my brother, complaining of my situation, and aware of my state, my feelings were acute in this respect, and my instances earnest and repeated that my correspondence should be private. Delicacy towards my family, if only that, dictated this. I received no attention. The same bigotted credulity that abandoned my person and soul to the doctor's management, abandoned also the secrets of my heart to his impertinent examination. I cannot describe the hatred with which the recollection of this conduct still inspires me: then I hated, I despised, I was enraged, I became hardened. I loathed myself for keeping any terms with my relations and those around me. In the end, I scoffed at religion; I blasphemed the name and nature of God. The doctor alone benefited; for his benefit it was designed. Liable to his subtle misrepresentation, I concealed and disguised my feelings, or wrote for his inspection, braving his malice and duplicity. My real distresses I left to time or chance to take away, or to unravel. I was brutalized.

Thus, in a state of derangement, I was abandoned to my fate, and so condemned, that I could not seek health by sane conduct. I could not recover sanity, but by ways which can alone be justified by insanity; from which I shrunk, even insane: ways, which the very nature of a sound understanding, the very nature of humane feeling, make impossible. But this is one example only. When I grew older in my afflictions, I found that no patient could escape from his confinement in a truly sound state of mind, without lying against his conscience, or admitting the doctrine, that deception and duplicity are consistent with a sound conscience. Those who do otherwise are not sane, they are living a lie. But what does that signify? they are good subjects, and the doctor's best friends. . . .

IV

They who have not been confined in a lunatic asylum, cannot conceive the dreadful and cruel suspense that delay, and not only the neglect, but the refusal of every day civilities, together with inattention to just and obvious complaints, occasion. They do not know our wants and fears, because they do not know the danger we are in. They may judge our danger, however, from what these men do; and from what they have done, they may judge what they dare to do: being encompassed, even more than a king, with a hollow impunity, and clothed in the deepest hypocrisy. They who have not endured this confinement do not know how the very suspicion of being a lunatic, coupled with being cut off from all pecuniary resources, shuts the minds of others against sympathy, impedes the proffer of assistance and the exercise of protection, and aught but the show of pity. Neither how it embarrasses the suppliant in his applications for redress, awakens anxiety, excites mistrust, and closes the door of his hopes; whilst he finds himself left defenceless to the sarcasm and persecutions of those he is accusing. This is an awful peril for a man in a sound mind to be exposed to, lest he become deranged; lest he be tempted to violence, *the object* of his tormentors, which would then be construed into an open act of insanity; and if not immediately accepted as damning proof, by imbecile magistrates, at least cruelly try the mind, by tantalizing the expectations. How much more fearful is such a trial for one who knows that he cannot plead innocence of lunacy; one who, in mind and bodily health, is weak, and thereby more exposed than another to follow a wrong course; exposed to suffer even from treatment which men in sound health might almost laugh at, still more from that which he dreads from having experienced it, and against which he is exasperated; and also, still more liable than the other to lose that gift, lately lost, so dear now, being newly restored to him,—the gift of a sound mind, and convalescent health; perishing again from want of wholesome communion, shattered by assault, or insidiously undermined. . . .

V

So little care was taken by my relations to be precise or explanatory in their conduct towards me, that the previous letter I received from my mother, desiring me a private apartment, merely contained a refusal to remove me from the madhouse of Dr. F.: the next told me that a private apartment was being prepared for me in a madhouse elsewhere. By that time I had been again insulted and injured by the forced use of the shower-bath and cold bath. I considered my life in danger under insolent and violent servants, malignant, prejudiced, and nettled physicians. . . .

I now took up this attitude against my family. I argued that although I was unsettled in my judgment and still partially lunatic, it did not give mankind or them any legal right to exercise a brutal and tyrannical control over my will, without respect to the nature of my calamity, and to the degree of restoration I had attained to. Instead of being treated as I was, *de haut en bas*, with complete contumely, no argument or address being made to my understanding, I conceived that my being a lunatic required on the contrary the more scrupulousness on their part, the more caution, openness, and explanation. That it was their duty to make my way more straight and clear before me because I was by my disease already sufficiently prone to delusion, and even to unprovoked suspicion. So at least the doctors desire you to believe, but I question if the suspicions of lunatics are not often most sane, and engendered necessarily by the underhand dealings of others towards them. . . .

I determined therefore for safety, for example's sake, and for revenge to appeal to the law against my physician.

... In order to succeed I desired first legal assistance to set forth my case and to save my rights; secondly to be taken to London to be for a short time under the care of a surgeon who had known me from a child, that he witnessing my state of mind and body, and hearing my complaints, might be able to argue and to give evidence concerning the necessity of requiring me to use the cold bath, at that inclement season, the propriety of using force considering the degree of understanding I was restored to, and the danger to my health of body from the shock and cold, and to my mind from the needless excitement. These requests were denied.

I then wrote to my mother, stating to her, that if she really was not aware of the cruelty of my situation, she had been deceived by Dr. F., and then might justly join me in demanding legal satisfaction, but that if she did not do so, I could not be reconciled to her, and must hold her also responsible to me at law, for she was certainly the most culpable. Moreover, that though I knew I was still lunatic, yet I knew too, from sad experience, that I was capable of taking care of myself in a more reasonable manner than the wretched physicians she confided in; that I was not a lunatic incapable of controlling myself, although I felt so sensible of my need of observation that I would not accept my liberty if it were given to me, but should place myself immediately under the eye of some one I could rely upon; but that if she insisted on placing me, where under pretence of observation, I should be defenceless, open to violence, impertinent intrusion, indelicate treatment, and deprived of tranquillity, peace, rest, and security, I should claim my freedom, though lunatic, as one not mischievous, and hold her responsible for my future detention. . . .

I might as well have appealed to the winds. I received letters from my elder brother and his wife, canting about submission, patience, and the Holy Spirit; to which I replied in mockery and disdain. I knew that my patience had been proved in a fire they could not have stood under for a moment; that it had not given way until they had neglected my representations, and made me desperate; and they talked to me of patience, ignorant of facts and circumstances, whose business it was to have humbled themselves and to have applied patiently for information to me. . . .

VI

I cannot say what I feel at my correspondence having been always left subject to the inspection of my physician; I am astonished, I speak as a man, at the indelicacy of my family—at their want of respect to my honour and to their own; I am astonished that I, recovering from derangement, should have been more sensible and reasonable in this respect than they were, who quenched sound feeling in obsequiousness. But I desire others to reflect how disgusting it is for lunatic doctors to challenge, and for relations to allow them this title. What! Mr. Newington to be the keeper of my conscience—to be the meddler in secrets between my Maker and myself—which I might feel compelled to divulge and yet only confide with propriety to a minister of religion, or to relations, or to friends!

I obliged to confide my feelings and desires to a stranger —feelings which it required even great delicacy to communicate properly to my nearest connexions!—or to be compelled to hold my peace in doubt, mistrust, or difficulty! By what authority do these men exercise this power —a power which even a clergyman, if he were a patient's guardian, would not be entitled to; on what grounds can they claim a confidence, which ties of kindred, or of friendship and respect, can alone confer? What is the result of their so doing? That a patient cannot return to a really sound state of mind; or else he must forego all useful communication by letter with his relations: since the very conditions these men force their patients to submit to, they can only be excusable in submitting to from insanity or dulness equal to their doctor's stupidity. These are like owls set to judge over the sanity of larks and nightingales. These are like swine or sloths set to judge over the manners of greyhounds and fleet coursers.

The reasons given for this interference are, that the patient may write something improper to his relations; but since highly important letters may be destroyed, who is to be on this plea the judge? and if he does, is it not equally improper for the doctor to see the writings? Therefore on this plea the letters should be burnt without reading. This is absolute prudery—an affectation of delicacy, and of respect for the feelings, on the part of men who prove that they have little or none. Surely, as far as the patient is concerned, he should be saved from the apprehension of having exposed himself before a *stranger*. The second reason, is that the doctor may know the state of the patient's mind, and require some clue to his disorder; and it is of a piece with all their charlatanerie, to affect a great care where they have no business to meddle, and to take the very course to disturb the peace of their patient's mind under pretence of restoring it. . . .

VII

If to resent neglect, insult, and ruffian-like violence, is a proof of madness, I was insane under Mr. Charles Newington. If to call by such terms the treatment I received under Dr. Fox, and to believe that it could not have been proper or wholesome for a nervous patient, was a delusion, I am still the puppet of a disordered fancy. If a desire and a determination to expose such a system, and to punish the conductors of it by lawful means, and a hope to be able to obtain their conviction for having compelled me to submit to a course of discipline contrary both to medical and surgical science, was an unjust, or even immoderate desire, I am still of unsound mind. If to postpone all selfish considerations, and to overcome the natural desire for avoiding publicity, in order to vindicate my rights, to uphold the law, to relieve the oppressed and to destroy the oppressor, and to set the Church up in proper authority in these matters, are symptoms of my being unfit to walk at large in my beloved country, hold up your hands, my readers, hold up your hands for Mr. C. Newington.

If my exasperation against my family, and even against my mother, caused by long ill treatment, and by my confinement needlessly protracted in improper circumstances, made it wholesome or reasonable, or necessary, to *continue the causes of that exasperation*; if my requiring of her to join me in prosecuting a man who had evidently deceived her, and my opinion, in consequence of her refusal, that I was *bound* to include her in my prosecution—if even that cool judgment degenerating at times into a desire to do so from vindictive motives, proved me to be of a disordered understanding—if my being unable to correspond in temperate language with those who in fact were mocking and oppressing me, whatever were their designs or intentions; if my sense of that inability which made me protest against being compelled to carry on direct correspondence, and to claim the interference of my friends—if my disinclination to meet my relations, until they acknowledged their errors, arising from a similar consciousness of the impropriety of doing so—if my refusal to see or to correspond with my brothers, who under these circumstances had referred me to the magistrates of a strange county—if my attempt to effect my escape, and the frank expression of my determination to do so at any risk, and without regard to the life of those robbing me of my liberty;—lastly, if my opinion, my desire, and my resolution to hold Mr. C. Newington responsible to me at law for acting upon these infamous pretences, and to try my cause with him also at law, proved me to be a madman, and justified him and the enlightened magistrates who visited the asylum, in the detention of my person—in prolonging my civil confinement—in excluding me from church, and in banishing me from society; then I have no right to be at large now, and I am still a dangerous and unworthy member of society. . . .

I was shocked and *amazed* at the terrible system to which, in common with so many, I was subjected; without help, without hope. I resolved—I was necessitated—to pit my strength and abilities against that system, to fail in no duty to myself and to my country; but at the risk of my life, or my health, and even of my understanding, to become thoroughly acquainted with its windings, in order to expose and unravel the wickedness and the folly that maintained it, and to unmask the plausible villainy that carries it on. I do not think that I was wrong. The work that I am now writing may, I hope, *rescue* many wretched persons now ill treated and oppressed under it, and enlighten many generations. . . .

VIII

But if persons . . . should still affirm that my conduct was immoderate and unreasonable, and that my resolution to escape from imprisonment, even at the risk of being compelled to take another's life, was outrageous, to them I answer, that if I was conceited, obstinate, and violent, it did not prove me unnatural or insane. I had been provoked, and I had the right on my side.

But to others whose judgment may be misled by such observations, I say that I regret extremely the division that took place between my family and myself; but I ask, was moderation to be only on one side? I put the question plainly; is any Englishman to submit even to one month's confinement, purely out of complaisance to his family? and was I to submit to months and months, and interminable months of confinement, the end of which was shrouded in mist, whilst I was kept in cruel suspense, and refused any reason or any explanation? Was I to do this from deference to *my* family, who had abandoned me to the ill treatment I met with in Dr. Fox's madhouse, the recollection of which was fresh upon me? Was I to pander to others' curiosity, to explain facts to those who made no sort of inquiry; to deal frankly with those who perverted what I said against me; admitting that it was *just* that I should be confined still, because *I had been* insane—when for THAT VERY CAUSE, it was most cruel and unnatural for my relations to detain me unnecessarily; when for that very reason they ought to have strained a point to improve my circumstances, and to make my situation more lively and more cheerful? No, no! Let not moderation be all on one side. Let there be a little thought for my feelings also. . . .

Such was my position at the end of April, 1832. I knew of no reasons for my continued confinement; and if any had been given me, I had forgotten them, or they had been communicated in a manner which made me think lightly of them. Mr. Newington also repeatedly assured me that I was NOT a lunatic but a NERVOUS patient, and that he was only afraid I should be made ill again by society! My mind looked forward then to a weary confinement in loathsome circumstances, and in a degrading position, until this man's conceit and vanity, or cupidity were satisfied.

I could not imagine that honest and liberal minds, possessing such power of judgment, and such diversity of talent as belong to my family, could confine me as insane because I wore ringlets and a beard—or because I had certain views of instituting legal proceedings against Dr. Fox and Dr. Newington, or even against them. I cannot now conceive how any honest minds could come to such a resolution.[1] At the same time, I could not believe it possible that a family so just and truly amiable could confine me merely to compel me to relinquish my objects. To question my relations seemed to me to be a reflection upon myself. I had such faith in their simplicity and honesty, that I was rather driven to doubt my own self. . . .

My family have not much originality of idea, or independence of mind. They thought, with the world, that lunacy was an impenetrable mystery; that lunatic doctors were the only persons capable of meddling with it; that they were entitled to submission, if not to implicit confidence. They never thought to question these premises. They thought also that it was their duty to conceal the misfortune that had happened to me, and that *no one in his senses* could wish to have it exposed. Simple, faithful, and conscientious in their own dealings, and living retired,

[1] It would be a short way to settle all causes, to have the appellant shut up as a madman.

even my brothers not being aware of one half of what I now know goes on in the world around them, they were not prepared to guard against such a system of duplicity and chicanery—of revolting insult, and murderous violence —of racket and confusion, as I was subjected to. They could not believe it possible, or, if possible, so wholly unnecessary. They will not believe it true, nor how much they have wronged me; and therefore, even now, like many others, they may consider me, for publishing this work, yet scarcely of sound mind. But now these things are true—therefore I cannot keep silence. Necessity is laid upon me, and I must bear witness of these things. And yet who is on my side? where shall I find energy to reform these abuses?

6

MADNESS AND BLACKNESS, 1840

From *The American Journal of Insanity*

The following selection* is an instructive introduction to the history of "psychiatric epidemiology." The reader may draw his own conclusions from the census figures as well as from the remarks on them by the anonymous correspondent to the New York *Observer*.

STARTLING FACTS FROM THE CENSUS

(From the New York *Observer*)

Messrs. Editors—In the interesting article on the increase of our population, published in your paper of June 12th, you remark in the words of The Commercial: "Either the free colored population are voluntarily emigrating at a rate beyond what is generally supposed, or there is something in their social condition that is entirely inimical to their physical prosperity."

Many arguments might be adduced to prove that the latter, and not the former alternative is the real fact.— And as a remarkable illustration of this truth, I send you a copy of a few items from a statistical table which I compiled some years ago from the U.S. Census of 1840, and published in a country newspaper, without obtaining much

* From "Startling Facts from the Census," *The American Journal of Insanity*, 8:153–55 (Oct.), 1851.

STATISTICAL TABLE FROM THE U.S. CENSUS OF 1840

States	Total White population	Insane and Idiots	Proportion	Total Color'd population	Insane and Idiots	Proportion
Maine	500,438	537	1 in 950	1,355	94	1 in 14
New Hampshire	284,036	486	1 in 584	538	19	1 in 28
Massachusetts	729,030	1,071	1 in 662	8,669	200	1 in 43
Vermont	291,218	398	1 in 731	730	13	1 in 56
Connecticut	301,856	498	1 in 606	8,159	44	1 in 185
Rhode Island	105,587	203	1 in 520	3,243	13	1 in 249
New York	2,378,890	2,110	1 in 1,108	50,031	194	1 in 257
New Jersey	351,588	369	1 in 952	21,718	73	1 in 293
Pennsylvania	1,676,115	1,946	1 in 861	37,952	187	1 in 256
Delaware	58,561	52	1 in 1,126	19,524	28	1 in 697
Maryland	317,717	387	1 in 821	151,515	141	1 in 1,074
Virginia	740,968	1,052	1 in 704	498,829	381	1 in 1,309
North Carolina	484,370	580	1 in 835	268,549	221	1 in 1,215
South Carolina	259,084	376	1 in 689	335,314	137	1 in 2,440
Georgia	407,695	294	1 in 1,387	283,697	134	1 in 2,117
Ohio	1,502,022	1,195	1 in 1,257	17,345	165	1 in 105
Kentucky	590,253	795	1 in 742	189,575	180	1 in 1,053
Louisiana	158,457	55	1 in 2,873	193,954	45	1 in 4,310

notice, although it exhibits, in a most striking light, the amazing prevalence of insanity and idiocy among our free colored population over the whites and the slaves.

It is a matter of regret, that the U.S. Census of 1840, groups both these classes of unfortunates together, as if they were involved in one and the same calamity. And it is also to be regretted that there is no discrimination of the prevalence of these maladies among the free blacks and the slaves. The writer made an effort to have these imperfections obviated in taking the last census in 1850; but he has reason to apprehend, from what he has seen of the returns, that his feeble voice did not engage the attention of the "Commissioners" who were intrusted with the responsible duty of preparing the forms; though they solicited suggestions from those who felt an interest in the subject.

The census of our own State, taken in 1845, carefully distinguishes between idiots and lunatics; from which it appears, that their ratio in the State of New York is about 4 to 5, or more nearly 16 to 21, on the whole population; but it makes no distinction between the white and colored population in regard to the existence of these maladies. It is obvious, however, from the following schedule, that there is an awful prevalence of idiocy and insanity among the free blacks over the whites, and especially over the slaves. Who would believe, without the fact, in black and white, before his eyes, that *every fourteenth colored person in the State of Maine is an idiot or lunatic?* And though there is a gradual improvement in their condition, as we proceed west and south yet it is evident that the free States are the principal abodes of idiocy and lunacy among the colored race.

In the preceeding list, I have aimed to give a view of this subject on the territory occupied by the 13 original States. I have added Ohio and Kentucky merely to show that the same contrast between the old free and slave states exists in the new. . . . And in Louisiana, where a large majority of the population is colored, and four-fifths of them slaves, there is but one of these poor unfortunates to 4,310 who are sane. In fact, the want of sense or reason appears to be a rare visitation upon those who are held in slavery. This is an ample theme for the speculations of the physiologist and the moralist.

7

DEMOCRACY AS MENTAL DISEASE

From *The American Journal of Insanity*

> The following excerpt* is an early example of the frankly political use of the psychiatric imagery and vocabulary.

A New Form of Insanity.—In Berlin, a curious subject for a thesis has been found by a student in medicine, the son of M. Groddeck, the deputy, seeking his degree. M. Groddeck has discovered a new form of epidemic, whose virus has of late circulated throughout the Continental Nations with a rapidity contrasting strongly with the solemn and stately march of cholera. Its development, indeed, has been all but simultaneous in the great European Capitals, but we know not that it has before occurred to any one to treat it medically. M. Groddeck's thesis, publicly maintained, is entitled *"De morbo democratico, nova insaniae forma."* (On the democratic disease, a new form of insanity.)—The Faculty of Medicine, with the usual dislike of Faculties of Medicine to new discoveries, refused admission, it appears, to this dissertation, but the Senate of the University, on M. Groddeck's appeal, reversed their decision.—*Athenaeum*, March 23, 1850.

* From *The American Journal of Insanity*, 8:195 (Oct.), 1851.

8

"IN CASE YOU REFUSE . . ."

From the Records of the Dorothea Dix Hospital, Raleigh, N.C.

The following brief document is the record of the admission of the first Negro patient to the Dorothea Dix Hospital in Raleigh, North Carolina, in 1865. Construction of the hospital was authorized by the General Assembly in 1848, as a result of Miss Dix's efforts. The hospital was opened in 1856.

It is of interest to note that the superintendent of the "Lunatic Asylum" was here ordered to admit a patient under threat of penalties for refusal to comply. To be sure, Raleigh was then occupied by the Union army and the city was under martial law.*

> Provost Marshalls Office
> Raleigh, N.C.
> April 18, 1865

Dr. Edward Fisher, Lunatic Asylum
Raleigh, N.C.

Sir

You will receive and care for the insane Negro sent herewith.

---

* Dr. Robert Rollins, Superintendent of the Dorothea Dix Hospital, discovered this record among the archives of the hospital. I am indebted to him for his kindness and generosity in granting me permission to include this material, never previously published, in this volume.

In case you refuse the guard has instructions to bring you to me forthwith.

> Millard Nasser
> Col. & Prov. Mar.

The cover sheets are entitled: "African—Isaac—April 18, '65—Wake County" and "Isaac admitted 18th April '65—The servant of Wm. Holleman."

The records indicate that the cause of admission was given as "the war"; that the patient was said to be suffering from "mania"; and that he was discharged, "cured," on May 17, 1865.

PART TWO

THE GROWTH OF PSYCHIATRIC POWER (1865—1920)

1

MADNESS AND MARRIAGE

E. P. W. Packard

Mrs. E. P. W. Packard was incarcerated at the State Insane Asylum in Jacksonville, Illinois from 1860 till 1863. Her case was the first, and is probably still the most famous, exposé of what has since become known as "false commitment" to a mental hospital. Although her story is mentioned in most texts on the history of psychiatry, it seems safe to assume that few psychiatrists and even fewer nonpsychiatrists have read Mrs. Packard's intensely interesting and well-documented book on her ordeal and on the legal, religious, and social circumstances that made it possible. Moreover, despite all the evidence regarding the reasons for Mrs. Packard's commitment, many psychiatric historians continue to treat her shabbily. Thus, Albert Deutsch casts doubt on her "sanity" and dismisses her efforts at reform as counterproductive. "Whether Mrs. Packard was mentally sound or not at the time of her commitments or confinement is a moot question," he writes. "It appears to be established that she suffered from certain delusions and had been a patient at the Worcester State Hospital in Massachusetts for a brief period when a girl."* And in the style of the true psychiatric believer that he was, Deutsch offers

* Albert Deutsch, *The Mentally Ill in America*, Second Edition, (New York: Columbia University Press, 1952), pp. 424–25.

this comment about the results of Mrs. Packard's labors: ". . . she succeeded in getting the Illinois legislature to enact, in 1867, a law 'for the protection of personal liberty,' which prohibited the commitment of any person to an institution for the insane without trial by jury. In this case, the remedy proved worse than the condition it was supposed to cure. The requirement of a jury trial did not protect the insane at all, nor the sane for that matter, since it left the decision as to insanity in the hands of a lay jury ignorant of the medical aspects of mental disease. . . . Needless to say, the Illinois law met with unanimous opposition of the psychiatric and allied professions."[†]

Ironically, we are now again treated to Packard-like exposés of psychiatric "abuses" (some in a Soviet setting, as if the Communists had invented this evil as well!), and to the same old legalistic remedies for it that were tried a century ago. It seems inevitable that until psychiatric slavery is abolished, the "care" of psychiatric slaves would shift back and forth between the medical and legal professions.

I[1]

I made no physical resistance to this order, but told my husband I should not go voluntarily into an asylum, and leave my six children, and my previous babe, without some kind of trial.

He replied, "I am doing as the laws of Illinois allow me to do. You have no protection in law but myself, and I am protecting you now. It is for your good I am doing this; I want to save your soul! You don't believe in total depravity, and I want to make you right."

[†] Ibid., p. 307.
[1] From E. P. W. Packard (Mrs.), *Modern Persecution or Insane Asylums Unveiled*, Vol. I. (Hartford: Case, Lockwood & Brainard, Printers and Binders, 1873), pp. 53–54.

"Husband, have I not a right to my opinion?"

"Yes; you have a right to your opinions if you think right."

"But does not the Constitution defend the right of private judgment to all American citizens?"

"Yes, to all citizens it does defend this right. But you are not a citizen; while a married woman, you are a legal nonentity, without even a soul in law. In short, you are dead as to any legal existence, while a married woman, and therefore have no legal protection as a married woman."

I could not then credit this statement, but now *know* it to be too sadly true, for the statute of Illinois expressly states that a man may put his wife into an insane asylum without evidence of insanity. The law now stands on 96th page, section 10, of Illinois statute-book, under the general head of "Charities!" It was passed Feb. 15th, 1851, and reads thus:

"Married women and infants, who, in the judgment of the medical superintendent (meaning the Superintendent of the Illinois State Hospital for the Insane) are evidently insane of distracted, may be entered or detained in the hospital on the request of the husband of the woman or the guardian of the infant, *without* the evidence of insanity required in other cases."

Hon. S. S. Jones, of St. Charles, Illinois, thus remarks upon this Act: "Thus we see a corrupt husband, with money enough to corrupt a Superintendent, can get rid of a wife as effectually as was ever done in a more barbarous age. The Superintendent may be corrupted either with money or influence, that he thinks will give him position, place or emoluments. Is not this a pretty statute to be incorporated into our laws no more than thirteen years ago? Why not confine the husband at the instance of the wife, as well as the wife at the instance of the husband? The wife evidently had no voice in making the law."

II[2]

In preparing a report of this Trial, the writer has had but one object in view, namely, to present a faithful history of the case as narrated by the witnesses upon the stand, who gave their testimony under the solemnity of an oath. The exact language employed by the witnesses has been used, and the written testimony given in full, with the exception of a letter, written by Dr. McFarland, to Rev. Theophilus Packard, which letter was retained by Mr. Packard, and the writer was unable to obtain a copy. The substance of the letter is found in the body of the report, and has been submitted to the examination of Mr. Packard's counsel, who agree that it is correctly stated.

This case was on trial before the Hon. Charles R. Starr, at Kankakee City, Illinois, from Monday, January 11th, 1864, to Tuesday the 19th, and came up on an application made by Mrs. Packard, under the *Habeas Corpus Act*, to be discharged from imprisonment by her husband in their own house.

The case has disclosed a state of facts most wonderful and startling. Reverend Theophilus Packard came to Manteno, in Kankakee county, Illinois, seven years since, and has remained in charge of the Presbyterian Church of that place until the past two years.

In the winter of 1859 and 1860, there were differences of opinion between Mr. Packard and Mrs. Packard, upon matters of religion, which resulted in prolonged and vigorous debate in the home circle. The heresies maintained by Mrs. Packard were carried by the husband from the fireside to the pulpit, and made a matter of inquiry by the church, and which soon resulted in open warfare; and her views and propositions were misrepresented and animad-

---

[2] This report was written by Stephen R. Moore, Attorney at Law, who was Mrs. Packard's counsel in her successful suit for *habeas corpus* against her husband. From E. P. W. Packard (Mrs.), *Modern Persecution or Married Woman's Liabilities*, Vol. II. (Hartford: Case, Lockwood & Brainard, Printers and Binders, 1873), pp. 22–37.

verted upon, from the pulpit, and herself made the subject of unjust criticism. In the Bible-Class and in the Sabbath School, she maintained her religious tenets, and among her kindred and friends, defended herself from the obloquy of her husband.

To make the case fully understood, I will here remark, that Mr. Packard was educated in the Calvinistic faith, and for twenty-nine years has been a preacher of that creed, and would in no wise depart from the religion of his fathers. He is cold, selfish, and illiberal in his views, possessed of but little talent, and a physiognomy innocent of expression. He has large self-will, and his stubbornness is only exceeded by his bigotry.

Mrs. Packard is a lady of fine mental endowments, and blest with a liberal education. She is an original, vigorous, masculine thinker, and were it not for her superior judgment, combined with native modesty, she would rank as a "strong-minded woman." As it is, her conduct comports strictly with the sphere usually occupied by woman. She dislikes parade or show of any kind. Her confidence that Right will prevail, leads her to too tamely submit to wrongs. She was educated in the same religious belief with her husband, and during the first twenty years of married life, his labors in the parish and in the pulpit were greatly relieved by the willing hand and able intellect of his wife.

Phrenologists would also say of her, that her self-will was large and her married life tended in no wise to diminish this phrenological bump. They have been married twenty-five years, and have six children, the issue of their intermarriage, the youngest of whom was eighteen months old when she was kidnapped and transferred to Jacksonville. The older children have maintained a firm position against the abuse and persecutions of their father towards their mother, but were of too tender age to render her any material assistance.

Her views of religion are more in accordance with the liberal views of the age in which we live. She scouts the Calvinistic doctrine of man's total depravity, and that God has foreordained some to be saved and others to be damned. She stands fully on the platform of man's free agency and accountability to God for his actions. She believes that man, and nations, are progressive; and that in His own good time, and in accordance with His great purposes, Right will prevail over Wrong, and the oppressed will be freed from the oppressor. She believes slavery to be a national sin, and the church and the pulpit a proper place to combat this sin. These, in brief, are the points in her religious creed which were combated by Mr. Packard, and were denominated by him as "emanations from the devil," or "the vagaries of a crazed brain."

For maintaining such ideas as above indicated, Mr. Packard denounced her from the pulpit, denied her the privilege of family prayer in the home circle, expelled her from the Bible Class, and refused to let her be heard in the Sabbath School. He excluded her from her friends, and made her a prisoner in her own house.

Her reasonings and her logic appeared to him as the ravings of a mad woman—her religion was the religion of the devil. To justify his conduct, he gave out that she was insane, and found a few willing believers, among his family connections.

This case was commenced by filing a petition in the words following, to wit:

STATE OF ILLINOIS,
Kankakee County

To the Honorable Charles R. Starr, *Judge of the 20th Judicial Circuit in the State of Illinois.*

William Haslet, Daniel Beedy, Zalmon Hanford, and Joseph Younglove, of said county, on behalf of Elizabeth P. W. Packard, wife of Theophilus Packard, of said county, respectfully represent unto your Honor, that said Elizabeth P. W. Packard, is unlawfully restrained of her liberty, at Manteno, in the county of Kankakee, by her husband, Rev. Theophilus Packard, being forcibly confined and imprisoned in a close room of the dwelling-house of her said husband, for a long time, to wit, for the space of six weeks, her said husband refusing to let her visit her neighbors and refusing her neighbors to visit her; that they believe her said husband is about to forcibly convey her from out the State; that they believe there is no just cause or ground for restraining said wife of her liberty; that they believe that said wife is a mild and amiable woman. And they are advised and believe, that said husband cruelly abuses and misuses said wife, by depriving her of her winter's clothing, this cold and inclement weather, and that there is no necessity for such cruelty on the part of said husband to said wife; and they are advised and believe, that said wife desires to come to Kankakee City, to make application to your Honor for a writ of *habeas corpus*, to liberate herself from said confinement or imprisonment, and that said husband refused and refuses to allow said wife to come to Kankakee City for said purpose; and that these petitioners make application for a writ of *habeas corpus* in her behalf, at her request. These petitioners therefore pray that a writ of *habeas corpus* may forthwith issue, commanding said Theophilus Packard to produce the body of said wife, before your Honor, according to law, and that said wife may be discharged from said imprisonment.

(Signed),

William Haslet
Daniel Beedy
Zalmon Hanford
J. Younglove

J. W. Orr } Petitioners' Attorneys
H. Loring

Stephen R. Moore—*Counsel*

STATE OF ILLINOIS
Kankakee County

William Haslet, Daniel Beedy, Zalmon Hanford, and Joseph Younglove, whose names are subscribed to the above petition, being duly sworn, severally depose and say, that the matters and facts set forth in the above petition are true in substance and fact, to the best of their knowledge and belief.

> William Haslet
> Daniel Beedy
> Zalmon Hanford
> J. Younglove

Sworn to and subscribed before me, this 11th day of January, A.D. 1864

> MASON B. LOOMIS, J.P.

Upon the above petition, the Honorable C. R. Starr, Judge as aforesaid, issued a writ of *habeas corpus*, as follows:

STATE OF ILLINOIS
Kankakee County

The People of the State of Illinois, To Theophilus Packard:

We command you, That the body of Elizabeth P. W. Packard, in your custody detained and imprisoned, as it is said, together with the day and cause of caption and detention, by whatsoever name the same may be called, you safely have before Charles R. Starr, Judge of the Twentieth Judicial Circuit, State of Illinois, at his chambers, at Kankakee City in the said county, on the 12th instant, at one o'clock, P.M., and to do and receive all and singular those things which the said Judge shall then and there con-

MADNESS AND MARRIAGE 61

sider of her in this behalf, and have you then and there this writ.

Witness, Charles R. Starr, Judge aforesaid, this 11th day of January, A.D. 1864.

(REVENUE STAMP.)
CHARLES R. STARR, (SEAL.)
Judge of the Twentieth Judicial Circuit
of the State of Illinois.

Indorsed: "By the *Habeas Corpus Act*."

To said writ, the Rev. Theophilus Packard made the following return:

The within named Theophilus Packard does hereby certify, to the within named, the Honorable Charles R. Starr, Judge of the Twentieth Judicial Circuit of the State of Illinois, that the within named Elizabeth P. W. Packard is now in my custody, before your Honor. That the said Elizabeth is the wife of the undersigned, and is and has been for more than three years past insane, and for about three years of that time was in the Insane Asylum of the State of Illinois, under treatment, as an insane person. That she was discharged from said Asylum, without being cured, and is incurably insane, on or about the 18th day of June, A.D. 1863, and that since the 23rd day of October, the undersigned has kept the said Elizabeth with him in Manteno, in this county, and while he has faithfully and anxiously watched, cared for, and guarded the said Elizabeth, yet he has not unlawfully restrained her of her liberty; and has not confined and imprisoned her in a close room, in the dwelling-house of the undersigned, or in any other place, or way, but, on the contrary, the undersigned has allowed her all the liberty compatible with her welfare and safety. That the undersigned is about to remove his residence from Manteno, in this State, to the town of Deerfield, in the county of Franklin, in the State of Massachusetts, and designs and intends to take his said wife Elizabeth with him. That the undersigned has never misused or abused the said Elizabeth, by depriving her of her winter's clothing, but, on the contrary, the undersigned has always treated the said Elizabeth with kindness and affection, and has provided her with a sufficient quantity of winter clothing and other clothing; and that the said Elizabeth has never made any request of the undersigned, for liberty to come to Kankakee City, for the purpose of suing out a writ of *habeas corpus*. The undersigned hereby presents a letter from Andrew McFarland, Superintendent of the Illinois State Hospital, at Jacksonville, in this State, showing her discharge, and reasons of discharge, from said institution, which is marked "A," and is made of part of this return. And also presents a certificate from the said Andrew McFarland, under the seal of said hospital, marked "C," refusing to re-admit the said Elizabeth again into said hospital, on the ground of her being incurably insane, which is also hereby made a part of this return.

THEOPHILUS PACKARD.

Dated January 12, 1864

The Court, upon its own motion, ordered an issue to be formed, as to the sanity or insanity of Mrs. E. P. W. Packard, and ordered a venire of twelve men to aid the Court in the investigation of said issue. And thereupon a venire was issued.

The counsel for the respondent, Thomas P. Bonfield, Mason B. Loomis, and Hon. C. A. Lake, moved the court to quash the venire, on the ground that the court had no right to call a jury to determine the question, on an application to be discharged on a writ of *habeas corpus*. The court overruled the motion; and thereupon the following jury was selected:

John Stiles, Daniel G. Bean, V. H. Young, F. G. Hutchinson, Thomas Muncey, H. Hirshberg, Nelson Jarvais, William Hyer, George H. Andrews, J. F. Mafit, Lemuel Milk, G. M. Lyons.

Christopher W. Knott was the first witness sworn by the

respondent, to maintain the issue on his part, that she was insane; who being sworn, deposed and said:

I am a practicing physician in Kankakee City. Have been in practice fifteen years. Have seen Mrs. Packard; saw her three or four years ago. Am not much acquainted with her. Had never seen her until I was called to see her at that time. I was called to visit her by Theophilus Packard. I thought her partially deranged on religious matters, and gave a certificate to that effect. I certified that she was insane upon the subject of religion. I have never seen her since.

Cross-examination—This visit I made her was three or four years ago. I was there twice—one-half hour each time. I visited her on request of Mr. Packard, to determine if she was insane. I learned from him that he designed to convey her to the State Asylum. Do not know whether she was aware of my object or not. Her mind appeared to be excited on the subject of religion; on all other subjects she was perfectly rational. It was probably caused by overtaxing the mental faculties. She was what might be called a monomaniac. Monomania is insanity on one subject. Three-fourths of the religious community are insane in the same manner, in my opinion. Her insanity was such that with a little rest she would readily have recovered from it. The female mind is more excitable than the male. I saw her perhaps one-half hour each time I visited her. I formed my judgment as to her insanity wholly from conversing with her. I could see nothing except an unusual zealousness and warmth upon religious topics. Nothing was said in my conversation with her, about disagreeing with Mr. Packard on religious topics. Mr. Packard introduced the subject of religion the first time I was there; the second time, I introduced the subject. Mr. Packard and Mr. Comstock were present. The subject was pressed on her for the purpose of drawing her out. Mrs. Packard would manifest more zeal than most people upon any subject that interested her. I take her to be a lady of fine mental abilities, possessing more ability than ordinarily found. She is possessed of a nervous temperament, easily excited, and has a strong will.

I would say that she was insane, the same as I would say Henry Ward Beecher, Spurgeon, Horace Greeley, and like persons, are insane. Probably three weeks intervened between the visits I made Mrs. Packard. This was in June, 1860.

Re-examined—She is a woman of large, active brain, and nervous temperament. I take her to be a woman of good intellect. There is no subject which excites people so much as religion. Insanity produces, oftentimes, ill-feelings towards the best friends, and particularly the family, or those more nearly related to the insane person—but not so with monomania. She told me, in the conversation, that the Calvinistic doctrines were wrong, and that she had been compelled to withdraw from the church. She said that Mr. Packard was more insane than she was, and that people would find it out. I had no doubt that she was insane. I only considered her insane on that subject, and she was not bad at that. I could not judge whether it was hereditary. I thought if she was withdrawn from conversation and excitement, she could have got well in a short time. Confinement in any shape, or restraint, would have made her worse. I did not think it was a bad case; it only required rest.

J. W. Brown, being sworn, said:

I am a physician; live in this city; have no extensive acquaintance with Mrs. Packard. Saw her three or four weeks ago. I examined her as to her sanity or insanity. I was requested to make a visit, and had an extended conference with her; I spent some three hours with her. I had no difficulty in arriving at the conclusion, in my mind, that she was insane.

Cross-examination—I visited her by request of Mr. Packard, at her house. The children were in and out of the room; no one else was present. I concealed my object in visiting her. She asked me if I was a physician, and I told her no; that I was an agent, selling sewing machines, and had come there to sell her one.

The first subject we conversed about was sewing machines. She showed no sign of insanity on that subject.

The next subject discussed, was the social condition of the female sex. She exhibited no special marks of insanity on that subject, although she had many ideas quite at variance with mine, on the subject.

The subject of politics was introduced. She spoke of the condition of the North and the South. She illustrated her difficulties with Mr. Packard, by the difficulties between the North and the South. She said the South was wrong, and was waging war for two wicked purposes: first, to overthrow a good government, and second, to establish a despotism on the inhuman principle of human slavery. But that the North, having right on their side, would prevail. So Mr. Packard was opposing her, to overthrow free thought in woman; that the despotism of man may prevail over the wife; but that she had right and truth on her side, and that she would prevail. During this conversation I did not fully conclude that she was insane.

I brought up the subject of religion. We discussed that subject for a long time, and then I had not the slightest difficulty in concluding that she was hopelessly insane.

Question. Dr., what particular idea did she advance on the subject of religion that led you to the conclusion that she was hopelessly insane?

Answer. She advanced many of them. I formed my opinion not so much on any one idea advanced, as upon her whole conversation. She then said that she was the "Personification of the Holy Ghost." I did not know what she meant by that.

Ques. Was not this the idea conveyed to you in that conversation: That there are three attributes of the Deity—the Father, the Son, and the Holy Ghost? Now, did she not say, that the attributes of the Father were represented in mankind, in man; that the attributes of the Holy Ghost were represented in woman; and that the Son was the fruit of these two attributes of the Deity?

Ans. Well, I am not sure but that was the idea conveyed, though I did not fully get her idea at the time.

Ques. Was not that a new idea to you in theology?
Ans. It was.

Ques. Are you much of a theologian?

Ans. No.

Ques. Then because the idea was a novel one to you, you pronounced her insane.

Ans. Well, I pronounced her insane on that and other things that exhibited themselves in this conversation.

Ques. Did she not show more familiarity with the subject of religion and the questions of theology, than you had with these subjects?

Ans. I do not pretend much knowledge on these subjects.

Ques. What else did she say or do there, that showed marks of insanity?

Ans. She claimed to be better than her husband—that she was right—and that he was wrong—and that all she did was good, and all he did was bad—that she was farther advanced than other people, and more nearly perfection. She found fault particularly that Mr. Packard would not discuss their points of difference on religion in an open, manly way, instead of going around and denouncing her as crazy to her friends and to the church.

She had a great aversion to being called insane. Before I got through the conversation she exhibited a great dislike to me, and almost treated me in a contemptuous manner. She appeared quite lady-like. She had a great reverence for God, and a regard for religious and pious people.

Re-examined. Ques. Dr., you may now state all the reasons you have for pronouncing her insane.

Ans. I have written down, in order, the reasons which I had, to found my opinion on, that she was insane. I will read them.

1. That she claimed to be in advance of the age thirty or forty years.

2. That she disliked to be called insane.

3. That she pronounced me a copperhead, and did not prove the fact.

4. An incoherency of thought. That she failed to illuminate me and fill me with light.

5. Her aversion to the doctrine of the total depravity of man.

6. Her claim to perfection, or near perfection in action and conduct.

7. Her aversion to being called insane.

8. Her feeling towards her husband.

9. Her belief that to call her insane and abuse her, was blasphemy against the Holy Ghost.

10. Her explanation of this idea.

11. Incoherency of thought and ideas.

12. Her extreme aversion to the doctrine of the total depravity of mankind, and in the same conversation, saying her husband was a specimen of man's total depravity.

13. The general history of the case.

14. Her belief that some calamity would befall her, owing to my being there, and her refusal to shake hands with me when I went away.

15. Her viewing the subject of religion from the osteric standpoint of Christian exegetical analysis, and agglutinating the polsynthetical ectoblasts of homogeneous asceticism.

The witness left the stand amid roars of laughter; and it required some moments to restore order in the court room.

Joseph H. Way, sworn, and said:

I am a practicing physician in Kankakee City, Illinois. I made a medical examination of Mrs. Packard a few weeks since at her house; was there perhaps two hours. On most subjects she was quite sane. On the subject of religion I thought she had some ideas that are not generally entertained. At that time I thought her to be somewhat deranged or excited on that subject; since that time I have thought perhaps I was not a proper judge, for I am not much posted on disputed points in theology, and I find that other people entertain similar ideas. They are not in accordance with my views, but that is no evidence that she is insane.

Cross-examined. I made this visit at her house, or his house, perhaps, at Manteno. I conversed on various subjects. She was perfectly sane on every subject except religion, and I would not swear now that she was insane. She seemed to have been laboring under an undue excitement on that subject. She has a nervous temperament, and is easily excited. She said she liked her children, and that it was hard to be torn from them. That none but a mother could feel the anguish she had suffered; that while she was confined in the Asylum, the children had been educated by their father to call her insane. She said she would have them punished if they called their own mother insane, for it was not right.

Abijah Dole, sworn, and says:

I know Mrs. Packard; have known her twenty-five or thirty years. I am her brother-in-law. Lived in Manteno seven years. Mrs. Packard has lived there six years. I have been sent for several times by her and Mr. Packard, and found her in an excited state of mind. I was there frequently; we were very familiar. One morning early, I was sent for; she was in the west room; she was in her night clothes. She took me by the hand and led me to the bed. Libby was lying in bed, moaning and moving her head. Mrs. Packard now spoke and said, "How pure we are." "I am one of the children of heaven; Libby is one of the branches." "The woman shall bruise the serpent's head." She called Mr. Packard a devil. She said Brother Dole, these are serious matters. If Brother Haslet will help me, we will crush the body. She said Christ had come into the world to save men, and that she had come to save woman. Her hair was disheveled. Her face looked wild. This was over three years ago.

I was there again one morning after this. She came to me. She pitied me for marrying my wife, who is a sister to Mr. Packard; said, I might find an agreeable companion. She said if she had cultivated amativeness, she would have made a more agreeable companion. She took me to another room and talked about going away; this was in June, before they took her to the State Hospital. She sent for me again; she was in the east room; she was very cordial. She wanted me to intercede for Theophilus, who was at Marshall, Michigan; she wanted him to stay there, and it was thought not advisable for him to stay. We wished him to come away, but did not tell her the reasons. He was with a Swedenborgian.

After this I was called there once in the night. She said she could not live with Mr. Packard, and she thought she had better go away. One time she was in the Bible-class. The question came up in regard to Moses smiting the Egyptian; she thought Moses had acted too hasty, but that all things worked for the glory of God. I requested her to keep quiet, and she agreed to do it.

I have had no conversation with Mrs. Packard since her return from the Hospital; she will not talk with me because she thinks I think she is insane. Her brother came to see her; he said he had not seen her for four or five years. I tried to have Mrs. Packard talk with him, and she would not have anything to do with him because he said she was a crazy woman. She generally was in the kitchen when I was there, overseeing her household affairs.

I was Superintendent of the Sabbath School. One Sabbath, just at the close of the school, I was behind the desk, and almost like a vision she appeared before me, and requested to deliver or read an address to the school. I was much surprised; I felt so bad, I did not know what to do. (At this juncture the witness became very much affected, and choked up so that he could not proceed, and cried so loud that he could be heard in any part of the court-room. When he became calm, he went on and said,) I was willing to gratify her all I could, for I knew she was crazy, but I did not want to take the responsibility myself, so I put it to a vote of the school, if she should be allowed to read it. She was allowed to read it. It occupied ten or fifteen minutes in reading.

I cannot state any of the particulars of that paper. It bore evidence of her insanity. She went on and condemned the church, all in all, and the individuals composing the church, because they did not agree with her. She looked very wild and very much excited. She seemed to be insane. She came to church one morning just as services commenced, and wished to have the church act upon her letter withdrawing from the church immediately. Mr. Packard was in the pulpit. She wanted to know if Brother Dole and Brother Merrick were in the church, and wanted them to have it acted upon. This was three years ago, just before she was taken away to the hospital.

Cross-examined. I supposed when I first went into the room that her influence over the child had caused the child to become deranged. The child was ten years old. I believed that she had exerted some mesmeric or other influence over the child, that caused it to moan and toss its head. The child had been sick with brain fever; I learned that after I got there. I suppose the mother had considerable anxiety over the child; I suppose she had been watching over the child all night, and that would tend to excite her. The child got well. It was sick several days after this; it was lying on the bed moaning and tossing its head; the mother did not appear to be alarmed. Mr. Packard was not with her; she was all alone; she did not say that Mr. Packard did not show proper care for the sick child. I suppose she thought Libby would die.

Her ideas on religion did not agree with mine, nor with my view of the Bible.

I knew Mr. Packard thought her insane, and did not want her to discuss these questions in the Sabbath School. I knew he had opposed her more or less. This letter to the church was for the purpose of asking for a letter from the church.

Question. Was it an indication of insanity that she wanted to leave the Presbyterian Church?

Answer. I think it strange that she should ask for letters from the church. She would not leave the church unless she was insane.

I am a member of the church—I believe the church is right. I believe everything the church does is right. I believe everything in the Bible.

Ques. Do you believe literally that Jonah was swallowed by a whale, and remained in its belly three days, and was then cast up?

Ans. I do.

Ques. Do you believe literally that Elijah went direct up

to Heaven in a chariot of fire—that the chariot had wheels, and seats, and was drawn by horses?

Ans. I do—for with God all things are possible.

Ques. Do you believe Mrs. Packard was insane, and is insane?

Ans. I do.

III[3]

On the 18th day of January, 1864, at 10 o'clock, p.m. the jury retired for consultation, under the charge of the sheriff. After an absence of seven minutes, they returned into court, and gave the following verdict:

> STATE OF ILLINOIS,
> Kankakee County
>
> We, the undersigned, Jurors in the Case of Mrs. Elizabeth P. W. Packard, alleged to be insane, having heard the evidence in the case, are satisfied that said Elizabeth P. W. Packard is SANE.
>
> John Stiles, *Foreman*
> Daniel G. Bean
> F. G. Hutchinson
> V. H. Young
> G. M. Lyons
> Thomas Muncey
> H. Hirshberg
> Nelson Jervais
> William Hyer
> Geo. H. Andrews
> J. F. Mafit
> Lemuel Milk

Cheers rose from every part of the house; the ladies waved their handkerchiefs, and pressed around Mrs. Packard, and extended her their congratulations. It was some-

[3] Ibid., pp. 57–60.

time before the outburst of applause could be checked. When order was restored, the counsel for Mrs. Packard moved the court, that she be discharged. Thereupon the court ordered the clerk to enter the following order:

STATE OF ILLINOIS
Kankakee County

> It is hereby ordered that Mrs. Elizabeth P. W. Packard be relieved from all restraint incompatible with her condition as a sane woman.
> C. R. Starr,
> Judge of the Twentieth Judicial District
> of the State of Illinois.

January 18, 1864.

Thus ended the trial of this remarkable case. During each day of the proceedings the court-room was crowded to excess by an anxious audience of ladies and gentlemen, who are seldom in our courts. The verdict of the jury was received with applause, and hosts of friends crowded upon Mrs. Packard to congratulate her upon her release. . . .

On Monday morning, and before the defense had rested their case, Mr. Packard left the State, bag and baggage, for parts unknown, having first mortgaged his property for all it is worth to his sister and other parties.

We cannot do better than close this report with the following editorial from the Kankakee *Gazette*, of January 21, 1864:

MRS. PACKARD

The case of this lady, which has attracted so much attention and excited so much interest for ten days past, was decided on Monday evening last, and resulted, as almost every person thought it must, in a complete vindication of her sanity. The jury retired on Monday evening, after hearing the arguments of the counsel; and after a brief consultation, they brought in a verdict that Mrs. Packard is a SANE woman.

Thus has resulted an investigation which Mrs. Packard has long and always desired should be had, but which her cruel husband has ever sternly refused her. She has always asked and earnestly pleaded for a jury trial of her case, but her relentless persecutor has ever turned a deaf ear to her entreaties, and flagrantly violated all the dictates of justice and humanity.

She has suffered the alienation of friends and relatives—the shock of a kidnapping by her husband and his posse when forcibly removed to the Asylum—has endured three years incarceration in that Institution—upon the general treatment in which there is severe comment in the State, and which, in her special case, was aggravatingly unpleasant and ill-favored—and when at last returning to her home found her husband's saintly blood still congealed; a winter of perpetual frown on his face, and the sad, dull monotony of "Insane! Insane!" escaping his lips in all his communications to and concerning her—her children, the youngest of the four at home being less than four years of age, over whose slumbers she had watched, and whose wailings she had hushed with all a mother's care and tenderness—taught to look upon her as insane, and not to respect the counsels or heed the voice of a maniac just loosed from the Asylum, doom sealed by official certificates.

Soon her aberration of mind led her to seek some of her better clothing carefully kept from her by her husband, which very woman-like act was seized by him as an excuse for confining her in her room, and depriving her of her apparel, and excluding her lady friends. Believing that he was about to again forcibly take her to an asylum, four responsible citizens of that village made affidavit of facts which caused the investigation as to her sanity or insanity. During the whole trial she was present, and counseled with her attorneys in the management of the case.

Notwithstanding the severe treatment she has received for nearly four years past, the outrages she has suffered, the wrong to her nature she has endured, she deported herself during the trial as one who is not only not insane, but as one possessing intellectual endowments of a high order, and an equipoise and control of mind far above the majority of human kind.

The heroic motto: "suffer and be strong," is fairly illustrated in her case. While many would have opposed force to his force, displayed frantic emotions of displeasure at such treatment, or sat convulsed and "maddened with the passion of her part," she meekly submitted to the tortures of her bigoted tormentor, trusting and believing in God's Providence the hour of her vindication and her release from thraldom would come. And now the fruit of her suffering and persecution has all the autumn glory of perfection. . . .

Feeling the accusations of his guilty conscience, seeing meshes of the net with which he had kept her surrounded were broken, and a storm-cloud of indignation about to break over his head in pitiless fury, the intolerant Packard, after encumbering their property with trust deeds, and despoiling her of her furniture and clothing, left the country. Let him wander! with the mark of infamy upon his brow, through far-off states, where distance and obscurity may diminish till the grave shall cover the wrongs it cannot heal.

It is to be hoped Mrs. Packard will make immediate application for a divorce, and thereby relieve herself of a repetition of the wrongs and outrages she has suffered by him who for the past four years has only used the marriage relation to persecute and torment her in a merciless and unfeeling manner.

IV[4]

In Dr. McFarland's tenth biennial report of 1866, he utters severe criticisms on an act passed by the Legislature of 1865, and complains of the injustice of such legislation as allows persons accused of insanity to have a fair trial before imprisonment.

The act which he thus ignores, provides, as Dr. McFarland says:

[4] Ibid., pp. 214–15.

"Any person whose condition requires his or her being sent to the hospital, shall be personally present in the court while the examination goes on, being served with notice, stimulated by counsel, invited to cross-examine witnesses, and placed, in all instances, and in every respect as the active defendant in the case. This act is so cruel in its effect upon those for whose interest it must be presumed to have been introduced, that silence is impossible, until attention is called to it. And his voice would be for the summary repeal of the act in question, to protest against the existence of which is the plain duty of this report. What antagonisms of the most painful kind are wantonly engendered; what violations of delicacy and often of decency, what outrages upon mental and physical suffering must be the result while this enactment exists. And these are only slight specimens of the wrongs of which this act will be the prolific stock."

We wish to ask any candid person a few simple, commonplace questions in reference to the above extract:

Which course would be the most likely to engender antagonism—the consignment of a relative to an indefinite term of imprisonment, without allowing them any hearing or any chance at self-defense—or, by allowing them a fair trial and opportunity of self-defense before imprisonment?

Which would be the most probable "prolific stock" of wrongs to humanity—the imprisonment of an individual on the decision of twelve impartial men, after a fair hearing of both parties, or, on the decision of one interested man, on the simple testimony of others, without proof?

Is it no more probable that *one* man may possibly be corrupted by motives of interest and policy to make an unjust decision, than that *twelve* men could be thus corrupted?

Dr. McFarland asserts that "a wrong under the old law, under which nine-tenths of all the patients have been received, is as nearly a moral impossibility as can well exist."

Is it a moral impossibility to get a sane person into that institution, while a statute exists, which expressly permits a certain class of persons to be there imprisoned without evidence of insanity, and without any trial—which statute suspends the personal liberty of this class of citizens wholly upon the decision of one fallible man?

And "is it as nearly a moral impossibility as can well exist," that this one man may possibly err in judgment?

2

EXPERT TESTIMONY IN JUDICIAL PROCEEDINGS*

John Ordronaux

> The author of this essay—who was identified as both a physician and an attorney and a "State Commissioner in Lunacy"—pleads against the battle of psychiatric experts in court and for replacing this practice with reliance solely on the testimony of "impartial" court-appointed experts. Although the language is in places old-fashioned, the argument here presented is exactly the same as that advanced by many modern experts on forensic psychiatry. This selection not only demonstrates convincingly that the contemporary psychiatric plea for court-appointed experts is ripe with age and has nothing whatever to do with the so-called discoveries of modern psychiatry, but also illustrates the implacable hostility that institutional psychiatry has always shown, and continues to show, toward the fundamental principles of Anglo-American law, and especially toward the Rule of Law.

There is a growing tendency to look with distrust upon every form of skilled testimony, and to abandon it to the risks of polemical detraction and obloquy. Nor is this strange. . . . If science, for a consideration, can be induced to prove anything which a party litigant needs, in

* From John Ordronaux, "On Expert Testimony in Judicial Proceedings," *The American Journal of Insanity*, 30:312–22 (Jan.), 1874.

order to sustain his side of the issue, then science is fairly open to the charge of venality and perjury, rendered the more base by the disguise of natural truth in which she robes herself. In fact, the calling of experts has now come to be regarded as the signal for a display of forensic pyrotechnics, beneath whose smoke and lurid glare, law, common sense and unalloyed justice, are swept away in a whirlwind of muddy metaphysics. . . .

That these facts, in relation more particularly to expert testimony, are attracting public attention everywhere, and silently preparing the way for some speedy demand upon the law-making power to cast out the old fetich of procedure by which courts are still fettered, is becoming matter of daily observation. And the sign is so good and augurs so well for the redemption of the law from the embarrassing clogs of tradition, that we feel it a duty to hasten the time of this enfranchisement, by bringing the matter forward with all the power of presentation of which we are capable.

In their last annual report to the Legislature, the Managers of the New York State Lunatic Asylum feel themselves called upon to allude to the subject in the following very pertinent observations:

> It may not be amiss to observe that this matter of the testimony of experts, especially in cases of alleged insanity, has gone to such an extravagance that it has really become of late years a profitable profession to be an expert witness, at the command of any party and ready for any party, for a sufficient and often an exorbitant fee; thus destroying the real value of the testimony of unbiased experts. Vaunted and venal expertness is usually worthless for evidence; and yet such testimony is getting to be in great demand. One expert, whether real or assumptive, is set up against another; and finally it will result that, by competition, pretending inexpertness, will prevail, by numbers, against the real expertness of those few thoroughly qualified men whose judgement is the

mature experience collected from years of daily study and practical observation. Obviously it does not become States, or great tribunals, or public justice, that the testimony which settles matters of weight should be trifled with as it is for an emolument; and experts should only be called, as formerly they were, by the court itself, on its own judgment of the necessity requiring them; and when called at all, they should be the sworn advisers of the court and jury, and not witnesses summoned in the particular behalf of any party; nor should they be permitted to receive either fee or reward from any party, but only from the court or the public. Capable judges are competent to say, in any case, whether the court requires evidence of experts for its information in matters of technical knowledge or science, and also to say who shall be particularly summoned for his acknowledged expertness; and should, therefore, have the control of that sort of testimony, which is only allowable to enlighten the court and jury, and not to be the ordinary captious weapon of attorneys and counselors, nor to be the theoretical, one-sided opinions of sciolists, founded on some hypothetical case which deflects more or less from the actual truth of the real case in question.

That some remedy is called for in the interests of both humanity and justice all are ready to admit, and that the remedy should be so far reaching in its effects, as the disorder it is intended to alleviate, is equally apparent. The difficulty of making any change, however, has been generally over-estimated, from the assumption that it would necessarily derange well-established principles of jurisprudence. But this is a danger more imaginary than real, and like many other figments of the imagination grows smaller the nearer we approach to it. . . .

The most cursory glance shows us that the Common Law

procedure relating to the whole field of expert testimony, whether in the method of summoning, of examining, or of presenting such testimony to the jury is paradoxical in principle and self-contradictory in practice. The very term witness, when applied to an expert, is at the start a legal paradox. It owes its origin to the custom of allowing experts to be summoned by either party litigant, and in the exclusive interest of that side from which they either have received, or expect to receive a retainer. Consequently, and in that capacity, they come upon the stand with minds prepared to favor only that view of the case which they are retained to sustain. . . .

The expert being in no proper sense of the word a witness, should have his status definitely determined, should be free from alliances with either party, and give his opinions only upon an agreed statement of facts. In other words he should arbitrate and not testify. So long as he is introduced as a party witness, the opposite side have the right to confront and necessarily to cross-examine him, but how unphilosophical, not to say ridiculous even, is the idea of an expert being cross-examined for the purpose of testing his professional knowledge, by a layman. The entire effect and benefit of his participation in any trial is thus mutilated, deformed and nullified by the legal paradox which assumes him to be a witness. . . .

In whatever direction we look, we see how inevitably these conflicting principles arise from the first departure in recognizing the true position of the expert. Having once been summoned as an ordinary witness by one party, he is fore-doomed to that position throughout his entire service in court; is cross-examined as such and his opinions before the jury lose proportionally the weight which, but for this, would attach itself to them. No jury can be expected to place absolute confidence in the statement of a witness called exclusively in the interest of one party. They will balance probabilities even in the matter of his professional accuracy, whenever his opinions conflict with their own preconceived ideas upon the subject. To that extent, therefore, they will sit in judgment upon his opinion, rather than accept it as a specified adjudication in a matter admitted to be beyond their knowledge and comprehension. Nor is it laying too much emphasis upon the results of such repudiation of skilled testimony to affirm, that it begets an overweening self-confidence in jurors, which is not slow to extend from the opinions of experts to those of the court.

3

THE PSYCHIATRIC ASSASSINATION OF KING LUDWIG II OF BAVARIA

Werner Richter

Because of his fate at the hands of psychiatrists, historians often refer to Ludwig II of Bavaria (1864–86) as the "mad king." The sad story of Ludwig makes clear, however, that he was actually not particularly "mad" even by traditional psychiatric standards.* The significance of his "commitment" lies in that this was, to my knowledge, the first successful public psychiatric assassination of a prominent person. This event thus marks the beginning of an era that was to see the ever-increasing popularity of accusation by psychiatric diagnosis and execution by psychiatric incarceration. As I discussed this case in detail elsewhere,† it should suffice to note here, first, that none of the psychiatrists who declared Ludwig mentally ill had examined him; and second, that two days after his incarceration at the Berg Castle, which had been converted into a sort of private madhouse for the exclusive use of the king, Ludwig tried to drown himself in the lake adjoining the castle, and when Dr. Gudden, the psychiatrist who held him prisoner, attempted to stop him, he drowned Gudden and then himself.

* From Werner Richter, *The Mad Monarch: The Life and Times of Ludwig II of Bavaria*, trans. by William S. Schlamm (Chicago: Henry Regnery, 1954), pp. 250–51.
† See Thomas S. Szasz, *Law, Liberty, and Psychiatry: An Inquiry into the Social Uses of Mental Health Practices* (New York: Macmillan, 1963), pp. 48–53.

In the morning hours of June 8, 1886, Dr. Bernhard von Gudden, Director of the District Asylum for the Insane in Upper Bavaria, and Professor of Psychiatry at the University of Münich, finished the draft of a medical finding on which he had been working most of the night. An hour or so later, he went into closed session with two other directors of public institutions for the insane, Dr. Hagen and Dr. Hubrich, and with Professor Grashey. Around noon all four distinguished psychiatrists signed Gudden's finding which ended on these three conclusions:

"1) His Majesty is psychically disturbed in an advanced degree, suffering from the kind of mental sickness which psychiatrists know well and call paranoia (insanity).

"2) In view of this form of sickness and its gradual and progressive development over a great number of past years, His Majesty must be declared incurable, for a further deterioration of his mental powers appears certain.

"3) Because of his sickness the exercise of His Majesty's free will is rendered completely impossible and His Majesty must be considered hindered in the execution of government, which impediment will last, not only longer than a year, but for his entire lifetime."

These unequivocal sentences of the psychiatrists signified the removal of Ludwig II not only from Bavaria's throne but from community with the living.

4

THE "BOODLE GANG"*

S. V. Clevenger

Shobal Vail Clevenger (1843–1920) was one of the very few honest superintendents of a state mental hospital in the history of American psychiatry. He neither embezzled hospital funds, nor created fictitious statistics flattering to the institution, as had been the rule for superintendents. Moreover—and he was, to the best of my knowledge, the only physician in such a position who ever did this—he denounced the whole state mental hospital system as harmful to the patients consigned to its care. Accordingly, he was dismissed, after only three months of service, as superintendent of the Eastern Illinois Hospital for the Insane at Kankakee, Illinois; and his name is not mentioned in any text on the history of psychiatry.

Clevenger led a colorful, and in the end a tragic, life. After serving in the Union Army during the Civil War, he became chief engineer of the Southern Dakota Railway. He turned to medicine only in his thirties, receiving his M.D. degree from the Chicago Medical College, now Northwestern University. During most of his medical career he was in private practice in Chicago, and served as alienist and neurologist on the staffs of the Alexian Brothers and Michael

* From S. V. Clevenger, "Treatment of the Insane," *Journal of the American Medical Association*, 27:894–901 (Oct. 24), 1896.

Reese Hospitals; he was also a lecturer on art anatomy at the Chicago Art Institute, on physics at the Chicago College of Pharmacy, and on medical jurisprudence at the Chicago College of Law. He was the author of several books and numerous journal articles.†

In a now-forgotten biography of Clevenger, Victor Robinson wrote: "History cannot always be written without indignation. And it is because Shobal Vail Clevenger has aroused our indignation at atrocities, continued until this very day against the most helpless of human beings, that we have passed weightier names by, and have written instead this story of Chicago's shame, thus contributing to medical history a type which we shall ever cherish—the Don Quixote of Psychiatry."‡

Toward the end of his life, when Clevenger increasingly saw his rejection by the medical and psychiatric community of his day as a fate similar to that which befell Semmelweis—he remarked with resignation in a letter to a friend that "It's interfering with vested interests that the world does not forgive."*

At the county asylum the warden refused to buy a few dollars' worth of needed medicines on account of their expense, but the next drug account itemized 48 cases of beer, 10 barrels of whiskey, 20,000 cigars, and much wine, brandy and fancy liquors were also covered by the item "sundry drugs." The periodical celebrations of the county commissioners and their friends in the dance-hall and dining room of the asylum necessitated rapid and constant replenishing of that portion of the dispensary stock. Five dollars per capita would have covered the amount of meat eaten by 600 at the county asylum, yet in 1884 the bills were $15,763.04, and in 1885 amounted to $18,934.11, av-

---

† Deaths, *Journal of the American Medical Association*, 74:963 (Apr. 3), 1920.
‡ Victor Robinson, *The Don Quixote of Psychiatry* (New York: Historico Medical Press, 1919), p. 334.
* Ibid., p. 330.

eraging $26. and $31. per patient, while 9 cents per pound was charged for hogs' heads in a filthy condition, some of which held iron rings in the noses. Mike Wasserman, one of the convicted boodle commissioners of unsavory memory, when once shown the iron ring in a pig's snout found in the soup of a patient, remarked: "Well, what would you have; gold watches?"

The bookkeeping of a large asylum can be made so elaborate as to be meaningless: Voluminous ledgers and auxiliary books have been known to be pure shams. Requisitions supposed to be sent to the storekeeper by attendants were not approved by supervisors or anyone else, and the storekeeper had every chance of misappropriating goods, and under the loose system of issue no proof could be secured of his guilt. Small quantities of butterine issued have been charged up as butter in large quantities; the actual ration of some of the dements consisting in forty grains of butterine, one five-hundredth of a pound of inferior tea and a small plate of corn-meal mush, and patients have fought over their scanty fare, the most helpless being often wholly deprived of food. . . .

It is with the greatest difficulty that the expense account of county institutions can be approximated. Concealment is the rule and in the words of a county commissioner, "the county expenditures is nobody's business." Collusion among all asylum officers is not to be presumed, for many of them are kept in ignorance of financial matters and can only see results in a general way against which they can not protest.

Estimating possibilities in the State institutions, it is practicable for $150,000 to be abstracted from $500,000 biennially appropriated for a single institution, through perquisites of $30,000 to the one who heads the division of offices, sometimes a member of the legislature who has controlled a large number of votes for the State election; one trustee, who acts without salary and merely for the honor of the appointment, by diligently attending to the hospital business can secure $50,000; a less influential trustee can save $20,000 by cooperating with his companion in the matter of auditing accounts, while the one whose vote is not needed can be placated with $5,000. The storekeeper has opportunities to earn $10,000 on his $75 per month salary. An industrious business manager can net $25,000; the bookkeeper through occasional opportunities can add $1,500 to his savings, and $8,500 can be secured by others in various ways from the wastage and shrinkage fields of the place. The treasurer is openly known to receive the interest on the asylum funds, though there is no legal provision for so doing. Probably $3,000 per annum is thus earned, and if in the meanwhile the State is in need of funds it can readily borrow by paying interest. . . .

The intriguery, waste, extravagance, plotting, rioting, neglect of duty, insolence of employees, disregard of the needs of patients and of medical care, the "doping" of patients by attendants, and frequent instances of personal abuse, the insufficient cooking of insufficient food, with the thorough "cooking" of statistics and accounts, the high death rate and low recovery rate, the crowding of several violent patients in one room, and multitudes of other discreditable affairs, must be witnessed to understand how deep-rooted and arrogant a hold the political spoils system has upon the country. . . . The privations, sufferings and frequent murders of insane patients are strictly logical outcomes of the pernicious system which fills our legislatures, State, county and city offices with gamblers and saloon-keepers, who swagger about in vulgar jewelry and attire, openly congratulating one another upon some recent success in prostituting public and private interests. . . .

Reports of the State Board of Public Charities for Illinois are filled with accounts of the insane in various counties being treated more as animals than as men and women, neglected, abused, chained, locked up in nakedness and filth, no medical or personal attendance, packed in rooms too small for their numbers, with poor ventilation and foul odors, no separation of the sexes, insufficient food, and myriad other such matters are officially mentioned in these reports to the governor and legislature, without influencing the least improvement.

The charges sustained in the 1886 investigation of the Cook County asylum were:

1. Cruelly insufficient provision for the insane in the county asylum in all respects, when more than ample funds are alleged to have been used by the management of said asylum for the care of the insane.

2. Abuse of said insane by said management, said abuse being direct and indirect, by personal violence and neglect.

Subsequent to this report to the governor, a county court investigation on the petition of Julia Willard, May 13, 1889, was made in which witnesses detailed murders and abuse of patients, their starvation and the brutal nature of the management. Patients were made to work for the profit of attendants, their clothing was stolen and sold to saloon-keepers; fighting, rioting, feasting and drunkenness of politicians were narrated, with no apparent differences in the conditions since the State board report of 1878, except in enlarged opportunities for brutality. . . .

In 1895, as a sample of many instances, two attendants were on trial in Chicago for kicking a patient to death; an "investigation" was made by the commissioners, who duly whitewashed themselves, and by publishing hundreds of columns of newspaper interviews, and vaporings generally, managed to confuse everyone and tire out the public. A New York legislative inquiry into the killing of a patient came to nothing through the report of the committee being stolen. . . .

In the *Chicago Inter Ocean*, Nov. 4, 1884, appeared an appeal from a physician at the county asylum stating the atrocities there and asking "all respectable men to be sure that the county commissioners for whom they voted owed no allegiance to gamblers and thieves."

The doctor was promptly shot at and several other attempts were made upon his life and as he kept up the fight ten years he was finally pronounced to be insane by politicians in general, and certainly from the standpoint of a community which condones robbery of the helpless, the one who refuses opportunity to steal from them must be out of his environment and practically a crank.

5

WARD NO. 6

Anton Pavlovich Chekhov

Anton Pavlovich Chekhov (1860–1904) is widely regarded as one of the greatest Russian writers and dramatists. Though trained as a physician, he practiced medicine only for a short time, and devoted himself instead to literary work.

Like many great literary figures, Chekhov was not only an acute observer of human nature and social conditions, but also a social critic. In 1890 he visited the convict island of Sakhalin, publishing his impressions of the journey a year later (*Saghalien Island*). This book is credited with having had a major influence in ameliorating the barbaric penal practices then prevalent in Russia.

"Ward No. 6," published in 1892, is considered one of his best short stories. The impression it produced on Lenin has been recorded by his sister. According to her, the story "had such an oppressive effect on him that he felt like going out of his room and taking a breath of air; while he was reading it, it seemed to him that he had himself been locked up in Ward No. 6."*

Praised immediately upon its appearance by most critics, the story was interpreted as a symbolic allusion

---

* Gleb Struve, "Introduction to 'Ward No. 6,'" in *Seven Short Stories by Chekhov*, trans. by Barbara Makanowitzky, (New York: Bantam Books, 1963), p. 107.

—the mental hospital representing contemporary Russian society. Some years after its first appearance, the editor of an official provincial newspaper asked for permission to reprint the story in his paper in order to call attention to the abuses rampant in the psychiatric section of the local hospital. Chekhov's publisher turned down the request. On the whole, however, Chekhov was said to have been surprised by the leniency with which the Czarist censors had treated his story. In the selection that follows, I made some cuts in "Ward No. 6,"† to abbreviate an otherwise rather lengthy "short" story. If, as a result, the continuity of the narrative has been impaired somewhat, I am to be blamed, not Chekhov.

I

Fresh faces are rarely seen in Ward No. 6. The doctor has long ago stopped admitting new mental cases, and there are but few people in this world who like to visit madhouses. Once every two months Semen Lazarich, the barber, calls at the wing. Of how he clips the insane, and how Nikita assists him, and into what confusion the patients are thrown at every appearance of the intoxicated, smiling barber—of that we will not speak.

Save for the barber no one looks in at the wing. The patients are condemned to see no one but Nikita, day in and day out.

However, a rather strange rumor has recently spread through the hospital building.

Someone has started a rumor that, apparently, the doctor has taken to visiting Ward No. 6.

† Anton Pavlovich Chekhov, "Ward No. 6" [1892], trans. by Bernard Guilbert Guerney, in Charles Neider, Editor, *Short Novels of the Masters* (New York: Holt, Rinehart & Winston, 1962), pp. 286–428.

II

A strange rumor!

Doctor Andrew Ephimich Raghin is, after his own fashion, a remarkable man. They say that in his early youth he was exceedingly pious and had been preparing himself for a career in the church, and that, after he had finished studying in the gymnasium in 1863, he had intended to enter a seminary; but his father, a doctor of medicine and a surgeon, had apparently jeered at him caustically and had declared categorically that he would not consider him his son if he joined the psalm-snufflers. How true that is I do not know, but Andrew Ephimich has confessed more than once that he had never felt any call for medicine and, in general, for the applied sciences. . . .

When Andrew Ephimich came to this town to take his post, the "eleemosynary institution" was in a dreadful state. It was hard to breathe in the wards, the corridors, and the hospital courtyard because of the stench. The hospital orderlies, the nurses, and their children, all used to sleep in the same wards with the sick. Everybody complained there was no living on account of the cockroaches, the bedbugs, and mice. There was never a shortage of erysipelas in the surgical division. For the whole hospital there were but two scalpels and not a single thermometer; the bathtubs were used as storage bins for potatoes. The superintendent, the woman who had full charge of the linen and so forth, and the assistant doctor—they all robbed the sick; while it was told of the old doctor, Andrew Ephimich's predecessor, that he bootlegged the hospital alcohol and had set up for himself a whole harem of nurses and female patients. The people in the town were very familiar with these irregularities and even exaggerated them, yet regarded them with equanimity; some justified them by the fact that the only ones who filled the hospital beds were burghers and mushiks, who could not possibly be dissatisfied, since they lived far worse at home than they did at the hospital: no use pampering them with delicacies, you know! Others said, in justification, that the town found it beyond its means to maintain a good hospital without any aid from the county: thank God there was even a bad one. As for the county, it would not open a hospital either in the city or near it, giving the excuse that the town already had a hospital of its own.

After an inspection of the hospital Andrew Ephimich came to the conclusion that this institution was immoral and in the highest degree harmful to the health of the inhabitants. The most intelligent thing to do, in his opinion, would be to turn the patients loose and close the hospital. But he reasoned that his will alone was not enough for this, and that it would be useless; were the physical and moral uncleanliness driven from one place it would pass on to some other; one had to wait until the thing had thoroughly aired itself. In addition to that, if the people opened a hospital and tolerated it in their midst, it meant that they found it necessary; the prejudices and all those everyday vilenesses and abominations were necessary, since in the course of time they become worked over into something useful, even as manure is worked over into black loam. There is nothing on this earth so good that it had not some vileness at its prime source.

After accepting the post Andrew Ephimich evidently took a rather indifferent attitude toward the irregularities. He merely requested the orderlies and the nurses not to pass their nights in the wards, and put in two wall-cases of surgical instruments; as for the superintendent, the woman in charge of linen, the assistant doctor, and the surgical erysipelas, they all stayed put.

Andrew Ephimich is exceedingly fond of intelligence and honesty, yet he has not sufficient character and belief in his rights to establish an intelligent and honest life about him. To order, to forbid, to insist—these things he is utterly unable to do. It seems as if he had taken a vow never to raise his voice and never to use the imperative mood. To say "Let me have this," or "Bring me that," is for him a difficult matter; when he wants to eat he coughs irresolutely and says to the cook: "What about some tea, now?" or:

"What about dinner?" As for telling the superintendent to stop stealing, or driving him out, or doing away altogether with this needless, parasitical post—that is something altogether beyond his strength. Whenever Andrew Ephimich is being taken in or flattered, or a palpably and vilely doctored account is submitted for his signature, he turns as red as a boiled lobster and feels himself guilty, yet he signs the account just the same; whenever the patients complain to him about being starved or about the boorish nurses he becomes confused and mumbles guiltily: "Very well, very well—I'll look into that later. . . . Probably there's some misunderstanding here—"

At first Andrew Ephimich had worked very assiduously. He received patients from morning until dinner-time, performed operations, and even practiced obstetrics. The ladies said of him that he was conscientious and diagnosed complaints excellently—especially those of women and children. But as time went on the work markedly bored him with its monotonousness and obvious futility. Today you received thirty patients; on the morrow, before you knew it, they ran up to thirty-five; the day after there would be forty, and so on from day to day, from year to year, yet the date-rate in the town did not decrease and the sick never ceased coming. It was a physical impossibility, in the time between morning and noon, to extend any real aid to the forty patients who came; therefore, willy-nilly, the result was plain humbug. During the fiscal year twelve thousand out-patients had been received; therefore, it simply stood to reason that twelve thousand people had been humbugged. As for placing those seriously ill into the wards, and treating them in accordance with all the rules of science, that also was impossible—for although there were rules there was no science; on the other hand, were one to abandon philosophy and follow the rules pedantically, as other physicians did, you would need for that, first and foremost, cleanliness and ventilation instead of filth, wholesome food instead of soup cooked out of stinking sauerkraut, and decent assistants instead of thieves.

And besides, why hinder people from dying, since death

is the normal and ordained end of every being? What did it matter if some haggling shopkeeper or petty government clerk did live five or ten years extra? But if one saw the aim of medicine as the alleviation of suffering through drugs then, involuntarily, the question bobbed up: Wherefore should sufferings be alleviated? In the first place, they say that sufferings lead man to perfection and, in the second, should mankind really learn to alleviate its sufferings through pills and drops, it would abandon altogether religion and philosophy, in which it has found up to now not only a defense against all tribulations but even happiness. Pushkin, just before death, experienced dreadful tortures; that poor fellow Heine, lay for several years stricken by paralysis—why, then, shouldn't some Andrew Ephimich or Matrena Savishna ail for a bit, since their lives are devoid of all content and would be altogether vacuous and like the life of an amoeba, were it not for their sufferings?

Crushed by such reflections Andrew Ephimich let his spirits sink and became irregular in his attendance at the hospital.

III

Here is the way his life goes on. Usually he gets up about eight in the morning, dresses, and has his tea. Then he sits down in his study to read, or goes to the hospital. Here, in the hospital, in a narrow, dark little corridor, sit the ambulatory patients, waiting to be received. Orderlies, their boots clattering on the brick floor, and nurses hurry past them; gaunt patients walk by in their robes; dead bodies and filled bed-pans are carried by; the children are crying; there is a windy draft. Andrew Ephimich knows that for the ague-stricken, for the consumptives, and, in general, for all the susceptible patients such a setting is excruciating, but what can one do?

In the reception room he is met by Serghei Sergheich, the assistant doctor, a small, stout man with a clean-shaven, well-groomed puffy face, with soft, stately manners and wearing a new, roomy suit: he looks more like a senator than an assistant doctor. He has an enormous practice in town, wears a white cravat and considers himself better informed than the doctor, who has no practice whatsoever. Placed in one corner of the reception room is an icon, in a case, with a ponderous lampad glowing before it; standing near it is a lectern in a white slipcover; hanging upon the walls are portraits of arch-priests, a view of Holy Mount Monastery and wreaths of dried corn-flowers. Serghei Sergheich is religious and loves churchly pomp. The holy image has been placed here at his expense; of Sundays, in this reception room, one patient or another reads an acathistus at his orders, at which all stand, while after the reading Serghei Sergheich makes the round of all the wards with a censer and thurifies them with frankincense. . . .

At these clinical sessions Andrew Ephimich does not perform any operations whatsoever; he has long since grown disused to them and the sight of blood agitates him unpleasantly. When he has to open a baby's mouth to look down its throat, and the baby squalls and defends itself with its tiny hands, his head swims from the noise in his ears and tears appear in his eyes. He hastens to prescribe some medicine and waves his hands at the peasant woman to take the baby away in a hurry.

During such a session he soon becomes bored with the timidity of the patients and their lack of sense, with the proximity of the pompous Serghei Sergheich, with the portraits on the walls and with his own questions which he has been putting, without ever varying them, for more than twenty years by now. And, after having received five or six patients, he leaves. The assistant doctor receives the rest without him.

With the pleasant reflection that, thank God, he has had no private practice for a long, long time now, and that no one will interrupt him, Andrew Ephimich upon getting home immediately sits down at the desk in his study and falls to reading. Half his salary goes for the purchase of books, and out of the six rooms in his quarters three are piled up with books and old periodicals. . . .

Always standing near his book is a small decanter of

vodka, while lying right on the cloth, without any plate, is a pickled cucumber or a pickled apple. Every half hour, without taking his eyes off the book, he pours out a pony of vodka and drinks it down, then without looking, he gropes for the cucumber and takes a small bite.

At three o'clock he cautiously approaches the kitchen door, coughs and says:

"Dariushka, what about some dinner?"

After dinner, rather badly cooked and sloppily served, Andrew Ephimich paces through his rooms, with his arms crossed on his breast, and meditates. Four o'clock chimes, then five, but he is still pacing and meditating. At rare intervals the kitchen door creaks and Dariushka's red, sleepy face peeks out:

"Isn't it time for your beer, Andrew Ephimich?" she asks solicitously.

"No, not yet," he answers. "I'll wait . . . I'll wait a while—" . . .

IV

Whenever the clock strikes Andrew Ephimich throws himself back in his armchair and closes his eyes for a little thought. And unintentionally, under the influence of the fine thoughts he had read out of his books, he casts a glance over his past and his present. The past is execrable: better not recall it. As for the present, it is filled with the same sort of thing as the past. He knows that even as his thoughts go careering with the cooled earth around the sun, in the great barrack-like structure of the hospital, alongside of the quarters he occupies, people are languishing amid disease and physical uncleanliness; someone is perhaps not sleeping but warring with insects; someone is being infected with erysipelas or moaning because of a bandage too tightly applied; the patients are, perhaps, playing cards with the nurses and drinking vodka. During the fiscal year twelve thousand people had been humbugged; this whole hospital business, just as the case was twenty years ago, is built upon thievery, squabbles, slanders, nepotism, and upon crass charlatanry, and the hospital, just as hitherto, represents an institution immoral and in the highest degree harmful to the inhabitants. He knows that behind the barred windows of Ward 6 Nikita is beating the patients. . . .

On the other hand, he knows exceedingly well that a fairy-tale change has taken place in medicine during the last twenty-five years. When he had been studying at the university it had seemed to him that medicine would shortly be overtaken by the same fate as alchemy and metaphysics; but now, when he reads of nights, medicine amazes him and arouses wonder and even rapture in him. And really, what unexpected brilliancy there is here, and what a revolution! Thanks to antiseptics, surgeons perform such operations as the great Pirogov had deemed impossible. . . . Ordinary country doctors have the courage to perform resections of the knee-joint; out of a hundred Caesarian sections one case only ends in mortality; as for gallstones, they are considered such a trifle that no one even writes about them. Syphilis can be radically cured. And what about the theory of heredity, and hypnotism, the discoveries of Pasteur and Koch, hygiene and its statistics? What about the county medical centers in Russia? Psychiatry, with its present classification of derangements, its methods of investigation and treatment—why, by comparison with what used to be, it towers nothing short of the Elbruz. The heads of the insane are no longer doused with cold water, nor are they strapped into straitjackets; they are maintained humanely and, actually (so the newspapers write), theatrical entertainments and balls are arranged for them. Andrew Ephimich knows that, judged by present-day views and tastes, such an abomination as Ward No. 6 is possible only a hundred and twenty-five miles from any railroad, in a miserable little town where the mayor and all the councilmen are semiliterate burghers who regard a physician as a high priest who must be believed without any criticism, even though he were to pour molten lead into your mouth; in any other place the public and the newspapers would long since have left not one stone of this little Bastille standing upon another.

"But what of it?" Andrew Ephimich asks himself, opening his eyes. "What of all this? There are antiseptics, and Koch, and Pasteur, yet in substance the business hasn't changed in the least. Ill-health and mortality are still the same. Balls and theatrical entertainments are arranged for the insane—but just the same, they're not allowed to go free. Therefore, everything is bosh and pother and, substantially, there's no difference between the best clinic in Vienna and my lazarhouse."

However, sorrow and a feeling resembling envy hinder him from being indifferent. This, probably, is due to fatigue. His ponderous head droops toward the book; he places his hands under his face, to make it more comfortable, and reflects:

"I am serving an evil cause, and receive my salary from people whom I dupe: I am not honest. But then I, by myself, am nothing; I am but a particle of a necessary social evil: all the district bureaucrats are harmful and receive their salaries for nothing. Therefore, it is not I who am to blame for my dishonesty but the times. . . . Were I to be born two hundred or so years from now, I would be an honest man."

When three o'clock strikes he puts out the lamp and goes to his bedroom. He does not feel sleepy. . . .

V

On a certain evening in spring, when there was no longer any snow on the ground and the starlings were singing in the hospital garden, the doctor stepped out to see his friend the postmaster to the gate. Precisely at that moment the Jew Moisseika was entering the yard, returning from his foraging. He was hatless and had shallow galoshes on his bare feet, and was holding a small sack with the alms.

"Gimme a copper!" He turned to the doctor; he was shivering from the cold and smiling.

Andrew Ephimich, who never refused anybody, gave him a tenkopeck silver coin.

"How bad that is," he thought, glancing at the bare legs, with red, bony ankles. "Why, it's wet out."

And, moved by a feeling which resembled both pity and squeamishness, he set out for the hospital wing after the Jew, glancing now at his bald spot, now at his ankles. At the doctor's entrance Nikita jumped up from his mound of rubbish and drew himself up at attention.

"How do, Nikita," Andrew Ephimich said softly. "What about issuing a pair of boots to this Jew, or something of that sort—for he's likely to catch cold."

"Right, Your Honor. I'll report it to the superintendent."

"Please do. Ask him in my name. Say I asked him to do it."

The entry door was open into the ward. Ivan Dmitrich, lying on his bed and propped up on an elbow, was listening uneasily to the unfamiliar voice, and suddenly recognized the doctor. His whole body began to quiver with wrath, he sprang up and, with a red, angry face, his eyes bulging, ran out into the middle of the ward.

"The doctor has come!" he cried out, and burst into laughter. "At last! Gentlemen, I felicitate you—the doctor is honoring you by his visit! You damned vermin!" he screeched, and stamped his foot in such fury as no one in the ward had ever seen before. "This vermin ought to be killed! No, killing him is not enough! He ought to be drowned in the privy!"

Andrew Ephimich, who had heard this, peeped out into the ward from the entry and asked gently:

"For what?"

"For what?" cried out Ivan Dmitrich, walking up to him with a threatening air and convulsively drawing his robe about him. "For what? You thief!" he uttered with revulsion and shaping his lips as if he wanted to spit. "Quack! Hangman!"

"Calm yourself," said Andrew Ephimich with a guilty smile. "I assure you I have never stolen anything; as for the rest, you probably exaggerate greatly. I can see that you are angry at me. Calm down if you can, I beg of you, and tell me without any heat what you are angry at me for."

"Well, why do you keep me here?"

"Because you are unwell."

"Yes—unwell. But then scores, hundreds of madmen are going about in full freedom, because your ignorance is incapable of distinguishing them from normal people. Why then must I and all these unfortunates sit here, like so many scapegoats for everybody? You, your assistant doctor, the superintendent, and all your hospital riff-raff are, as far as morals are concerned, immeasurably beneath each one of us: why, then, are we sitting here and not the whole lot of you? Where's the logic in that?"

"A moral attitude and logic have nothing to do with all this. Everything depends on chance. He who has been placed in here stays here, while he who hasn't been placed here goes about in full freedom: that's all there is to it. In the fact that I am a doctor and you are a psychopathic case there is neither morality nor logic, but only trivial chance." . . .

"Let me out," said Ivan Dmitrich, and his voice quavered.

"I can't."

"But why? Why?"

"Because that isn't in my power. Judge for yourself: what good would it do you if I were to let you out? Go ahead. The people in town and the police will detain you and send you back."

"Yes, yes, that's true enough," Ivan Dmitrich managed to say, and rubbed his forehead. "This is horrible! But what am I to do? What?"

The voice of Ivan Dmitrich, and his youthful, clever face with its grimaces proved to the doctor's liking. He felt an impulse to be kind to him and to calm him. He sat down next to him on the bed, thought a while, and said:

"You ask, what's to be done? The best thing to do in your situation is to escape from here. But, regrettably, that is useless. You would be detained. When society fences itself off from criminals, psychopaths, and people who are generally embarrassing, it is insuperable. There is but one thing left for you: to find reassurance in the thought that your staying here is necessary."

"It isn't necessary to anybody."

"Since prisons and madhouses exist, why, somebody is bound to sit in them. If not you, then I; if not I, then some third person. Bide your time: when in the distant future prisons and madhouses will have gone out of existence, there will be no more bars on windows, nor hospital robes. Of course, sooner or later, such a time will come."

Ivan Dmitrich smiled mockingly.

"You jest," said he, puckering his eyes. "Such gentry as you and your helper, Nikita, have nothing to do with the future; but you may rest assured, my dear sir, that better times will come! I may be expressing myself in a banal way —laugh, if you like—but the dawn of a new life will shine forth, truth will rise triumphant—and then it will be our turn to rejoice. I will not live to see the day, I will have perished even as animals perish—but then somebody's grandchildren will live to see it. I hail them with all my soul, and I rejoice—I rejoice for them! Onward! God be with us and help us, my friends!"

Ivan Dmitrich, his eyes shining, stood up and, stretching his arms out toward a window, continued with excitement in his voice:

"From behind these window-bars I bless you! May truth prevail! I rejoice!"

"I can't find any particular cause for rejoicing," said Andrew Ephimich, whom Ivan Dmitrich's gesture had struck as theatrical while, at the same time, it had been very much to his liking. "There will be a time when jails and madhouses will no longer exist and truth, as you were pleased to put it, will rise triumphant; but then, the substance of things will not have changed; the laws of nature will still remain the same. Men will ail, will grow old, and die, even as they do now. No matter how magnificent a dawn may be illuminating your life, after all is said and done you will be nailed up in a coffin just the same and then pitched into a hole in the ground."

"But what of immortality?"

"Oh, come, now!"

"You do not believe; but then I do. Dostoyevsky or Voltaire makes somebody say that if there were no God, men would have to invent Him. And I believe profoundly that if there is no immortality, some great human mind will, sooner or later, invent it."

"Well put," Andrew Ephimich let drop, with a smile of pleasure. "It's a good thing, your having faith. With such a faith one can live as smug as a bug in a rug even bricked up in a wall. Did you receive your education anywhere in particular?"

"Yes; I attended a university, but did not graduate."

"You are a thinking and meditative person. You are capable of finding tranquility within your own self, in any environment. Free and profound reasoning, which strives toward a rationalization of life, and a complete contempt for the foolish vanities of this world: there you have two blessings, higher than which no man has known. And you can possess them, even though you live behind triple bars. Diogenes lived in a tun—yet he was happier than all the princes of this earth."

"Your Diogenes was a blockhead," Ivan Dmitrich said morosely. "Why do you talk to me of Diogenes and of some rationalization or other?" he suddenly became angry and sprang up. "I love life—love it passionately! I have a persecution mania, a constant, excruciating fear; yet there are moments when I am overwhelmed by a thirst for life, and then I am afraid of going out of my mind. I want to live— I want to terribly, terribly!" . . .

VI

Ivan Dmitrich was lying in the same pose as yesterday, his hands clutching his head and with his legs tucked up. One could not see his face.

"Good day, my friend," said Andrew Ephimich. "You aren't sleeping?"

"In the first place I am not your friend," Ivan Dmitrich spoke into his pillow, "and, in the second, you are putting yourself out for nothing: you won't get a single word out of me."

"How odd—" Andrew Ephimich muttered in embarrassment. "Yesterday we were conversing so peacefully, but suddenly you took offense for some reason and at once cut our conversation short. Probably I must have expressed myself clumsily, somehow, or perhaps have come out with some idea incompatible with your convictions—"

"Oh yes,—catch me believing you, just like that," said Ivan Dmitrich, raising himself and regarding the doctor mockingly and in disquiet; his eyes were red. "You can go and do your spying and interrogating somewhere else, but there's nothing for you to do here. I understood even yesterday what you had come here for."

"What a strange fancy!" smiled the doctor. "That means you take me for a spy?"

"Yes, I do. Either a spy or a doctor assigned to testing me—it's all one."

"Oh, come, you must excuse me for saying so, but really —what an odd fellow you are!"

The doctor seated himself on a tabouret next to the madman's bed and shook his head reproachfully.

"Well, let's suppose you are right," he said. "Let's suppose that I am treacherously trying to trip you up on something you say, so as to betray you to the police. You are arrested and then brought to trial. But then, will you be any worse off in the courtroom and in prison than you are here? And even if they send you away to live in some remote part of Siberia, or to penal servitude—would that be worse than sitting here, in this hospital wing? I don't think it would be. What, then, is there to fear?"

Evidently these words had an effect on Ivan Dmitrich. He sat up, reassured.

It was five in the afternoon—the time when Andrew Ephimich, as a rule, was pacing through his rooms, and Dariushka was asking him if it weren't time for his beer. It was calm, clear out of doors.

"I happened to go out for a walk after dinner, and just dropped in on you, as you see," said the doctor. "It's actually spring out."

"What month is it now? March?" asked Ivan Dmitrich.

"Yes—the end of March."

"Is it muddy out?"

"No, it's not so bad. You can see the paths in the garden."

"It would be fine to drive a carriage now, somewhere outside the town," said Ivan Dmitrich, rubbing his red eyes, just as though he were coming out of his sleep, "then to come home to a warm cozy study and . . . to take treatments for headaches from a decent doctor. . . . It's a long while since I have lived like a human being. But everything here is abominable! Unbearably abominable!"

After the excitement of yesterday he was fatigued and listless, and spoke unwillingly. His fingers were shaky, and one could see by his face that his head ached badly.

"Between a warm, cozy study and this ward there is no difference whatsoever," said Andrew Ephimich. "A man's tranquility and contentment lie not outside of him but within his own self."

"Just how do you mean that?"

"The ordinary man expects that which is good or bad from without—from a carriage and a study, that is; whereas a thinking man expects it from his own self."

"Go and preach that philosophy in Greece, where it is warm and the air is filled with the fragrance of oranges, but here it is not in keeping with the climate. Whom was I speaking with about Diogenes? Was it you, by any chance?"

"Yes, it was with me—yesterday."

"Diogenes had no need of a study and of warm quarters —it's hot enough there as it is. Just lie in your tub and eat oranges and olives. But had he chanced to live in Russia he would be begging his head off for a room not only in December but even in May. Never fear, he would be perishing from the cold."

"No. It is possible not to feel the cold, as well as every pain in general. Marcus Aurelius has said: 'Pain is a living conception of pain; exert thy will, in order to change this conception; put it away from thee, cease complaining, and the pain shall vanish,' which is true enough. A sage, or simply a thinking, meditative man, is distinguished precisely by his holding suffering in contempt; likewise, he is always content, and is not astonished by anything."

"That means I am an idiot, since I suffer, feel discontent, and am astonished at human baseness."

"You are wrong in saying so. If you will think deeply and often, you will comprehend how insignificant are all these matters which perturb you. One must strive toward a rationalization of life; therein lies the true good."

"Rationalization—" Ivan Dmitrich made a wry face. "The inward, the outward.... Pardon me, I don't understand it. All I know," he said, getting up and regarding the doctor angrily, "is that God created me out of warm blood and nerves—yes! And organic tissue, if it be imbued with life, must react to every irritant. And I do react! To pain I respond by screaming and tears; to baseness, by indignation; to vileness, by revulsion. According to me that, precisely, is what they call life. The lower the organism, the less sensitive it is, and the more weakly does it respond to irritation, and the higher it is the more receptively and energetically does it react to reality. How can one be ignorant of that? You are a doctor—and yet you don't know such trifles! In order to despise sufferings, to be always content and never astonished at anything, one must reach such a state as this—" and Ivan Dmitrich indicated the obese muzhik, bloated with fat—"or else one must harden one's self through sufferings to such a degree as to lose all sensitivity to them: that is, in other words, cease to live. Pardon me, I am no sage and no philosopher," Ivan Dmitrich went on with irritation, "and I understand nothing of all this. I am in no condition to reason."

"On the contrary, you reason splendidly."...

VII

This conversation went on for about an hour more and, evidently, made a profound impression on Andrew Ephimich. He took to dropping in at the hospital wing every day. He went there of mornings and after dinner, and often the dusk of evening would find him still conversing with Ivan Dmitrich. At first Ivan Dmitrich had fought shy of him; he suspected him of some evil design and frankly expressed his hostility; later on, however, he became used to him and changed his harsh attitude to a condescending ironical one.

It was not long before a rumor spread all through the hospital that Doctor Andrew Ephimich had taken to frequenting Ward No. 6. Nobody—neither the assistant doctor, nor Nikita, nor the nurses—could understand why he went there, why he sat there for hours on end, what he spoke about, and why he did not write out any prescriptions. His actions seemed queer. Many times Michael Averianich failed to find him at home, something that had never happened before, and Dariushka was very much put out because the doctor drank his beer no longer at the designated time, and occasionally was actually late for dinner.

Once (this was already toward the end of June) Doctor Hobotov dropped in at Andrew Ephimich's about something; not finding him at home, he set out to look for him in the courtyard; there he was told that the old doctor had gone to see the psychopathic cases. As he entered the wing and paused in the entry, Hobotov heard the following conversation:

"We shall never sing the same tune, and you won't succeed in converting me to your belief," Ivan Dmitrich was saying in irritation. "You are absolutely unfamiliar with reality and you have never suffered but, like a leech, have merely found your food in the proximity of the sufferings of others, whereas I have suffered ceaselessly from my birth to this very day. Therefore I say frankly: I consider myself superior to you and more competent in all respects. It isn't up to you to teach me."

"I do not at all presume to convert you to my belief," Andrew Ephimich let drop quietly and with regret because the other did not want to understand him. "And that's not where the gist of the matter lies, my friend. It does not lie in that you have suffered, whereas I have not. Sufferings and joys are transitory; let's drop them—God be with them.

But the gist of the matter does lie in that you and I do reason; we see in each other someone who can think and reason, and this makes for unity between us, no matter how divergent our views may be. If you only knew how fed up I have become with the general insanity, mediocrity, stolidity, and what a joy it is each time I converse with you! You are an intelligent man, and I find you delightful."

Hobotov opened the door an inch or so and peered into the ward: Ivan Dmitrich in his nightcap and Doctor Andrew Ephimich were sitting side by side on the bed. The madman was grimacing, shuddering and convulsively muffling himself in his bathrobe, while the doctor sat motionless, with his head sunk on his chest, and his face was red, helpless and sad. Hobotov shrugged his shoulders, smiled sneeringly and exchanged glances with Nikita. Nikita, too, shrugged his shoulders.

The next day Hobotov came to the wing with the assistant doctor. Both stood in the entry and eavesdropped.

"Why, it looks as if our grandpa has gone off his nut completely!" Hobotov remarked as they were leaving the wing.

"The Lord have mercy upon us sinners!" sighed the benign-visaged Serghei Sergheich, painstakingly skirting the small puddles so as not to soil his brightly polished shoes. "I must confess, my dear Eugene Fedorovich, I have been long anticipating this!"

VIII

After this Andrew Ephimich began to notice a certain atmosphere of mysteriousness all around him. The orderlies, the nurses, and the patients, whenever they came across him, glanced at him questioningly and then fell to whispering among themselves. Masha, the superintendent's little daughter, whom he liked to come upon in the garden, whenever he approached her now with a smile to pat her little head, would run away from him for some reason or other. Michael Averianich, the postmaster, whenever he was listening to the doctor no longer said "Absolutely correct!" but kept mumbling "Yes, yes, yes . . ." in incomprehensible confusion and regarded him thoughtfully and sadly; for some reason he took to advising his friend to leave vodka and beer alone, but in doing so did not speak directly, since he was a man of delicacy, but in hints, telling him now about a certain battalion commander, a splendid person, now about a regimental chaplain, a fine fellow, both of whom had been hard drinkers and had fallen ill; after leaving off drink, however, they had gotten perfectly well. Andrew Ephimich's colleague, Hobotov, dropped in on him two or three times; he, too, advised him to leave spirituous drinks alone and, without any apparent reason, recommended him to take potassium bromid.

In August Andrew Ephimich received a letter from the mayor, requesting the doctor to call on him concerning a very important matter. On arriving at the appointed time in the city offices Andrew Ephimich found there the head of the military, the civilian inspector of the county school, a member of the city council, Hobotov, and also some gentleman or other, stout and flaxen-fair, who was introduced to him as a doctor. This doctor, with a Polish name very hard to pronounce, lived some twenty miles out of town, on a stud-farm, and happened to be passing through the town just then.

"There's a little report here, dealing with your department," said the member of the city council to Andrew Ephimich, after they had all exchanged greetings and seated themselves around a table. "Eugene Fedorovich here tells us the pharmacy is in rather cramped quarters in the main building, and that it ought to be transferred into one of the wings. Of course, that's nothing—one can transfer it, right enough; but the main thing is, the wing will require alterations."

"Yes, it can't be done without alterations," said Andrew Ephimich, after a little thought. "If the corner wing, for instance, were to be fitted out as a pharmacy, it would, I suppose, require five hundred rubles, at a minimum. An unproductive expenditure."

They were all silent for a little while.

"I have already had the honor of submitting a report ten years ago," Andrew Ephimich went on in a quiet voice, "that this hospital, in its present state, appears to be a luxury for this town beyond its resources. It was built in the forties—but at that time the resources were different from what they are now. The town is spending too much on unnecessary buildings and superfluous posts. I think that, under different conditions, two model hospitals could be maintained for the same money."

"There, you just try and set up different conditions!" the member of the city council said with animation.

"I have already had the honor of submitting a report: transfer the medical department to the supervision of the county."

"Yes: transfer the money to the county—and the county will steal it," the flaxen-fair doctor broke into laughter.

"Which is the way of things," concurred the member of the city council, and laughed in his turn.

Andrew Ephimich threw a listless and dull glance at the flaxen-fair doctor and said:

"We must be just."

They were again silent for a little while. Tea was served. The head of the military, who for some reason was very much embarrassed, touched Andrew Ephimich's hand across the table and said:

"You have forgotten us altogether, Doctor. However, you are a monk; you don't play cards, you don't like women. You just feel bored with us fellows."

They all began speaking of how boresome life was for a decent person in this town. No theater, no music, while at the last evening dance given at the club there had been about twenty ladies and only two gentlemen. The young people did not dance but were clustered around the buffet all the time or playing cards. Andrew Ephimich slowly and quietly, without looking at anybody, began saying what a pity, what a profound pity it was that people in town were expending their life energy, their hearts and their minds, on cards and gossiping, but neither could nor would pass their time in interesting conversation and in reading, they would not avail themselves of the pleasures which the mind affords. The mind alone is interesting and remarkable; as for everything else, it is petty and base. Hobotov was listening attentively to his colleague and suddenly asked:

"Andrew Ephimich, what's today's date?"

Having received his answer he and the flaxen-fair doctor proceeded, in the tone of examiners conscious of their lack of skill, to ask Andrew Ephimich what day it was, how many days there were in the year, and whether it was true that there was a remarkable prophet living in Ward No. 6.

In answering the last question Andrew Ephimich turned red and said:

"Yes, he is ill, but he is an interesting young man."

No further questions were put to him.

As the doctor was putting on his overcoat in the foyer, the head of the military put his hand on his shoulder and said with a sigh:

"It's time we old fellows were given our rest!"

When he had come out of the city offices Andrew Ephimich grasped that this had been a commission to examine his mental faculties. He recalled the questions that had been put to him, turned red and for some reason felt, for the first time now, bitterly sorry for medicine.

"My God!" he reflected, recalling how the physicians had been putting him through a test just now. "Why, they were attending lectures on psychiatry not so long ago, they had to pass examinations—whence, then, comes this all-around ignorance? They haven't the least conception of psychiatry!"

And, for the first time in his life, he felt himself insulted and angered.

That same day, in the evening, Michael Averianich dropped in on him. Without exchanging greetings, the postmaster walked up to him, took both of his hands, and said in an agitated voice:

"My dear friend, prove to me that you believe in my good intentions and consider me your friend . . . My friend!" And, preventing Andrew Ephimich from saying anything, he went on, still agitated: "I love you because of your culture and the nobility of your soul. Do listen to me, my dear fellow. The ethics of science obligate doctors to conceal the truth from you but, military fashion, I tell the truth and shame the devil—you are not well! Excuse me, my dear fellow, but that's the truth: all those around you have noticed it long ago. Just now Doctor Eugene Fedorovich was telling me that for the sake of your health you absolutely must take a rest and have some diversion. Absolutely correct! Excellent! In a few days I'll take a leave of absence and go away for a change of air. Prove to me that you are my friend—let's go somewhere together! Let's go—and recall the good old days!"

"I feel myself perfectly well," Andrew Ephimich said, after thinking a while. "But as for going somewhere, that's something I can't do. Do let me prove my friendship for you in some other way."

To be going off somewhere, for some unknown reason, without books, without Dariushka, without beer, breaking off sharply the order of life established through twenty years—the very idea struck him, at the first moment, as wild and fantastic. But he recalled the conversation that had taken place in the city offices and the oppressive mood which he had experienced on his way home from there, and the thought of going away for a short time from the town where stupid people considered him mad appealed to him.

"But where, in particular, do you intend going?" he asked.

"To Moscow, to Petersburg, to Warsaw! I spent five of the happiest years of my life in Warsaw. What an amazing city! Let's go, my dear fellow!"

IX

A week later it was suggested to Andrew Ephimich that he take a rest—that is, that he hand in his resignation, something which he regarded apathetically—and after another week he and Michael Averianich were already seated in a posting tarantass, bound for the nearest railroad station. The days were cool, clear, with blue skies and a transparent vista. The one hundred and twenty-five miles to the station they covered in two days, and on the way stopped over twice for the night. When, at the posting stations, their tea was served in badly washed tumblers, or too much time was spent in harnessing the horses, Michael Averianich turned purple, his whole body shook, and he shouted "Quiet, you! Don't you dare to argue!" And when he was seated in the tarantass he kept talking without a minute's rest about his journeys through the Caucasus and the Kingdom of Poland. How many adventures there had been, and what encounters! He spoke loudly and, as he spoke, such an astonished look came into his eyes that one might have thought he was lying. To top it off, in the heat of his story-telling he breathed right in Andrew Ephimich's face and laughed in his very ear. This embarrassed the doctor and hindered him from thinking and concentrating.

For reasons of economy they went by third class on the train, in a car where smoking was not permitted. The passengers were halfway decent. Michael Averianich in a short while became well acquainted with all of them and, passing from seat to seat, declared loudly that such exasperating roads ought not to be patronized. All-around knavery! Riding horseback, now, was an altogether different matter: you could cover sixty-five miles in a single day and still feel yourself hale and hearty. As for the poor crops we've been having, that was due to the Pinsk swamps having been drained. As a general thing, everything was at sixes and sevens—frightfully so. He grew heated, spoke loudly, and gave no chance to the others to say anything. This endless chatter, alternating with loud laughter and expressive gestures, wearied Andrew Ephimich.

"Which one of us two is the madman?" he reflected with vexation. "Is it I, who am trying not to disturb the passengers in any way, or is it this egoist, who thinks he is more intelligent and interesting than all those here, and therefore will not give anybody any rest?"

In Moscow Michael Averianich donned a military frock-coat without any shoulder-straps and trousers with red piping. He went through the streets in a military cap and a uniform overcoat, and the soldiers saluted him. To Andrew Ephimich he now seemed a man who out of all the seignorial ways that had been his had squandered all that was good and had retained only that which was bad. He loved to be waited on, even when it was unnecessary. Matches might be lying on the table right in front of him, and he saw them, yet he would shout to a waiter to bring him some; he was not at all embarrassed about walking around in nothing but his underwear before a chambermaid; he addressed all waiters indiscriminately—even the old men—as patent inferiors and, if angered, called them blockheads and fools. This, as it seemed to Andrew Ephimich, was seignorial, yet vile. . . .

The doctor went about, saw the sights, ate and drank, yet he had but one feeling: that of vexation at Michael Averianich. He longed for a rest from his friend, to get away from him, to hide himself, whereas his friend considered it his duty not to let the doctor go a step from his side and to provide him with as many diversions as possible. When there were no sights to see he diverted him with conversations. Andrew Ephimich stood this for two days, but on the third he informed his friend that he was ill and wanted to stay in all day. His friend said that in that case he, too, would stay. Really, one had to rest up, otherwise you would run your legs off. Andrew Ephimich lay down on the divan, with his face towards its back and, with clenched teeth, listened to his friend, who assured him ardently that France was inevitably bound to smash Germany, sooner or later, that there were ever so many swindlers in Moscow, and that you can't judge the good points of a horse just by its looks. The doctor's ears began to buzz and his heart to pound but, out of delicacy, he could not find the resolution to ask his friend to go away or to keep still. Fortunately, Michael Averianich grew bored with being cooped up in the hotel room and, after dinner, he went out for a stroll.

Left alone, Andrew Ephimich gave himself up to a feeling of repose. How pleasant to lie motionless on a divan and realize that you were alone in the room! True happiness is impossible without solitude. The Fallen Angel must have betrayed God probably because he had felt a desire for solitude, which the angels know naught of. Andrew Ephimich wanted to think over that which he had seen and heard during the last few days, yet he could not get Michael Averianich out of his head.

"And yet he took a leave of absence and went on this trip with me out of friendship, out of magnanimity," the doctor reflected with vexation. "There's nothing worse than this friendly guardianship. There, now, it would seem he is kindhearted and magnanimous and a merry fellow, and yet he's a bore. An unbearable bore. In precisely the same way there are people whose words are always intelligent and meritorious, yet one feels that they are dull people."

During the days that followed Andrew Ephimich claimed he was ill and did not leave the hotel room. He lay with his face toward the back of the divan and was on tenter-hooks whenever his friend was diverting him with conversations, or rested when his friend was absent. He was vexed with himself for having gone on this trip, and he was vexed with his friend, who was becoming more garrulous and familiar with every day. No matter how hard the doctor tried he could not succeed in attuning his thoughts to a serious, exalted vein.

"This is that reality Ivan Dmitrich spoke of, which is getting me down so," he mused, angry at his own pettiness. "However, that's nonsense. I'll come home, and then things will go in their old way again." . . .

When the friends got back to their town it was already November and its streets were deep in snow. Andrew Ephimich's place had been taken by Hobotov, who was still living in his old rooms while waiting for Andrew Ephimich to come and clear out of the hospital quarters. The homely woman whom he called his cook was already living in one of the hospital wings.

New gossip concerning the hospital was floating through

the town. It was said that the homely woman had quarreled with the superintendent and that the latter, it would seem, had crawled on his knees before her, begging forgiveness.

On the very first day of his arrival Andrew Ephimich had to look for rooms for himself.

"My friend," the postmaster said to him timidly, "pardon my indiscreet question: what means have you at your disposal?"

Andrew Ephimich counted his money in silence, and said:

"Eighty-six rubles."

"That's not what I am asking you about," Michael Averianich got out in confusion, without having understood the doctor. "I am asking you, what means you have in general?"

"Why, that's just what I'm telling you: eighty-six rubles. Outside of that I have nothing."

Michael Averianich considered the doctor an honest and noble man, but just the same suspected him of having a capital of twenty thousand at the least. But now, having learned that Andrew Ephimich was a pauper, that he had nothing to live on, he for some reason burst into tears and embraced his friend.

X

Andrew Ephimich was living in a small house with only three windows, belonging to Belova, a burgher's widow. There were just three rooms in this little house, without counting the kitchen. Two of them, with the windows facing the street, were occupied by the doctor, while Dariushka and the burgher's widow with her three children lived in the third room and the kitchen. . . .

He got up at eight, as before, and after tea would sit down to read his old books and periodicals. By now he had no money for new ones. Either because the books were old, or perhaps because of the change in his environment, reading no longer had as profound a hold on him and tired him out. In order not to spend his time in idleness he was compiling a catalogue *raisonné* of his books and pasting small labels on their backs, and this mechanical, finicky work seemed to him more interesting than reading. The monotonous, finicky work in some incomprehensible fashion lulled his thoughts; he did not think of anything, and the time passed rapidly. Even sitting in the kitchen and cleaning potatoes with Dariushka, or picking the buckwheat grits clean, seemed interesting to him. On Saturdays and Sundays he went to church. Standing close to the wall, with his eyes almost shut, he listened to the chanting and thought of his father, of his mother, of his university, of different religions; he felt at ease and pensive and later, as he left the church, he regretted that the service had ended so soon.

He went twice to the hospital to call on Ivan Dmitrich, to have a chat with him. But on both occasions Ivan Dmitrich had been unduly excited and bad-tempered; he begged to be left in peace, since he had long since wearied of empty chatter, and said that he begged from accursed, vile men but one reward for all his sufferings: solitary confinement. Was it possible that he was being denied even that? On both occasions as Andrew Ephimich was wishing him good night in parting, the madman had snarled back and said:

"Go to the devil!"

And now Andrew Ephimich did not know whether to go to him a third time or not. And yet the wish to go was there. . . .

He was very angry at himself for having spent on the trip the thousand rubles he had hoarded. How handy that thousand would come in now! He felt vexed because people would not leave him in peace. Hobotov considered it his duty to visit his ailing colleague at infrequent intervals. Everything about him aroused aversion in Andrew Ephimich: his well-fed face, and his vile, condescending tone, and the word "colleague," and his high boots; but the most repulsive thing was that he considered himself obliged to treat Andrew Ephimich, and thought that he really was giving him treatment. At his every visit he brought a vial of potassium bromid and some rhubarb pills.

And Michael Averianich, too, considered it his duty to drop in on his friend and divert him. On each occasion he came into Andrew Ephimich's place with an assumed insouciance, laughed boisterously but constrainedly, and fell to assuring him that he looked splendid today and that matters, thanks be to God, were on the mend, and from this one could have concluded that he considered his friend's situation hopeless. He had not yet paid back the debt he had contracted in Warsaw and was crushed by profound shame, on edge, and consequently strove to laugh more loudly and to tell things as amusingly as he could. His anecdotes and stories now seemed endless and were torture to both Andrew Ephimich and to himself.

When he was present Andrew Ephimich would usually lie down on the divan, with his face to the wall, and listen with his teeth clenched; he felt the slag gathering over his soul, layer upon layer, and after his friend's every visit he felt that this slag was rising ever higher and seemed to be reaching his very throat.

In order to drown out these trivial emotions he made haste to reflect that he himself, and Hobotov, and Michael Averianich were bound to perish sooner or later, without leaving as much as an impress upon nature. If one were to imagine some spirit flying through space past the earth a million years hence, that spirit would behold only clay and bare crags. Everything—culture as well as moral law—would perish, and there would not be even a burdock growing over the spot where they had perished. What, then, did shame before the shopkeepers matter, or the insignificant Hobotov, or the oppressive friendship of a Michael Averianich? It was all stuff and nonsense.

But such reflections were no longer of any help. He would no sooner imagine the terrestrial globe a million years hence when, from behind a bare crag, Hobotov would appear in his high boots, or Michael Averianich, guffawing with constraint, and one could even catch his shamefaced whisper: "As for that Warsaw debt, my dear fellow—I'll pay you back one of these days. . . . Without fail!"

XI

One day Michael Averianich came after dinner, when Andrew Ephimich was lying on the divan. It so happened that Hobotov with his potassium bromid put in his appearance at the same time. Andrew Ephimich rose heavily, sat up, and propped both his hands against the divan.

"Why, my dear fellow," Michael Averianich began, "your complexion is much better than it was yesterday. Yes, you're looking fine! Fine, by God!"

"It's high time you were getting better, colleague—high time," said Hobotov, yawning. "No doubt you yourself must be fed up with this long drawn out mess."

"And get better we will!" Michael Averianich said gaily. "We'll live for another hundred years! We will that!"

"Well, not a hundred, maybe, but he's still good for another twenty," Hobotov remarked consolingly. "Never mind, never mind, colleague, don't despond. That'll do you, trying to pull the wool over my eyes."

"We'll show them what stuff we're made of!" Michael Averianich broke into loud laughter, and patted his friend's knee. "We'll show them yet! Next summer, God willing, we'll dash off to the Caucasus and ride all through it on horseback—*hup, hup, hup!* And when we get back from the Caucasus first thing you know, like as not, we'll be celebrating a wedding." Here Michael Averianich winked slyly. "We'll marry you off, my dear friend . . . we'll marry you off—"

Andrew Ephimich suddenly felt the slag reaching his throat; his heart began to pound frightfully.

"That's vulgar!" he said, getting up quickly and going toward the window. "Is it possible you don't understand that you're saying vulgar things?"

He wanted to go on suavely and politely but, against his will, suddenly clenched his fists and raised them above his head.

"Leave me alone!" he cried out in a voice that was not his own, turning purple and with his whole body quivering. "Get out! Get out, both of you! Both of you!"

Michael Averianich and Hobotov got up and stared at him, in perplexity at first, and then in fear.

"Get out, both of you!" Andrew Ephimich kept shouting. "You dolts! You nincompoops! I don't need either friendship—or your drugs, you dolts! What vulgarity! What vileness!"

Hobotov and Michael Averianich, exchanging bewildered looks, backed toward the door and stepped out into the entry. Andrew Ephimich seized the vial with the potassium bromid and hurled it after them; tinkling, the vial smashed against the threshold.

"Take yourselves off to the devil!" he cried out in a tearful voice, running out into the entry. "To the devil!"

When his visitors had left Andrew Ephimich, shivering as if in fever, lay down on the divan and for a long time thereafter kept repeating:

"Dolts! Nincompoops!"

When he had quieted down, the first thought that came to him was how frightfully ashamed Michael Averianich must feel now and how heavy at heart, and that all this was horrible. Nothing of the sort had ever happened before. What then, had become of the mind and of tact? What had become of rationalization and philosophic equanimity?

The doctor could not fall asleep all night from shame and vexation at himself and in the morning, about ten, he went to the post office and apologized to the postmaster.

"Let's not recall what has happened," said the touched Michael Averianich with a sigh, squeezing the doctor's hand hard. "Let bygones be bygones." . . . "It didn't even occur to me to be offended at you. Illness is no sweet bedmate, I understand that. Your fit frightened the doctor and myself yesterday, and we spoke about you for a long time afterwards. My dear fellow, why don't you tackle your illness in earnest? How can one act like that? Pardon my friendly candor," Michael Averianich sank his voice to a whisper, "but you are living in a most unfavorable environment: there isn't room enough, the place isn't clean enough, there's no one to look after you, you have no money for treatment. . . . My dear friend, the doctor and I implore you with all our hearts: heed our advice, go to the hospital! There the food is wholesome, and you'll be looked after, and will receive treatment. Even though Eugene Fedorovich—speaking just between you and me—has atrocious manners, he is nevertheless competent; he can be fully relied on. He gave me his word that he would take you under his care."

Andrew Ephimich was touched by this sincere interest and by the tears which suddenly began to glitter on the postmaster's cheeks.

"My worthiest friend, don't you believe them!" the doctor began whispering, placing his hand on his heart. "Don't you believe them! My illness consists solely of my having found, in twenty years, only one intelligent person in this whole town—and even that one a madman. There's no illness of any sort—but I have simply fallen into a bewitched circle, from which there is no way out. Nothing matters to me; I am ready for everything."

"Go to the hospital, my dear friend."

"Nothing matters to me—I'd even go into a hole in the ground."

"Give me your word, old fellow, that you will obey Eugene Federovich in everything."

"If you like: I give you my word. But I repeat, my worthiest friend, that I have fallen into a bewitched circle. Everything, even the sincere concern of my friends, now tends toward one thing: my perdition. I am perishing, and I have the fortitude to realize it."

"You will get well, old fellow."

"Why should you say that?" Andrew Ephimich asked with irritation. "There are few men who, toward the close of their lives, do not go through the same experience as mine right now. When you're told that you've got something in the nature of bad kidneys and an enlarged heart, and you start taking treatments, or you're told that you are a madman or a criminal—that is, in short, when people suddenly turn their attention upon you—know, then, that you have fallen into a bewitched circle out of which you will nevermore escape. You will strive to escape—and will go still further astray. Yield, for no human exertions will any longer save you. That's how it looks to me." . . .

That same day, before evening, Hobotov in his short fur-lined coat and his high boots appeared unexpectedly at Andrew Ephimich's and said, in such a tone as if nothing at all had happened yesterday:

"Well, I have come to you on a professional matter, colleague. I have come to invite you: would you care to go to a consultation with me? Eh?"

Thinking that Hobotov wanted to divert him by a stroll, or that he really wanted to give him an opportunity of earning a fee, Andrew Ephimich put on his things and went out with him into the street. He was glad to have this chance to smooth things over after having been at fault yesterday and of effecting a reconciliation, and at heart was thankful to Hobotov, who had not even hinted at yesterday's incident and, evidently, was sparing him. It was difficult to expect such delicacy from this uncultured man.

"But where is your patient?" asked Andrew Ephimich.

"In my hospital. I have been wanting to show him to you for a long while. . . . A most interesting case."

They entered the hospital yard and, skirting the main building, headed for the wing where the demented patients were housed. And all this, for some reason, in silence. When they entered the wing Nikita, as usual, sprang up and stood at attention.

"One of the patients here had a sudden pulmonary complication," Hobotov said in a low voice, entering the ward with Andrew Ephimich. "You wait here a little; I'll be right back. I'm going after my stethoscope."

And he walked out.

XII

It was already twilight. Ivan Dmitrich was lying on his bed, his face thrust into the pillow: the paralytic was sitting motionlessly, softly crying and moving his lips. The obese muzhik and the one-time mail sorter were sleeping. Everything was quiet.

Andrew Ephimich sat on Ivan Dmitrich's bed and waited. But half an hour passed, and instead of Hobotov it was Nikita who entered the ward, holding in his arms a bathrobe, somebody's underwear, and slippers.

"Please dress yourself, Your Honor," said he quietly. "Here's your little bed—please to come over here," he added, indicating a vacant bed, evidently brought in recently. "Never mind; you'll get well, God willing."

Andrew Ephimich grasped everything. Without uttering a word he went over to the bed Nikita had indicated and sat down; perceiving that Nikita was standing and waiting, he stripped to the skin, and a feeling of shame came over him. Then he put on the hospital underwear; the drawers were very short, the shirt was long, while the bathrobe smelt of smoked fish.

"You'll get well, God willing," Nikita repeated.

He picked up Andrew Ephimich's clothes in his arms, went out, and shut the door after him.

"It doesn't matter. . . ." Andrew Ephimich reflected, shamefacedly drawing the bathrobe closely about him, and feeling that in his new outfit he looked like a convict. "It doesn't matter. . . . It doesn't matter whether it's a frock-coat, or a uniform, or this hospital bathrobe—"

But what about his watch? And the notebook in his side-pocket? And his cigarettes? Where had Nikita carried off his clothes to? Now, likely as not, he would have no occasion until his very death to put on trousers, vest, and boots. All this was odd, somehow, and even incomprehensible, at first. Andrew Ephimich was convinced, even now, that between the widow Belova's house and Ward No. 6 there was no difference whatsoever; that everything in this world was nonsense and vanity of vanities, yet at the same time his hands were trembling, his feet were turning cold, and he felt eerie at the thought that Ivan Dmitrich would awake soon and see him in a hospital bathrobe. He stood up, took a turn about the room, and sat down again.

There, he had sat through half an hour, an hour, by now, and he had become deadly wearied. Could one possibly live through a day here, through a week, and even years, like these people? There, now, he had been sitting, had taken a turn about the room, and had sat down again; one could go and take a look out of the window, and again traverse the room from one corner to the other. But, after that, what? Sit just like that, all the time, like an image carved of wood, and meditate? No, that was hardly possible.

Andrew Ephimich lay down, but immediately got up, mopped the cold sweat off his forehead with the sleeve of his bathrobe—and felt that his whole face had begun to reek of smoked fish. He took another turn about the room.

"This must be some sort of misunderstanding—" he let drop, spreading his hands in perplexity. "I must have an explanation—there's some misunderstanding here—"

At this point Ivan Dmitrich awoke. He sat up and propped his cheeks on his fists. He spat. Then he glanced lazily at the doctor and, evidently, did not grasp anything at the first moment: shortly, however, his sleepy face became rancorous and mocking.

"Aha—so they've planted you here as well, my fine fellow!" he got out in a voice still hoarse from sleep, puckering up one eye. "Very glad of it! There was a time when you drank men's blood, but now they'll drink yours. Splendid!"

"This must be some sort of misunderstanding—" Andrew Ephimich got out, frightened at Ivan Dmitrich's words; he shrugged his shoulders and repeated: "Some sort of misunderstanding—" . . .

XIII

Andrew Ephimich went to the door and opened it, but Nikita immediately sprang up and blocked his way.

"Where are you going? You mustn't, you mustn't!" he said. "Time to go to sleep!"

"But I want to go for just a minute, to take a walk in the yard!" Andrew Ephimich was taken aback.

"Mustn't, mustn't—those are orders. You know that yourself."

Nikita slammed the door and put his back against it.

"But suppose I were to go out of here, what harm would that do anybody?" asked Andrew Ephimich, shrugging his shoulders. "I can't understand this! Nikita, I must go out!" —and there was a catch in his voice. "I've got to."

"Don't start any disorders—it's not right!" Nikita admonished him.

"This is the devil and all!" Ivan Dmitrich suddenly cried out and sprang up. "What right has he got not to let us out? How dare they keep us here? The law, it seems, says plainly that no man may be deprived of liberty without a trial! This is oppression! Tyranny!"

"Of course it's tyranny!" said Andrew Ephimich, heartened by Ivan Dmitrich's outcry. "I've got to, I must go out! He has no right to do this! Let me out, I tell you!"

"Do you hear, you stupid brute?" Ivan Dmitrich shouted, and pounded on the door with his fist. "Open up, or else I'll break the door down! You butcher!"

"Open up!" Andrew Ephimich shouted, his whole body quivering. "I demand it!"

"Just keep on talking a little more!" Nikita answered from the other side of the door. "Keep it up!"

"At least go and ask Eugene Fedorovich to come here! Tell him I beg of him to be so kind as to come—for just a minute—"

"He'll come of his own self tomorrow."

"They'll never let us out!" Ivan Dmitrich went on in the meantime. "They'll make us rot here! Oh Lord, is there really no hell in the other world, and these scoundrels will be forgiven? Where is justice, then? Open up, you scoundrel—I'm suffocating!" he cried out in a hoarse voice and threw his weight against the door. "I'll smash my head! You murderers!"

Nikita flung the door open, shoved Andrew Ephimich aside roughly, using both his hands and one knee, then swung back and smashed his fist into the doctor's face. It seemed to Andrew Ephimich that an enormous salty wave had gone over his head and dragged him off toward his bed; there really was a salty taste in his mouth; probably his teeth had begun to bleed. He began to thresh his arms, just as if he were trying to come to the surface, and grabbed at somebody's bed, and at that point felt Nikita strike him twice in the back.

Ivan Dmitrich let out a yell. Probably he, too, was being beaten.

After that everything quieted down. The tenuous moonlight streamed in through the barred windows, and lying on the floor was a shadow that looked like a net. Everything was frightening. Andrew Ephimich lay down and held his breath; he anticipated with horror that he would be struck again. Just as though someone had taken a sickle, had driven it into him and then twisted it several times in his breast and guts. From pain he hit his pillow and clenched his teeth and suddenly, amid all the chaos, a fearful, unbearable thought flashed clearly in his head: that exactly the same pain must have been experienced throughout the years, day in and day out, by these people who now, in the light of the moon, seemed to be black shadows. How could it have come about, during the course of twenty years, that he had not known, and had not wanted to know, all this? He did not know pain, he had had no conception of it—therefore he was not to blame, yet conscience, just as intractable and harsh as Nikita, made him turn cold from the nape of his neck to his heels. He sprang up, wanted to cry out with all his might and to run as fast as he could to kill Nikita, then Hobotov, and the superintendent, and the assistant doctor, and then himself; but never a sound escaped from his breast and his legs would not obey him; suffocating, he yanked at the breast of his bathrobe and shirt, tore them and crashed down unconscious on his bed.

XIV

On the morning of the next day his head ached, his ears hummed, and his whole body felt broken up. He did not blush at the recollection of his weakness of yesterday. Yesterday he had been pusillanimous, had been afraid even of the moon, had given sincere utterance to feelings and thoughts which he had not formerly even suspected of having within him. The thought, for instance, about the dissatisfaction of the small fry. But now nothing mattered to him.

He did not eat, did not drink; he lay without moving and kept silent.

"Nothing matters to me," he thought when questions were put to him. "I'm not going to bother answering . . . Nothing matters to me."

Michael Averianich came after dinner and brought him a quarter-pound packet of tea and a pound of marmalade candy. Dariushka also came and stood for a whole hour by his bed with an expression of stolid sorrow on her face. Doctor Hobotov, too, paid him a visit. He brought a vial of potassium bromid and ordered Nikita to fumigate the place with something.

Toward evening Andrew Ephimich died from an apoplectic stroke. At first he had felt a staggering ague-fit and nausea; something disgusting (so it seemed), penetrating his whole body, even into his fingers, started pulling from the stomach toward his head, and flooded his eyes and ears. Everything turned green before his eyes. Andrew Ephimich realized that his end had come, and recalled that Ivan Dmitrich, Michael Averianich and millions of men believe in immortality. And what if it should suddenly prove actual? But he felt no desire for immortality, and he thought of it only for an instant. A herd of reindeer, extraordinarily beautiful and graceful (he had read about them yesterday), ran past him; then a countrywoman stretched out her hand to him, holding a letter for registration. . . . Michael Averianich said something. Then everything vanished, and Andrew Ephimich forgot everything for all eternity.

6

MADNESS AND MORALITY

Karl Kraus

Karl Kraus (1874–1936), Austrian critic, journalist, and poet, started to publish in his early twenties and, when only twenty-five, founded and edited the periodical *Die Fackel* (*The Torch*). This review was first largely, and later entirely, written by him. The main objects of Kraus's satire were the middle classes and the "liberal" press. One of his students appraised him in these words: "Karl Kraus did not 'open any eyes.' But what is more important and more difficult, he taught open eyes to see." ("Karl Kraus hat niemanden 'die Augen geöffnet.' Er hat, was wichtiger und schwieriger ist, offene Augen sehen gelehrt . . .")*

I am indebted to my brother, Dr. George Szasz, for bringing these selections to my attention, and to Miss Maria Sachs for assisting with the translation.

THE CASE OF LOUISE VON COBURG[1]

I

We grieve for Louise von Coburg who has been destroyed by psychiatry, the courts and the police. . . .

---

* Friedrich Torberg, *Pamphlete, Parodien, Postscripta* (München-Wien: Langer-Müller Verlag, 1964), p. 411.

[1] "Irrenhaus Österreich," (*Die Fackel*, October, 1904), in Karl Kraus, *Sittlichkeit und Kriminalität* (München-Wien: Langer-Müller Verlag, 1963), pp. 75–93.

The police and the military have a new function: to channel the sexual drives in desired directions. As a result, there exists in Austria an office that may be called the Ministry of Jealousy. This Ministry does not rule by naked force: it does not poison or strangle. It uses psychiatry instead. Nor is this surprising in a country such as ours, where the ranks of humanity begin with the baron, and where, therefore, it would be madness to deceive a prince with a count. Moreover, as we consider the ranks of humanity as beginning with the barony, so we regard it as ending with psychiatry. Why, then, should not the psychiatrist's diagnosis suffice to deprive someone of his freedom? Nothing is impossible here, in our land of tips and favors.

II

For a long time the population of Austria has been classified according to two principles: the sane and the insane, the innocent and the criminal. The sane and the criminal are accommodated in certain lunatic asylums, whereas the mad and the innocent are placed in prisons. The court psychiatrist [Gerichtspsychiater] sees to it that these distinctions, which are often difficult to make, are properly arrived at. Many problems thwart their routine: the hardest task being to decide which is more ethical—to confine ten commoners in jail or one aristocrat in a mental hospital?

With the exception of a few scientists who are not taken seriously, psychiatrists are of two kinds: knaves and fools. An example of a psychiatrist who fits both categories at once is Herr Regierungsrat Hinterstoisser, the first to offer an expert opinion about poor Louise. For there are psychiatrists who willingly do things out of naive conviction what others can be induced to do only for bribes. One would, in other words, be wrong in believing that all the foul deeds in this world are caused by corruption, as if human baseness operated automatically with the insertion of a coin.

The great neuropathologist Benedikt is right when he speaks of a "biased declaration of insanity" in the Coburg case, and when he asserts, in the most widely read daily newspaper, that there are doctors "who gladly place the misuse of their knowledge and skills at the disposal of the ruling classes, in the expectation that they will be rewarded by positions, titles, medals, and riches."

Although such "bribery" can be readily proved in some cases, it is not necessary to go far afield looking for corruption when good old narrow-mindedness is so close at hand: trained for the stereotype, the psychiatrist is unprepared for real life and refuses to see that "one man's meat is another man's poison." . . . Yes, our pitiable state is partly caused by stupidity. But now at least we know that the "degradation of the intellectual and moral functions" of a princess are due to the lowering of the intellectual and moral functions of her physicians. Alas, journalists have fought with more success against corruption than the gods have against stupidity. In fact, corruption may yet prove to be our best antidote against stupidity: a bigger bribe may overcome high-ranking influence and might even help a just cause to triumph! Whereas profound stupidity carries deep convictions and cannot be bought off for any price. The greatest public menace, therefore, is the incorruptible psychiatric expert, as illustrated by the cases of Girardi and Louise von Coburg. We can be sure that Professor Wagner von Jauregg did not receive a penny from the Rothschilds and Coburgs to recognize, as a symptom of insanity, jealousy in one case, unfaithfulness in the other. . . . The very unselfishness with which such psychiatric outrages are perpetrated suggests that they spring from pathological imbecility rather than from any other source. If only such idiocies were not destined, in each and every case, to destroy a life!

III

I detest psychiatry because it feeds the individual's hunger for power; and because, like journalism, it carries within itself vast potentialities for its abuse. I see the psychiatrist, whose capacity for well-considered action and hence his talent for corruptibility I consider slight, as essentially feebleminded. I would describe the relationship between madmen and psychiatrists as a relationship between convex and concave folly.

The genius of insanity is opposed, usually, by the feeblemindedness of psychiatry. This psychiatric stupidity often turns into malice and even a maniacal desire to persecute. Such psychiatric interests are then sometimes placed in the services of the public prosecutor, sometimes in the service of combating so-called psychoses. In this connection, one should read the writings of the Hofrat von Krafft-Ebing who owes his international reputation to an interest in sexual perversions. And one should read also the "expert opinions" supplied by outstanding Viennese physicians to His Grace the Count Coburg—supplied by the psychiatrists as willingly and fitting as neatly as the gown supplied to Her Grace, the Countess, by her Paris couturiers, and, like the latter, no doubt left unpaid. The fact that to laymen the Princess appeared perfectly normal was to no avail; the noble lady's afflictions, according to His Grace, could be divined only by the experts.

What are the ostensible grounds for finding the Princess insane? A landslide in her youth, followed by a fall. And, more significantly, a shock to her nervous system caused by the death of Crown Prince Rudolf, as a result of which she "became addicted to the equestrian sport, which had formerly been foreign to her, in a manner incomprehensible to a sound mind." Finally, the married psychiatrists describe her "increasing antipathy, quite unmotivated, toward her husband, the Prince," as her most obvious "symptom." The fact that the Princess prefers the company of a "Lieutenant Mattassich" to that of the Duke of Sachsen-Coburg-Gotha is, in the eyes of the Vienna faculty, the penultimate proof that the Princess is insane and requires commitment.

The Princess perseveres in believing in her own personal integrity and in the innocence of her lover: this the experts call her most serious "symptom," and describe under the heading, "Medical History and Diagnosis." "She considers herself normal and mentally competent," reads the psychiatrists' report, "and her incarceration an enormous injustice." Now, isn't that foolish? Wouldn't the Princess be more sensible if she agreed that she was mentally sick?

The report continues: "She is often irritable and occasionally subject to fits of temper"; her confinement in a closed institution "she feels to be a great wrong"; Mattassich's imprisonment, she believes, "was brought about by lies and deception, and she dreams that, disguised as a man, she frees him from his prison." This is certainly suspicious.

On the other hand, the experts assure us that she bears her stay in the lunatic asylum with "equanimity." However, "there was no severe reaction when she learned of Mattassich having been sentenced." That too is suspicious. Agitation is a symptom of mental illness; calmness, too, is a symptom of mental illness!

But the Princess's most severe "symptom" of all is this: she is "conscious of her weakness of will." She said: "I am much too reasonable and fair, for I would rather suffer in silence than cause a scandal." Well, if that is how she is constituted—thought Herr von Krafft-Ebing—then she will not get out of the mental hospital as long as she lives! The layman might call it prudent self-control or timidity; the expert calls it "weak reaction" ["Reaktionsschwäche"]. Von Krafft-Ebing asserts that: "If one deprives a mentally healthy person of his freedom, violent reactions must be expected—such as, summoning all legal means of defense, escape attempts, emotional outbursts, finally suicide attempts." Herr von Krafft-Ebing has devised an infallible test of insanity: if the patient remains in the institution in which he has been imprisoned, then he is insane; if he escapes, he is sane. If the patient stays alive, he is insane; but if he kills himself, the autopsy will show that he was sane. Of course, Louise von Coburg makes it very easy for the psychiatrist to arrive at a diagnosis, even without attempting escape or suicide. "She spends a lot of time in bed, fritters away her time with her wardrobe, glances at the papers, and attends to trivialities without thinking seriously about her past and future, let alone taking steps to ameliorate her position. . . . She expresses a longing to see popular entertainment, to hear folk singers perform, and exhibits a lack of logic and weakness in debate." What a caricature of the female mind!

All this is so fantastic that one mistrusts his eyes: did Freiherr von Krafft-Ebing and Dean Vogl actually sign their names to this expert opinion? They accuse the Princess of a "lack of logic and a weakness in debate" and speak of a "weakened moral sense that made marriage appear a burden and even a chain," leading the "patient" to seek "diversions outside the home . . ." These knights in scientific armor then proceed to call the helpless Mattassich "a worthless person" whom the gracious lady should "abhor." The statement that the Princess tried to "excuse her behavior" sounds more insulting than psychiatric. Finally, the sentence about her "incorrigibility during the nearly one-year period of confinement" is hardly worth paying attention to compared with the other, much graver insults to modesty and common sense offered by the expert opinions of our own Wagner von Jauregg and three other psychiatrists from Berlin, Brussels, and Dresden.

The Princess's "completely unmotivated marital antipathy" turns up again and again in the psychiatric reports of the startled gentlemen. Soon it develops into the "odd hatred of the husband . . . that persists unchanged and is justified to us by the same meaningless arguments as before." Let us recall that before the first examining board the Princess had testified that her husband was "penurious, cowardly, and not overfond of cleanliness." We must realize, of course, that, in the eyes of the German professors, the last-mentioned complaint especially represents no reason for antipathy. On the other hand, we must accept that it will appear highly unnatural to those learned gentlemen that a Princess should be better informed about questions of fashion than about "the state of her business affairs."

IV

Today,[2] even Herr Wagner von Jauregg—who, like his predecessor Krafft-Ebing, diagnoses insanity merely from the fact that the committed person remains in the lunatic asylum—would be forced to admit that the Princess's "weakened" will has become vastly stronger. Of course, Herr Pierson, her warden, doesn't admit it even now. The cheated superintendent of the Lindenhof [Sanitarium] proclaims seeing the same "symptom" in the protest as the previous experts saw in the compliance: It is only her "morbid weakness of will" that made the Princess fall victim to Mattassich's efforts to free her! Some "experts"!

One would think that the close coincidence of two cases like those of Princess Coburg and of Count Csáky would be enough to make people feel fed up with this evil stew of malice, stupidity, conceit, and bootlicking that calls itself psychiatry. We are confronted with so-called medical authorities who regard "the permanent stay of a woman in a closed institution as absolutely essential" because all her "symptoms indicate that her husband refuses to pay the dress-maker's bills"; who testify, under oath, that head-scratching is a sign of psychological degeneration—even though they know that the patient suffers from a skin ailment; who dare refer to the report of the psychiatric profiteers at the Lindenhof, in which it was stated that "the Princess is no longer capable of so behaving in the outside world as to avert undesirable attention" . . . She had to be reminded that she must not scratch her head in a public restaurant—even though the same report acknowledges that a "skin inflammation, psoriasis, has existed for a long time . . ." What should one do with such "experts"? Lock *them* up?

How can such psychiatric humiliation be redressed or avenged? Here is what Mattassich writes in his memoirs:

[2] After a period of confinement Princess Louise von Coburg did escape—a fact assumed to be known by the readers of *Die Fackel*. (Ed.)

"When I was escorted from my rooms, the court psychiatrist of the city of Vienna, the Regierungsrat Dr. Hinterstoisser, the chief of police, and Dr. Bachrach were already waiting in the hall. After I had left the hotel, these gentlemen forced their way into the room of the Princess, who was in bed. Despite the entreaties of the lady-in-waiting, Countess Marie Fugger, they could not be persuaded to leave the room while the Princess dressed; she had to do so in their presence. The spokesman for the group was Dr. Bachrach. He informed the Princess that she must either return to her husband at the Coburg Palace, or must give her consent to enter a sanatorium. The Princess chose to go to the Sanatorium in Döbling, since under no conditions did she want to return to her husband. Dr. Bachrach then began to prowl around the room; seeking proof of adultery, he did not neglect to examine the Princess's bed. That was surely the vilest act that occurred. . . . The fact that the Princess then, during that shameless affront, did not break down, but, as eye-witness Countess Marie Fugger relates, although frightened to death immediately regained her composure is, perhaps, the best indication of her mental health [geistige Normalität]."

I believe every word of Herr Mattassich and of Louise von Coburg. On the basis of interviews which she had granted to several newspaper reporters, I consider this gracious lady not only in full possession of her faculties, but also a rare, indomitable spirit of great vitality. She adequately, and more than adequately, rebuts every argument of her infamous torturers. Indeed, thanks to the training acquired through six years' suffering, she could now supply a more convincing opinion of the mental states of Doctors Wagner, Jolly, Mellis, and Weber, than they ever could of hers. We laymen have ceased to be impressed by a "science" whose practitioners populate prisons with the insane, on the basis of a theory of "simulation"—and fill the lavish Sanatoria of the Ringstrassenkorso with criminals on the basis of a theory of "inheritance." Now, at last, we can laugh this pseudoscience in the face: On the liberated Princess, psychiatry wants to demonstrate to us its latest "discovery"—that insanity can simulate sanity! A feeble mind here offers proof of its weakness by demonstrating strength. But no! Psychiatrists haven't quite yet managed this.

Let us forget the proofs with which Louise von Coburg now defends her competence and her liberty. Her accusers absolve her. To dispel all doubt about whether or not she is sane, and whether or not she requires a guardian, we need only to refer to the main paragraph of the expert psychiatric opinion, headed "Results of Personal Observation by the Undersigned." Here lies truth. Perhaps a layman who *sees* the Princess cannot properly judge her condition; but surely, then, a layman who *does not see* her, but who reads the verdict of four experts who did see her, can make such a judgment!

In the first place, the evaluation must be deemed worthless insofar as it is based on the earlier report of the two hired "wardens," Pierson and Gebauer. At the same time, this document is an astounding confession: "Her entire bearing during our visits," we read, "was that of a gracious lady who is accustomed to making conversation and to discussing a number of subjects easily and adroitly, though without great depth." Of course, the experts are not deceived by this. "She had obviously prepared herself for these examinations and strived to make as good an impression as possible." So now the infuriated Herr Pierson seeks to destroy the good impression Louise von Coburg created by assuring us that she "has prepared herself for years" for the interviews with the psychiatrists! In other words, at first glance, even the experts might have been fooled. But not for long: "On closer examination of earlier events, and of the views which the Princess now holds about the present and the future, the picture of her defective mental state was revealed to us in all its clarity." What does this mean?

Does the Princess, after having uttered a few conventional phrases, again begin to "eat skin scabs, tear up her clothes, and throw potatoes at the visitor"? Oh no. She does much worse: She persists in asserting that she still does not love her husband, and describes her relationship to Mattassich as something "perfectly permissible." She says that she understands nothing of financial matters. And she "protests against having been declared feebleminded and expresses the hope that our observations will convince us that she should be released from guardianship."

In sum, then, what did Doctors Wagner, Jolly, Mellis, and Weber discover as a result of their "personal observation"? First, that the Princess still hates her husband; second, that she still loves Lieutenant Mattassich; and third, that she considers herself sane.

Is there nothing else? Is there not a single "medical" observation? Yes, there is one: that the Princess's skin rash (psoriasis) is on the point of disappearing.

The experts' conclusion: "The condition of morbid mental degeneration found at the time she was placed under guardianship continues unchanged. Because of this illness, and in the best interests of the noble patient, the continuing stay of the Princess in a closed institution is absolutely essential."

Never has a more audacious and more impudent attempt been made to fool the public.

V

We refuse to be fooled. To be sure, an army of flunkeys and parasites may manage to live for years on the profits that accrue from the insanity of a princess. To what extent the illustrious husband was motivated by pecuniary interests—there is an expectation of a Belgian inheritance running into the millions, and this cannot go to one mentally ill—need not concern us. Our interest should lie, rather, in the lack of integrity of the authorities, who are seemingly paralyzed by the magic words "from above," and for whom a noble wish is law.

For Dreyfus, there was at least an outcry of indignation, that became world-wide; but Louise von Coburg and Mattassich provoke no such interest or support. And yet, how do the two injustices compare? Who is the greater martyr—the victim of the interests of the state or the victim of the interests of private revenge enforced by the state?

To decent people, each official measure against the pair of lovers drove home a new lesson about the meaning of the word "official"—a lesson more threatening than the expert opinion of any group of psychiatrists or the verdict of any military court. The pure culture of gangsterism [die Reinkultur der Lumperei] which has resulted from this collaboration of legal and medical zealousness will not be easily surpassed. For who can match the evil power of the mighty Bachrach, who became a government councilor [Regierungsrat] by counseling those who govern about how to get rid of alimony-greedy spouses; and who disposes not just of babies but of the mothers? Is there, in some corner of the earth, a Bar Association that knows how to remain silent as well as ours? And is there, anywhere else, a public prosecutor like Kleeborn of whom it is said, by those who know whereof they speak, that he is subject to no superior authority because "he has made himself so well-liked at court through his services in the Coburg affair"? Many there are who know what they did. But we shall pray for forgiveness to You, O Lord, only for the psychiatrists!

FORENSIC PSYCHIATRY[3]

I

Of all the games people play, this one is the most amusing. . . . The law, of course, is a well-accepted game of blind man's bluff. But the game of blind asses is more novel. The donkeys are led in, see through the accused and say y-eah just as the prosecutor wants them to. However, inasmuch as they call their task, which they perform merrily in the company of their colleagues, "disposition of difficult cases," they do not consider themselves stupid asses but invite comparison with a more intelligent species of domestic animal: Our loyal psychiatrists are rather like good dogs—they protect house and yard, and "clean up" the

[3] "Gerichtspsychiatrie" (*Die Fackel*, February 1904), in Karl Kraus, *Sittlichkeit und Kriminalität* (München-Wien: Langer-Müller Verlag, 1963), pp. 293-97.

most difficult bones for their master. If a person walks at a rapid pace, they conclude that he is a thief. A dog's reliability does not lie in the reliability of his opinion, but in the fact that he gives one. In any case, its threatening bark helps create an impression of authority.

II

"He trembled, had cramps while going to sleep, felt sick in the morning. He became dissolute. His formerly sensitive appreciation of poetry and literature became dulled by alcohol. He lost his taste for the polished presentation of the Burgtheater and the opera, and, sinking ever lower morally, he gadded about in cheap dance halls with female acquaintances."

Well, then, we should not be surprised at anything. The court psychiatrists have here noted not only important symptoms, which *is* their duty—but have also supplied important presumptions, which *they regard* as their duty. The question to be decided is whether or not the accused Z. has committed fraud and embezzlement; to decide this, it is obviously essential to establish that he has lost his taste for the arty performances of the theater and the opera. It is clear proof of his moral inferiority!

Perhaps one could object that the problem is esthetic rather than psychiatric, and that the accused has in fact not demonstrated such poor taste in preferring the companionship of the young ladies of dance halls to the newer productions of our Burgtheater. Perhaps it is even fallacious to assume, as the psychiatrists seem to, that one sinks ever lower morally through associating with "female acquaintances" and through "frequenting dance halls." There are, after all, those who, having indulged in both "vices" have, nonetheless, not come one step closer to embezzling bank deposits. Conceivably, one might even be a veritable Don Juan and yet a thoroughly honorable man in business matters. Conversely, a celibate man may have little respect for the property of others. . . .

III

Consider the expert opinion of a group of Viennese court psychiatrists, rendered in the recent case of the son of a prominent manufacturer. The psychiatrists sought to justify their recommendation to hospitalize the young man by listing the following symptoms: "Even as a child he was excitable and disobedient; his behavior-reports at school were always bad; on his honeymoon, he was jealous without cause; lately, he made remarks about suicide, such as 'Eat, drink, and be merry, for tomorrow we die' [erst wird genossen, dann geschossen]. At the clinic, the patient states that he feels young and wants to live; and he had no serious intention of killing himself, but was only singing the lyrics of an operetta. He admits that, in retrospect, he might have been a little careless in showing himself in a theater loge in the company of . . ."

IV

Here is another case. A house maid is arrested for vagrancy. "Vagrancy" is the name the law gives to that time-honored trade in which a woman proposes to sell her body, without the protection of the police. The maid was arrested because she had no police permit. She claimed, instead, that she could prove police collaboration: the policeman propositioned her while he was escorting her. The policeman was instructed to sue for libel. The girl persisted in her claim. The accused, of course, has the right to lie; and the policeman, as a witness, has the right to stand on his oath of office. How, then, can the truth be ascertained?

Doubt was cast on the girl's truthfulness from several quarters; for example, a number of employers described her as having a sweet tooth. This kind of testimony right away convinced the judge that the mental condition of the accused needed to be examined by court physicians. Lo and behold, they gave an expert opinion that exonerated the policeman much more fully than conviction of the accused based only on the policeman's "oath of office" could possibly have. The poor girl was not guilty because she was not responsible for her actions!

After extended observation the experts found "that the accused was unable to solve simple arithmetic problems; that she did not know the name of the German Kaiser or what a leap year is; and that she claimed that the earth stood still." They concluded that although she was not completely devoid of her senses, she was "mentally very inferior and weak in intellect."

Of course, the purpose of this examination was merely to justify a preconception of guilt. Clearly the maid was mentally unbalanced: she was stupid enough to claim that a policeman had made her an immoral proposition. If *she* had made the immoral proposition to the policeman, she could at least have been convicted without a court psychiatrist having been called in. In that case, she would have been considered sufficiently responsible for her behavior to be considered responsible for her "vagrancy." Moreover, even if such a woman were accused of abortion or infanticide, she could scarcely succeed in impressing the psychiatrists with her ignorance. Even if she had remained in embarrassed silence when asked who the Emperor of Austria is! The court psychiatrists would simply say that she was *simulating* ignorance to avoid punishment! On this occasion, however, the psychiatrists asked who the German Kaiser was; when the girl said she did not know, not for a moment did they doubt the truthfulness of the accused whose untruthfulness was to be ascertained!

Finally, the view that the earth stood still should suffice to convince even the most skeptical psychiatrist that the accused is mentally sick. It is too bad that Galileo had to account for these things before the Inquisition and not before a Vienna district court. The earth does not stand still. We know this if only because forensic psychiatry, whose knowledge steadily expands, claims it to be so. Now only servant girls cling to the rejection of the Copernican system—which only proves that no policeman ever puts his hand up their skirts.

V

No doubt, the last few games have gone especially badly for the forensic psychiatrists. Those who were sitting on this decayed branch of the tree of knowledge have tumbled to the ground.

A madman recently expressed surprise that he had not yet become a psychiatrist. Nowadays real merit is always neglected. In any case, it would be too late: It is said that it had been decided, in authoritative quarters, to dissolve psychiatry as a science and a profession, and to allow it only a modest existence as a faith.

Enough of this humbug that has fooled mankind for so long!

7

THE COMMITMENT OF BISHOP MOREHOUSE

Jack London

John Griffith ("Jack") London (1876–1916) is popularly known as a great American storyteller—a literary entertainer who wrote novels of adventurous life and of wild and half-tamed animals. However, behind this Jack London, the hack writer and raconteur who, as he frankly admitted in his letters, wrote for money—there was another Jack London, whose sincerity and militancy made him at one time the American socialist best known outside of the United States. Today his socialism might be classified as a type of romantic communism: he saw his country headed toward a dictatorship at the hands of a capitalist "oligarchy," and believed that it could be saved only through socialism animated by Brotherly Love for the poor and the weak.

His first political work was *The War of the Classes* (1904). He became solidly established as a socialist writer with *The Iron Heel* (1907)*—written in 1904—when he was thirty years old, and was already one of the most widely read and successful writers in America. This book was ignored by American critics, but had a huge success in Europe. London intended *The Iron Heel* as an exposé of the American class system and class struggle in which, as he saw it, the rich ruth-

---

* Jack London, *The Iron Heel* (1907). Introduction by Max Lerner (New York: Sagamore Press Inc., 1957).

THE COMMITMENT OF BISHOP MOREHOUSE

lessly exploit and oppress the poor; in the process the ruling "oligarchy" establishes a tyranny over thought and behavior comparable to the tyrannies that were yet to come—in Russia and Germany. It was a bitterly anti-American book, which perhaps accounts for its European success. Interestingly, London included the mental hospital in the apparatus of social control employed by the capitalist "oligarchy" in its struggle to subdue the people. Thus, when Bishop Morehouse, one of the principal characters in the novel, becomes critical of the social system, he is incarcerated in an insane asylum. "If he [the Bishop] persisted in the truth as he saw it," wrote London, "he was doomed to an insane ward. And he could do nothing. His money, his position, his culture, could not save him. His views were perilous to society, and society could not conceive that such perilous views could be the product of a sane mind. Or, at least, it seems to me that such was society's attitude."† In his evaluation of the social role of institutional psychiatry, London was at once perceptive and prophetic.

The excerpts that follow are from *The Iron Heel*.‡ I have selected those portions of the novel which describe Bishop Morehouse's "deviation," and his punishment for it by means of psychiatric imprisonment. The novel, it should perhaps be added, is cast in the form of an autobiographical reminiscence, narrated by the widow of the hero, Ernest Everhard. The leader of American socialism and the organizer of the "Second Revolt," Everhard is captured and executed in 1932. After Everhard's execution, his widow retires to a small bungalow in Sonoma, California, where London himself had planned to spend his later years. *The Iron Heel* is the memoir of her experiences at the side of her great husband. Such is the frame upon which London chose to hang his vision of American fascism.

† Ibid., p. 163.
‡ Ibid., pp. 95–174.

I

"The Bishop is out of hand," Ernest wrote me. "He is clear up in the air. To-night he is going to begin putting to rights this very miserable world of ours. He is going to deliver his message. He has told me so, and I cannot dissuade him. To-night he is chairman of the I. P. H., and he will embody his message in his introductory remarks.

"May I bring you to hear him? Of course, he is foredoomed to futility. It will break your heart—it will break his; but for you it will be an excellent object lesson. You know, dear heart, how proud I am because you love me. And because of that I want you to know my fullest value, I want to redeem, in your eyes, some small measure of my unworthiness. And so it is that my pride desires that you shall know my thinking is correct and right. My views are harsh; the futility of so noble a soul as the Bishop will show you the compulsion for such harshness. So come to-night. Sad though this night's happening will be, I feel that it will but draw you more closely to me."

The I. P. H. held its convention that night in San Francisco. This convention had been called to consider public immorality and the remedy for it. Bishop Morehouse presided. He was very nervous as he sat on the platform, and I could see the high tension he was under. By his side were Bishop Dickinson; H. H. Jones, the head of the ethical department in the University of California; Mrs. W. W. Hurd, the great charity organizer; Philip Ward, the equally great philanthropist; and several lesser luminaries in the field of morality and charity. Bishop Morehouse arose and abruptly began:

"I was in my brougham, driving through the streets. It was night-time. Now and then I looked through the carriage windows, and suddenly my eyes seemed to be opened, and I saw things as they really are. At first I covered my eyes with my hands to shut out the awful sight, and then, in the darkness, the question came to me: What is to be done? What is to be done? A little later the question came to me in another way: What would the Master do? And with the question a great light seemed to fill the place, and I saw my duty sun-clear, as Saul saw his on the way to Damascus.

"I stopped the carriage, got out, and, after a few minutes' conversation, persuaded two of the public women to get into the brougham with me. If Jesus was right, then these two unfortunates were my sisters, and the only hope of their purification was in my affection and tenderness.

"I live in one of the loveliest localities of San Francisco. The house in which I live cost a hundred thousand dollars, and its furnishings, books, and works of art cost as much more. The house is a mansion. No, it is a palace, wherein there are many servants. I never knew what palaces were good for. I had thought they were to live in. But now I know. I took the two women of the street to my palace, and they are going to stay with me. I hope to fill every room in my palace with such sisters as they."

The audience had been growing more and more restless and unsettled, and the faces of those that sat on the platform had been betraying greater and greater dismay and consternation. And at this point Bishop Dickinson arose, and, with an expression of disgust on his face, fled from the platform and the hall. But Bishop Morehouse, oblivious to all, his eyes filled with his vision, continued:

"Oh, sisters and brothers, in this act of mine I find the solution of all my difficulties. I didn't know what broughams were made for, but now I know. They are made to carry the weak, the sick, and the aged; they are made to show honor to those who have lost the sense even of shame.

"I did not know what palaces were made for, but now I have found a use for them. The palaces of the Church should be hospitals and nurseries for those who have fallen by the wayside and are perishing."

He made a long pause, plainly overcome by the thought that was in him, and nervous how best to express it.

"I am not fit, dear brethren, to tell you anything about morality. I have lived in shame and hypocrisies too long to be able to help others; but my action with those women, sisters of mine, shows me that the better way is easy to find. To those who believe in Jesus and his gospel there can be no other relation between man and man than the relation of affection. Love alone is stronger than sin—stronger than death. I therefore say to the rich among you that it is their duty to do what I have done and am doing. Let each one of you who is prosperous take into his house some thief and treat him as his brother, some unfortunate and treat her as his sister, and San Francisco will need no police force and no magistrates; the prisons will be turned into hospitals, and the criminal will disappear with his crime.

"We must give ourselves and not our money alone. We must do as Christ did; that is the message of the Church to-day. We have wandered far from the Master's teaching. We are consumed in our own fleshpots. We have put mammon in the place of Christ. . . ."

The audience was agitated, but unresponsive. Yet Bishop Morehouse was not aware of it. He held steadily on his way.

"And so I say to the rich among you, and to all the rich, that bitterly you oppress the Master's lambs. You have hardened your hearts. You have closed your ears to the voices that are crying in the land—the voices of pain and sorrow that you will not hear but that some day will be heard. And so I say—"

But at this point H. H. Jones and Philip Ward, who had already risen from their chairs, led the Bishop off the platform, while the audience sat breathless and shocked.

II

Ernest laughed harshly and savagely when he had gained the street. His laughter jarred upon me. My heart seemed ready to burst with suppressed tears.

"He has delivered his message," Ernest cried. "The manhood and the deep-hidden, tender nature of their Bishop burst out, and his Christian audience, that loved him, concluded that he was crazy! Did you see them leading him so solicitously from the platform? There must have been laughter in hell at the spectacle."

"Nevertheless, it will make a great impression, what the Bishop did and said to-night," I said.

"Think so?" Ernest queried mockingly.

"It will make a sensation," I asserted. "Didn't you see the reporters scribbling like mad while he was speaking?"

"Not a line of which will appear in to-morrow's papers."

"I can't believe it," I cried.

"Just wait and see," was the answer. "Not a line, not a thought that he uttered. The daily press? The daily suppressage!"

"But the reporters," I objected. "I saw them."

"Not a word that he uttered will see print. You have forgotten the editors. They draw their salaries for the policy they maintain. Their policy is to print nothing that is a vital menace to the established. The Bishop's utterance was a violent assault upon the established morality. It was heresy. They led him from the platform to prevent him from uttering more heresy. The newspapers will purge his heresy in the oblivion of silence. The press of the United States? It is a parasitic growth that battens on the capitalist class. Its function is to serve the established by moulding public opinion, and right well it serves it.

"Let me prophesy. To-morrow's papers will merely mention that the Bishop is in poor health, that he has been working too hard, and that he broke down last night. The next mention, some days hence, will be to the effect that he is suffering from nervous prostration and has been given a vacation by his grateful flock. After that, one of two things will happen: either the Bishop will see the error of his way and return from his vacation a well man in whose eyes there are no more visions, or else he will persist in his madness, and then you may expect to see in the papers, couched pathetically and tenderly, the announcement of his insanity. After that he will be left to gibber his visions to padded walls."

"Now there you go too far!" I cried out.

"In the eyes of society it will truly be insanity," he replied. "What honest man, who is not insane, would take lost women and thieves into his house to dwell with him sisterly and brotherly? True, Christ died between two thieves, but that is another story. Insanity? The mental processes of the man with whom one disagrees, are always wrong. Therefore the mind of the man is wrong. Where is the line between wrong mind and insane mind? It is inconceivable that any sane man can radically disagree with one's most sane conclusions.

"There is a good example of it in this evening's paper. Mary McKenna lives south of Market Street. She is a poor but honest woman. She is also patriotic. But she has erroneous ideas concerning the American flag and the protection it is supposed to symbolize. And here's what happened to her. Her husband had an accident and was laid up in hospital three months. In spite of taking in washing, she got behind in her rent. Yesterday they evicted her. But first, she hoisted an American flag, and from under its folds she announced that by virtue of its protection they could not turn her out on to the cold street. What was done? She was arrested and arraigned for insanity. To-day she was examined by the regular insanity experts. She was found insane. She was consigned to the Napa Asylum."

"But that is far-fetched," I objected. "Suppose I should disagree with everybody about the literary style of a book. They wouldn't send me to an asylum for that."

"Very true," he replied. "But such divergence of opinion would constitute no menace to society. Therein lies the difference. The divergence of opinion on the parts of Mary McKenna and the Bishop do menace society. What if all the poor people should refuse to pay rent and shelter themselves under the American flag? Landlordism would go crumbling. The Bishop's views are just as perilous to society. Ergo, to the asylum with him."

But still I refused to believe.

"Wait and see," Ernest said, and I waited.

Next morning I sent out for all the papers. So far Ernest was right. Not a word that Bishop Morehouse had uttered was in print. Mention was made in one or two of the papers that he had been overcome by his feelings. Yet the platitudes of the speakers that followed him were reported at length.

Several days later the brief announcement was made that he had gone away on a vacation to recover from the effects of overwork. So far so good, but there had been no hint of insanity, nor even of nervous collapse. Little did I dream the terrible road the Bishop was destined to travel—the Gethsemane and crucifixion that Ernest had pondered about. . . .

III

It was after my marriage that I chanced upon Bishop Morehouse. But I must give the events in their proper sequence. After his outbreak at the I. P. H. Convention, the Bishop, being a gentle soul, had yielded to the friendly pressure brought to bear upon him, and had gone away on a vacation. But he returned more fixed than ever in his determination to preach the message of the Church. To the consternation of his congregation, his first sermon was quite similar to the address he had given before the Convention. Again he said, and at length and with distressing detail, that the Church had wandered away from the Master's teaching, and that Mammon had been instated in the place of Christ.

And the result was, willy-nilly, that he was led away to a private sanitarium for mental disease, while in the newspapers appeared pathetic accounts of his mental breakdown and of the saintliness of his character. He was held a prisoner in the sanitarium. I called repeatedly, but was denied access to him; and I was terribly impressed by the tragedy of a sane, normal, saintly man being crushed by the brutal will of society. For the Bishop was sane, and pure, and noble. As Ernest said, all that was the matter with him was that he had incorrect notions of biology and sociology, and because of his incorrect notions he had not gone about it in the right way to rectify matters.

What terrified me was the Bishop's helplessness. If he persisted in the truth as he saw it, he was doomed to an insane ward. And he could do nothing. His money, his position, his culture, could not save him. His views were perilous to society, and society could not conceive that such perilous views could be the product of a sane mind. Or, at least, it seems to me that such was society's attitude. . . . A week later we read in the newspaper of the sad case of Bishop Morehouse, who had been committed to the Napa Asylum and for whom there were still hopes held out. In vain we tried to see him, to have his case reconsidered or investigated. Nor could we learn anything about him except the reiterated statements that slight hopes were still held for his recovery.

"Christ told the rich young man to sell all he had," Ernest said bitterly. "The Bishop obeyed Christ's injunction and got locked up in a madhouse. Times have changed since Christ's day. A rich man to-day who gives all he has to the poor is crazy. There is no discussion. Society has spoken."

PART THREE

THE FLOWERING OF PSYCHIATRIC POWER (1920—   )

FROM THE SLAUGHTERHOUSE TO THE MADHOUSE

Ugo Cerletti

> Ugo Cerletti (1877–1963), a professor of psychiatry at the University of Rome, "discovered" electric shock treatment and introduced its use into psychiatry. The following excerpt* is from Cerletti's own account of the history of the development of electroshock therapy. It should suffice to note here that Cerletti does not mention having obtained permission from anyone for administering this experimental "treatment" to his "patient"; moreover, when the "patient" explicitly objected to the "treatment," Cerletti immediately administered another shock to him.†

Vanni informed me that at the slaughterhouse in Rome hogs were killed by electric current. Such information seemed to confirm my doubts regarding the danger of electric applications to man. I went to the slaughterhouse to observe this so-called electric slaughtering, and I saw that the hogs were clamped at the temples with big metallic tongs which were hooked up to an electric current (125

---

* Ugo Cerletti, "Electroshock Therapy," in A. M. Sackler, M. D. Sackler, R. R. Sackler, and F. Marti-Ibañez, Editors, *The Great Physiodynamic Therapies in Psychiatry: An Historical Reappraisal*, Chapter 4, pp. 91–120 (New York: Hoeber-Harper, 1956), pp. 92–94.

† For a more detailed commentary on this account, see Thomas S. Szasz, "From the Slaughterhouse to the Madhouse," *Psychotherapy*, 8:64–67 (Spring), 1971.

volts). As soon as the hogs were clamped by the tongs, they fell unconscious, stiffened, then after a few seconds they were shaken by convulsions in the same way as our experimental dogs. During this period of unconsciousness (epileptic coma), the butcher stabbed and bled the animals without difficulty. Therefore, it was not true that the animals were killed by the electric current: the latter was used, at the suggestion of the Society for the Prevention of Cruelty to Animals, so that the hogs might be killed painlessly.

It occurred to me that the hogs of the slaughterhouse could furnish the most valuable material for my experiments. And I conceived, moreover, the idea of reversing the former experimental procedure: while on dogs my aim had been the use of minimal quantity of current capable of inducing a seizure without harm to the animal, I now decided to establish the time duration, voltage, and the method of application that would be necessary to produce the death of the animal. Electric current would therefore be applied through the skull, in different directions, and through the trunk for several minutes. My first observation was that the animals rarely died, and then only when the duration of electric current flowed through the body and not through the head. The animals that received the severest treatment remained rigid during the flow of the electric current, then after a violent convulsive seizure they would lie on their sides for a while, sometimes for several minutes, and finally they would attempt to rise. After many attempts of increasing efficiency, they would succeed in standing up and making a few hesitant steps until they were able to run away. These observations gave me convincing evidence of the harmlessness of a few tenths of a second of application through the head of a 125-volt electric current, which was more than sufficient to insure a complete convulsive seizure.

At this point I felt we could venture to experiment on man, and I instructed my assistants to be on the alert for the selection of a suitable subject.

On April 15, 1938, the Police Commissioner of Rome

sent a man to our Institute with the following note: 'S.E., 39 years old, engineer, resident of Milan, was arrested at the railroad station while wandering about without a ticket on trains ready for departure. He does not appear to be in full possession of his mental faculties, and I am sending him to your hospital to be kept there under observation. . . .' The condition of the patient on April 18 was as follows: lucid, well-oriented. He describes with neologisms deliriant ideas of being telepathically influenced with related sensorial disturbances; his mimicry is correlated to the meaning of his words; mood indifferent to environment, low affective reserves; physical and neurologic examination negative; presents conspicuous hypacusis and cataract in L.E. A diagnosis of schizophrenic syndrome was made based on his passive behavior, incoherence, low affective reserves, hallucinations, deliriant ideas of being influenced, neologisms.

This subject was chosen for the first experiment of induced electric convulsions in man. Two large electrodes were applied to the frontoparietal regions, and I decided to start cautiously with a low-intensity current of 80 volts for 0.2 seconds. As soon as the current was introduced, the patient reacted with a jolt and his body muscles stiffened; then he fell back on the bed without loss of consciousness. He started to sing abruptly at the top of his voice, then he quieted down.

Naturally, we, who were conducting the experiment were under great emotional strain and felt that we had already taken quite a risk. Nevertheless, it was quite evident to all of us that we have been using a too low voltage. It was proposed that we should allow the patient to have some rest and repeat the experiment the next day. All at once, the patient, who evidently had been following our conversation, said clearly and solemnly, without his usual gibberish: 'Not another one! It's deadly!'

I confess that such explicit admonition under such circumstances, and so emphatic and commanding, coming from a person whose enigmatic jargon had until then been very difficult to understand, shook my determination to carry on with the experiment. But it was just this fear of yielding to a superstitious notion that caused me to make up my mind. The electrodes were applied again, and a 110-volt discharge was applied for 0.2 seconds.

2

THE DISCOVERY OF LOBOTOMY*

Egas Moniz

Antonio Caetano Abreum Freire Egas Moniz (1874–1955), a Portuguese neurologist and neurosurgeon, introduced prefrontal lobotomy into psychiatry in 1935, and, in 1949, received the Nobel Prize in physiology and medicine for it. This procedure is, so far as I know, the only medical treatment that has been formally condemned by the Vatican and banned in the U.S.S.R. The excerpts that follow are from Moniz's own work. It is significant that he does not even mention whether the "patients" he lobotomized were hospitalized voluntarily or involuntarily, or whether they or anyone else were asked for, or granted, permission for the operations.

It was owing to no sudden inspiration that I performed the surgical operation which I called "prefrontal leucotomy"....

A great adept of the doctrines of Ramon y Cajal, and based on the theory of the connections of the nerve cells, I often turned my attention to the origin of normal and pathological psychic activity and its dependence upon

* From Egas Moniz, *How I Came to Perform Prefrontal Leucotomy*, Congress of Psychosurgery (Lisboa: Edicoes Atica, 1948), pp. 7–18.

neuronal activity. The impulses pass through the neurones along the fibrils; in the synapses alterations are produced which react on many other cells.

All this came to my mind when I was engaged in solitary meditation.

To the cerebral activity of normal mental life I added the derangements which make their appearance in most psychoses and which had till then no anatomo-pathological explanation. I was especially impressed by the fact that the mental life of some lunatics—and I thought in particular of obsessed and melancholic patients—is limited to a small circle of ideas which overrule all others and keep recurring in their diseased brain, and I tried to find an explanation of this fact.

The nervous impulses come from everywhere: from the external world by the nerve terminals; from the chemical reaction taking place within the nerve tissue; from stimuli of the most diverse origins, many of which arise from the cellular life of the intracranial neuronal complexes. They give origin to currents which run at high speed along the nervous conductors, ascending to the brain from the peripheral nerves and the sympathetic nervous system, and along the fibres which connect the encephalic areas. . . .

Starting from these anatomical facts I arrived at the conclusion that the synapses, which are found in billions of cells, are the organic foundation of thought.

Normal psychic life depends upon the good functioning of the synapses and mental disorders appear as a result of synaptic derangements. . . .

All of these considerations led me to the following conclusion: it is necessary to alter these synaptic adjustments and change the paths chosen by the impulses in their constant passage so as to modify the corresponding ideas and force thought into different channels.

Induced by these reasons, after more than two years of meditation I decided to sever the connecting fibres of the neurones in activity. Being convinced of the importance of the prefrontal lobes in mental life, I chose this region for

THE DISCOVERY OF LOBOTOMY

attempt and it seems that it was well timed. By upsetting the existing adjustments and setting in movement other fibril-synaptic groups, I expected to be able to transform the psychic reactions and to relieve the patient thereby.

My purpose being to annihilate a great number of associations, I preferred to attack (en masse) the cell-connecting fibres of the anterior portion of both frontal lobes aiming at positive results. The method of destruction employed at first was alcohol injections followed by incisions with the leucotome, a small apparatus designed by us for this purpose. The white substance of the brain having limited circulation, the operation should be free from danger. Everything was done with the greatest care so as to protect the patient's life.

I take the liberty, if I may, of transcribing a short passage from my book "Tentatives Operatoires", which marks a decisive moment in my work:

"On the eve of my first attempt, in my justified anxiety at that moment, all fears were swept aside by the hope of obtaining favourable results.

"If we could suppress certain symptomatic complexes of psychic nature by destroying the cell-connecting groups we would prove definitely that the psychic functions and the brain areas which contributed to their elaboration were closely related. That would be a great step forward as a fundamental fact in the study of the psychic functions on an organic basis".

And this passage ended thus:

"We are certain that these experiments shall stir up keen discussion in the medical, psychiatric, psychological, philosophical, social and other fields. We expect that but hope at the same time that this discussion shall promote the progress of science and above all the benefit of mental patients."

We set to work with my valuable collaborator, Prof. Almeida Lima, to whom we are indebted for a great part of the pioneering works. The first alcohol injections in the white matter of the prefrontal lobe were given on the 12th of November 1935, and the first intervention with the leucotome took place on December 27th of the same year. We obtained cures and improvements but no failures to make us draw back.

3

THE SICK AND THE MAD

Frigyes Karinthy

Frigyes Karinthy (1887–1938) was one of the outstanding literary figures of modern Hungary. As a writer, he was precocious, prolific, and versatile. His first piece was published when he was fourteen. After graduation from the "Gymnasium," he studied mathematics and physics, and then medicine. After two years, he discontinued his medical studies and became a journalist and writer. He was a regular contributor to newspapers and magazines, was a literary critic and translator, and wrote poetry as well as fiction. His wife was a psychiatrist and many of Karinthy's writings show a thorough familiarity with psychiatry and psychoanalysis. In 1936, he developed symptoms of a brain tumor and was operated upon by Professor Olivecrona in Stockholm, Sweden. He made a temporary recovery, during which he recorded his experiences as a patient in the book, *Utazás a Koponyám Körül*.* He died from a hemorrhage into the regrowing tumor in 1938. From a collection of his short, mainly humorous, pieces, entitled *Betegek és Bolondok (The Sick and the Mad)*,† I have selected three

* *A Journey Round My Skull*, trans. by Vernon Duckworth Barker (New York & London: Harper & Brothers Publishers, 1939). To my knowledge, this is Karinthy's only work available in English.
† *Betegek és Bolondok (The Sick and the Mad)* (Budapest: Uj Idők Irodalmi Intézet R.T., 1946).

which seemed to me especially suitable for this volume. The translation is mine.

THE BAKER[1]

Why was Zoltán Fischer, the baker, locked up in the insane asylum?

The official report lies before me. The facts are clear. Nothing needs to be added to the report or taken away from it. It is enough to *record* it.

I wish to emphasize the necessity for writing down and publishing this case. Why? Because, according to official scientific psychiatry, there is absolutely nothing unusual or worth recording in this case: Zoltán Fischer was removed to the asylum for the simple reason that he was mentally ill, had a nervous breakdown—in short, because he went insane. Period. It's a purely clinical problem. We must therefore speak of it through the rhetoric of psychopathology; more specifically, through the so-called *anamnesis*. If, then, I propose to describe the case not in the special language of scientific psychiatry, but *in everyday language*, I realize that I commit a grave insult against the legally constituted authority of psychiatric medicine.

I respect the laws of science. If I make an exception here, it is because although the judgments and actions of psychiatry are clear, its explanations are not. If a person is mentally ill (excepting general paresis), his illness cannot be inferred from the objective condition of his brain or nervous system. . . . Nor can it be inferred from an examination of the brain and nervous system at autopsy. Psychiatric science is satisfied therefore with noting certain actions engaged in by the insane person, which are indeed unusual. That is the basis of the diagnosis. In other words, the psychiatrist *describes* the unusual actions of the so-called patient.

I shall do the same.

Recently, Zoltán Fischer, the baker, had been feeling restless. Or, as those around him said, he "behaved" as if

[1] "Pékmester" ("The Baker"), *Betegek és Bolondok*, pp. 16–21.

he were agitated: he was irritable, inattentive, moody. This disturbance is unusual only if we assume that the baker had nothing to be disturbed about. This is just what his "loved ones" maintained to be the case: business was good, and the baker had ample savings, a healthy family, and a well-functioning digestive tract. However, if we assume that the baker was disturbed by something *other* than his business, family, or digestion, his irritability and restlessness need not appear unusual. Let us suppose that Zoltán Fischer was mulling over some problem. When a person is preoccupied and in deep thought, it is quite natural for him to be irritable and restless; indeed, it would be unusual if he were not.

Well, then, it soon became apparent that the baker was *in fact* seriously considering a problem. His family, disturbed by the baker's condition, sent him to P. for a rest. (Aha! his family was *also* disturbed. Yet *they* were not committed to a mental hospital.) When Fischer returned from P. he appeared to be much improved. He was not restless or irritable.

This was because he was no longer preoccupied by the problem.

The trouble was now much more serious.

The baker began to *act*.

One morning, Zoltán Fischer began to distribute copies of a circular in the neighborhood. It was an announcement that the price of bread and rolls had been reduced drastically—so low, in fact, that they would bring no profit at all. The price was nominal, enough only to distinguish the goods from a free gift. Fischer also explained why he did this: "to help the poor people." As if to complete this "insane logic," he began himself to help deliver the products of his ovens.

At this point it became clear that here was a case for the insane asylum.

Had the baker believed that he was Napoleon, and had he addressed a petition to the government—it would have depended on the style and content of his appeal whether he would have been locked up (in a mental hospital or in a prison), or proclaimed the Great Leader. In any case, the diagnosis would have been uncertain.

The chances of commitment would have been greatly increased had the baker believed that he was a butcher. Being a butcher is not like being a Leader. The butcher must have certain skills. A group of butchers could thus determine whether Zoltán Fischer was in fact a competent butcher or whether his belief of being a butcher was a delusion.

In the present case, there was no such problem. It was a sure case for the madhouse. For the baker believed that he was a baker.

Of course, he considered himself to be a baker in a very basic sense: A baker, he believed, was a man who bakes bread and rolls for people who hunger after bread and rolls so that their hunger will be appeased.

This was the problem that had preoccupied and troubled Zoltán Fischer until he decided on a course of action while resting at P. If only he had continued to *think* and *worry*, but refrained from *acting*, he might never have been committed to a mental hospital.

For, so long as we cannot infer insanity from brain lesions, we must define it as follows: The insane person is an individual who *acts* on the basis of his *beliefs*, even if the actions to which he is so led are unusual in the time and place where he lives; he is especially insane if he acts in accordance with what *he considers right*, even if in so doing he will be said to harm himself or others.

Zoltán Fischer must have felt that there was something wrong with him, something very wrong, when he began to take the path which his reason and his conscience chose for him.

The report states that when the men in white coats came for him, he was not surprised. He did not resist. He acknowledged their arrival with composure, with a faint smile on his lips, almost a sigh of relief. He knew where they were taking him. He expected them.

"I am glad you are taking me to Leopoldfield [the name of the state mental hospital serving Budapest]." he said.

"It's a quiet place. I can get some sleep there. I am so sleepy."

Zoltán Fischer wanted to sleep. He was like the person who realizes that in trying to correct one mistake, the mistake of a lifetime, he has made another; such a person too wants to sleep.

I shall mention, but not belabor, a comparison. Our Master, who was also a baker, fed five thousand men with five loaves of bread. Yet, even in His day, five loaves of bread were thought to be enough for only five men.

Perhaps there is only one way to determine whether a good act is in fact good, *always* and *everywhere*: one must sleep on it. For three days, for three hundred years, if necessary, for three thousand years. In the story of the Redemption, I think we pay too much attention to the Crucifixion, and not enough to the Resurrection.

PSYCHIATRY[2]

"My dear colleague, I am here to consult you in an extraordinary case. You know why I have come to you? Because I trust you as a scientific psychiatrist; in fact, I trust you as much as I trust myself."

"I am honored, my dear colleague. And I must agree with you: in psychiatry, it's a dead heat between us."

"There can be no doubt about it. About mental illness, we always agree. I regard this as proof that psychiatry, correctly understood, is a mature science. This is why I have come to see you. Because 'Four eyes see better than two.' I want to discuss this interesting case with you. In strict confidence, of course."

"I am all ears, my dear friend."

"The question is simply this: Am I, your friend and colleague who is speaking to you, insane or not?"

"A very interesting question. It has occurred to me, too. So this is what you want to discuss with me?"

"Yes. At first, I thought that as the nation's foremost psychiatrist, I myself ought to decide this question. But

[2] "Tudomány" ("Science"), ibid., pp. 146-49.

then I decided that since it's an important case, I ought to have a consultant. Two doctors are always better than one. So I invited myself and you to this consultation."

"I approve. That is the correct medical procedure. Perhaps we ought to get right down to the case."

"I am at your service."

"So far, I do not have a firm opinion about the problem. I would be most anxious to hear your views about it."

"In my opinion, I am insane."

"That is certainly an important judgment, coming from an expert of your eminence."

"You flatter me, my dear colleague."

"Not at all. But let's get back to the problem. We agree —I think—about what constitutes the single most important diagnostic sign of insanity?"

"Of course. You have in mind what the French call *l'idée fixe;* the fixed idea. Is that not so?"

"Naturally. We must determine, then, whether or not you, my dear colleague, have any fixed ideas. I trust we agree what we mean by 'fixed idea'?"

"Of course we agree. A fixed idea is a delusion. An individual capable of perfectly logical reasoning holds a belief about himself that is completely false; for example, he thinks he is the Emperor, when in fact he is not."

"Correct. We both know, my dear friend, that save for his fixed idea, the insane person is perfectly reasonable. Let us see, then, if you have any fixed ideas. Because if you don't, if your reasoning is correct and logical, then you are not insane."

"I agree."

"Let's find out, then. Do you have any delusions, or fixed ideas, about yourself? What is your name?"

"Such and such."

"Correct. And who are you?"

"A psychiatrist."

"Correct. And where do you live?"

"At such and such address."

"Right again. It is already clear that you know perfectly

well who you are and what you are, because what you told me is correct. I would conclude that you have no delusions about yourself and are therefore not insane."

"But I think I am insane."

"But you don't have any delusions! You know what you are!"

"Yes, insane."

"No. We saw that you are not."

"You really think so?"

"Certainly. I have proved it to you."

"Oh, no, not so fast! For if I am really not insane, but believe that I am, then my belief is a delusion, a fixed idea."

"You are right!"

"You see, I told you: I have a delusion, therefore I am insane."

"Of course. If you have a delusion, you are insane."

"So, am I insane?"

"Well, since you have a delusion, evidently you are."

"Oh, no, there you go again! Now you say that if I have a delusion, I am insane. But you just said that I am insane. In that case, my belief is not a delusion, but a correct idea. Therefore I have no delusion. Therefore I am not, after all, insane. It is only a delusion that I am insane; hence I have a delusion; hence I am insane; hence I am right; hence I am not insane. Isn't psychiatry a magnificent science?"

"The most magnificent, my dearest colleague! But of course it's necessary to master it as well as only you and I have."

I STUDY THE SOUL[3]

Recently, I began to study mental illness.

For two semesters I attended lectures on neurosis, diagnosis, and psychotherapy by Professors Moravcsik, Ranschburg, and Freud. In all humility, I believe that I am es-

[3] "Tudományozom a Lelket" ("I Study the Soul"), ibid., pp. 155–58.

pecially sensitive and talented in diagnosing delusions and disturbances of mood. As one of my esteemed professors remarked, the human mind is best understood by studying the insane, just as the working of a watch is best understood by taking apart one that has stopped running.

In order to advance my psychological skills, I asked the chief psychiatrist of one of our insane asylums to allow me to spend some time in his institution. I wanted to observe the mental functioning of men who are actually mad.

The way to proceed, I told myself, is to talk individually to several of the patients, without any prior knowledge of what the doctors think about the case. I should arrive at my own, unprejudiced conclusions.

My psychiatrist friend took me to what the staff called the park of the paranoiacs. I asked him to leave me alone with the living dead. It was a classic scene: one madman stood immobile in a Napoleonic pose; another paced up and down talking gibberish; two others played chess, watched over by a kibitzer who seemed to be laughing uncontrollably.

My attention—guided by my hawk-like eyes and uncanny intuition—was attracted by a pale and haggard young man, wearing a white vest. He sat by the fence and looked tired. This poor man, I decided, was to be my first subject. I overcame the natural aversion which the sane feel toward the insane, approached him, and addressed him softly.

"How are you?"

He looks at me. The tired face shows no emotion. "I manage," he replies calmly.

Yes, a typical case. Burned out dementia praecox, perhaps with some depression. The sick man talks calmly and intelligently. One could not tell the difference between such a madman and a normal person until one happens to touch on his delusion. Well, he'll give himself away soon enough.

"How long have you been here?"

"Four years, damn it."

Aha! Typical. The patient knows where he is, but believes that he is held by some mistake. It's all an injustice.

He is perfectly well. He was brought here by force against his will. Poor man!

This calls for a careful interrogation. I must not antagonize him. In the meantime, I watch his pupils.

"Well, then, what is wrong with you, my friend?"

The patient makes a gesture of hopeless resignation. The typical gesture: He knows!

"What wrong with me? Ha? This is no life, I tell you. I have no Sundays, no holidays. I must get up at 5 o'clock in the morning. What kind of life is that?"

Here we go. He is beginning to talk about it.

"We have it hard, I tell you. It's a big responsibility. And what do we get for it? Yet we are responsible for everything—everything, I tell you! But I took the job, so I shall do my duty."

I tremble with inner joy. It's perfect. Big responsibility. Caesar-complex. He thinks he is an important statesman. Perhaps Bismarck. Or perhaps a great national leader on whose shoulders rests the fate of his countrymen.

I must be very careful. I must agree with everything he says. This is the correct approach.

"Do you trust yourself?" I asked him gently.

"Why shouldn't I? In two months I'll be promoted. It will be better then."

Good. It fits. He thinks he is the Crown Prince. In two months he'll be the King. This is his delusion. And how easily I discovered it. The poor boy. I'll try one more question.

"What kind of promotion do you expect?"

"What kind? Practically no kind at all! A mere twenty a month more. A pittance! A niggardly bunch . . . They don't deserve me . . . But they'll be sorry . . ."

He shakes his fist in anger. Panic overcomes me. I back away. The patient is enraged. As I retreat, I bump into a psychiatrist. I didn't even hear him approach. Thank God! Where would I be without him?

"Doctor"—I whisper in his ear as we walk away—"how did he get here?"

"Oh, John? He is a carpenter by trade. But work was

scarce. We hired him because he is a decent fellow. If only he wouldn't keep asking for a raise. He is one of our most reliable attendants."

I quit studying mental illness.

4

WARD 7

Valeriy Tarsis

Valeriy Tarsis (1906–), is a Russian literary critic, translator, and writer, who, in 1960, decided to send a manuscript critical of life in Khrushchev's Russia to England for publication. This work, *The Bluebottle*, was published in England in October 1962, and was followed by a number of other translations in the West.

The English edition came out under the pseudonym Ivan Valeriy. Tarsis had, however, opposed the use of a pseudonym and made no secret in Russia of having sent his book abroad. In August 1962, two months before the appearance of *The Bluebottle* in London, Tarsis was arrested and committed to the Koshchenko psychiatric hospital in Moscow. News of his fate soon reached the West, and was publicized by the British journalist Edward Crankshaw in *The Observer* (February 1963). In March 1963, Tarsis was released.

Ward 7* is Tarsis's account of what happened to him in the "mental hospital." It was written shortly after his release and smuggled to England in the summer of 1964. In this autobiographical novel, Valentine

---

* From *Ward 7: An Autobiographical Novel*, trans. by Katya Brown (London and Glasgow: Collins and Havrill Press, 1965), pp. 18–124.

Almazov, a Russian writer, is arrested and incarcerated in a psychiatric institution for the same offense as Tarsis had been; he is held in the notorious Russian asylum the "Villat Kanatchikov," which is actually the nickname among Russians of the Koshchenko Hospital; and he is released after protests from the West.

In February 1966, Tarsis was allowed to leave Russia and was deprived of his Soviet citizenship. He now resides in England.

I

"The madman is tormented by his thirst," an Indian sage had said (the wise are always madmen to philistines). "It grows ever sharper, it clings to him like bindweed, it follows him as he goes from life to life, like a monkey from tree to tree in search of refreshing fruit. I too was a monkey searching for fruit in the forest but finding only poisonous berries and breaking my bones but also the boughs."

Almazov's thirst was indeed unquenchable and so tormenting that he sometimes felt as if it would choke him. He kept notebooks of quotations in several languages and in his worst moments it gave him a strange and almost physical joy to read them aloud to himself. As powerful as incantations, they gave him not only comfort but the strength to live.

"Live as though you were on the point of death, as if every moment were an unexpected gift," he read in Marcus Aurelius.

This indeed had been his life for a long time past and especially in recent years, ever since he had realised that Communism was a form of Fascism and that Russian literature had ceased to exist: it was then that he handed over a batch of his manuscripts to a visiting British journalist whom he met by chance. His publishers urged him to use a pseudonym but he refused, although he knew what awaited him. He cared nothing for the official version of public opinion, and no genuine public opinion was left:

for years, no one in Russia had said what he really thought.

"If you knew the source of public judgments, you would cease to strive for approval and praise," Marcus Aurelius had said.

It was with bitter shame that Valentine recalled his years as a Party member. Why had it taken him so long to realise that his "comrades," particularly those who were officials, secretaries, members of the party bureau, were nothing but policemen? Now he held the proof of it. Acting openly as usual, he had made no secret of the fact that he had sent his manuscripts abroad. As soon as this was known, the secretary of his party committee rang him up. "Drop in tomorrow at noon, Valentine," he said in a honeyed voice. "Let's talk it over. We'll do our very best to *help you*."

Almazov went. The secretary met him in the hall. Bald and with vacant, watery eyes but usually talkative and self-assertive, he shuffled and rubbed his hands with an embarrassed air.

"Ah, my dear fellow! Come in . . . There are some comrades from State Security waiting to see you . . . I'm sure you understand. We thought we'd put our heads together about how to help you best . . . Let me introduce you . . ."

The two Chekists,[1] one short, fat and bald, the other tall, thin and grey, were wandering about the room, plainly ill at ease.

Almazov had one of those rare moments of illumination when a man suddenly sees clearly what, for years, was hidden from him. He scarcely heard what the agents were saying; their voices were drowned by the hammering in his head. How was it possible that for so many years he had mistaken this gang for a band of idealists?

"You are in a very serious predicament," mumbled the fat one. "If your book comes out abroad, we'll have to lock you up."

"It's certainly coming out, and others after it, so you'd

---

[1] Members of the Cheka, now known as the K.G.B.

better go ahead." Almazov grinned, "So Khrushchev's assurances of socialist legality are so much wind!"

"Why be coarse? We hope that you'll recall your manuscripts. This is plainly your duty as a communist . . ."

"Yes, I see . . ." He was thinking that he must hurry up and send the rest of his manuscripts abroad. So ended his affair with the Party; it had been a shameful *mésalliance*.

> He remembered the words of Oscar Wilde: But he never fell into the error of arresting his intellectual development by any formal acceptance of creed or system, or of mistaking, for a house in which to live, an inn that is but suitable for the sojourn of a night, or for a few hours of a night in which there are no stars and the moon is in travail.

Certainly, Almazov's night was dark enough, and starless, but he was filled with shame to think that, even for a time, he could have let himself mistake the Kremlin's pentagons for stars and a thieves' den for a house to live in.

But he had never indulged in the morbid contemplation of his sufferings. Now he knew that the sooner he shook the dust off his feet the better: he wrote to Khrushchev and asked permission to go abroad, frankly stating his reasons.

There was no answer for a long time. After a month or two, he assumed that as usual when bureaucrats are addressed without flattery there would be none. But the answer came. . . .

II

Almazov was writing variations on Leopardi's theme, the "tragedy of everyday life," when that very tragedy broke into his room in the person of two policemen, the head janitor who, like all head janitors, was employed by the police, and a nosy woman who, according to the head janitor, represented the "community" destined in the future to replace the organs of the State.[2]

"Sorry to trouble you, Valentine Ivanovich," said the senior of the two policemen, looking embarrassed. "But the police superintendent wants to have a word with you. He says, would you come and see him, it's urgent."

"What can the police want with me? I'm not a hooligan or a thief," said Almazov.

"I couldn't tell you, I'm afraid, I wasn't told. But as you know, the police is an organ of the State, so you have to come."

Clearly, Almazov was in trouble.

"I'll come with you," said his wife.

"Certainly," said the policeman.

In the front of the door was one of the blue cars with a red stripe which—to distinguish them from Stalin's black limousines known as "black ravens"—are popularly known as "plague cars."

At the police station Valentine was asked to wait. His escort had vanished. The policeman at the door was less polite and refused to answer any questions. Needless to say, there was no conversation with the superintendent. At the end of ten minutes, he was taken to a waiting ambulance in the yard. A woman doctor, employed as guard, said:

"You are Valentine Almazov? By order of the chief city psychiatrist you are being taken in for observation."

"Scoundrels!" Almazov muttered to his wife. "They even turn doctors into policemen! But don't worry, it only shows that they're getting frightened. They got me here by a trick. Communist bandits! They'll get what's coming to them in the end—the people will see to it."

He walked to the ambulance. Two young brutes like oxen stood in white overalls watching him.

It was raining. An hour earlier it had been fine, but now

---

[2] In the Soviet C.P. programme of 1961, it was announced that in view of the imminent advent of Communism the functions of the "State Organs" (e.g. the police) were being gradually taken over by the public.

the rain drummed on the roof of the ambulance and streamed down the windows. The two brutes sat sniffing; low clouds lumbered across the sky, like the rhinoceroses Valentine as a child had watched at the zoo, the city looked unfamiliar and hostile.

Almazov was brought to the transit point where, day and night, patients from the Moscow mental hospitals waited to be sent home. The two small rooms in the timber barrack were crowded. Clouds of cheap tobacco smoke drifted under the bare planks of the low ceiling. The floor was filthy with mud and spittle. An intolerable stench came from the door of the lavatory, hardly ever closed; an unshaded, fly-blown bulb threw faces into sinister relief; Almazov's wife was quietly weeping, while the doctor on duty—a middle-aged woman with a pained and exhausted expression—was looking past him into space and saying:

"It's too late to-day . . . Dr. Yanushkevich has gone home. He won't be in till to-morrow morning. What happened to you? Did you have a row with the neighbors? No? You have your own flat, you say . . . Is this your wife? . . . Yes, I see. Yes of course . . . You aren't the first and you won't be the last . . . You're lucky to be sent to an asylum. My husband was shot . . . The other day the regional party secretary came and condoled, he said the party would never forget what my husband did . . . That's what they all say . . . It's astonishing, isn't it? . . . Do they really think that we, widows and orphans, hundreds of thousands of us, will forget what the party did to us? . . ."

Almazov listened in silence. . . .

"Go and sit down, try to rest," said the doctor. "Try to keep your strength, you'll need it. Don't despair. But don't think of staging a protest—going on a hunger strike or writing to complain—it won't get you anywhere in our country, no one will pay the slightest attention. Even the Turks and the Greeks were moved when Nazim Hikmet and Glesos went on hunger strike, but here they'd only laugh at you. They're made of stone, they aren't human, they're nothing but hangmen . . ."

Almazov sat down on a bench. He felt he must be asleep and dreaming of Dante's Hell. . . .

III

In the morning Almazov was examined by the head city psychiatrist, exactly as a prisoner is examined by a magistrate. He was brought to Dr. Yanushkevich's consulting room under guard. The doctor made no attempt to treat him as a patient; illness was never even mentioned. Pink and smug, he seemed to take his role as prosecutor for granted. Valentine, now that he had got through the night, was calmer and ready to face his way of the cross.

"What's the game, eh?—writing anti-Soviet letters to foreign embassies?"

"Are you in the police? I thought that doctors at least were exempt."

"That's no way to talk."

"I don't wish to talk to a policeman."

"You are wasting my time. They can sort you out at Kanatchikov's." He called the guard. "Take him back."

"You are a poor interrogator, you haven't learned your job yet," Valentine put in as a parting shaft.

It was raining. The same woman doctor, who had been on duty the night before, saw him to the ambulance. He was driven away under the triple escort of whose training consisted in acting as guards. One of them asked him if he was quite comfortable.

Almazov was preoccupied with the notion, still new to him but for which he was finding more and more corroborating evidence—that, so far from being socialist, the system which had finally become established in Russia was a particularly vicious form of fascism.

"You remind me," he replied indifferently, "of the executioner who asks his victim: 'May I trouble you?'"

The students exchanged glances but said nothing. As Valentine was to discover later, mental patients had one important privilege. On condition that they remained calm (if they became violent they were given an injection), they could say whatever they chose and the staff were not allowed to answer back.

An hour after he arrived he was interviewed by the doctor in charge, Lydia Kizyak, who was the medical head of the section. Valentine immediately sensed in her the inhuman bureaucratic type usually admired as "one hundred per cent Soviet." There was a silence while they looked at each other as warily as two duellists.

Born in 1917, Lydia Kizyak was a worthy contemporary of the Revolution. Having made her career by hook or by crook, she clung to her position and was terrified of losing it.

She loved power, it was her only passion; yet she was as nervous as a cat.

"Well, let's get on with it," she began briskly. "Tell me about your illness, your family, your background. . . ."

"I forbid you to play the fool with me," Almazov said with deliberation. "I don't suppose you want a row, so we'd better agree on our terms of reference."

She fidgeted in her chair and looked round anxiously. There was no one else in the large interview room, but just then an orderly came in with a paper for her to sign. She signed it hastily and told him to deliver it and come straight back. Almazov gave her a withering glance.

"This is the position. I don't regard you as a doctor. You call this a hospital, I call it a prison, to which, in a typically fascist way, I have been sent without trial. So now, let's get everything straight. I am your prisoner, you are my jailer, and there isn't going to be any nonsense about my health or my relations, or about examination or treatment. Is that understood?"

"We'll have to use compulsory methods."

"You can try."

"All right. We'll see." . . .

IV

Almazov was relatively a newcomer. He was in Ward 7 and had bed No. 13 in the corner by the window. The window panes were opaque, immovable and invariably curtained, in order to make sure of obliterating the street with its young poplars, flower-beds, cats and passers-by, and with it the very notion of life going on outside. But if Almazov had long felt that the chaos of its daily existence had dried up every source of life in the country, he—like all the more sensible of his compatriots—possessed an inexhaustible spring of life in himself: his imagination, which had sustained him throughout the darkest years of his country's captivity, kept before him, day and night, the vision of the full, untrammelled, seething life in the free world; because he was cut off from it, he imagined it as much more beautiful than it really was.

For him as for his friends, the yardstick of beauty was freedom. After four terrible decades they, like other honest Russians, found that their sense of good and evil was blunted; to be more exact, everything appeared to them to be evil, and the good only a remote memory, a lost paradise in the minds of a few old men. . . .

At the moment Valentine was entangled in a political argument with Vasily Golin. A colourless individual of uncertain age and profession, all he knew about him was that he came from Kamyshin on the Volga. Golin had evolved a theory of the "liberation of the Soviet mind from the shackles of Stalinism" and was convinced that, once the present rulers were converted to it, everything would be set right.

"But don't you see," stormed Almazov, "that the conflict to-day is different from any other in history? It's nonsense to talk about peaceful co-existence—what is at stake is not a political regime or a system of balance of powers but the one all-important issue: whether man as an individual, as a person, is to exist or not. Personal freedom is the one unarguable good on earth. The communists have put forward another: not man but the collectivity, not the individual but the herd. But do you imagine that humanity will ever consent to be a speechless and mindless herd?— it would much sooner be destroyed! What the West and the whole free world is trying to prevent is *man* being turned back into a communised anthropomorphic ape. It took thousands of years for the individual to emerge from the herd. Now the atavistic instinct has revived—significantly, among the 'proletarians,' the spiritually destitute who, naturally, are led by blinkered fanatics. All great thinkers have been aristocrats of the spirit. . . .

"But I firmly believe that man will triumph and not the ape. But I believe that Russia will enter the new century liberated and renewed in spirit and that by then communism will only be a nursery bogy to frighten our grandchildren. This is why I take no stock in all these pious doctrines of modesty, self-sacrifice, peaceful co-existence, the reduction of all human gifts and potentialities to a single operation on the conveyor belt and of all mental and material needs to a pauper's ration. They are nothing but hypocritical puritanism masquerading as revolution, a new scholasticism more dead than the medieval, a new captivity more terrifying than Babylon . . ."

After breakfast it was time for aminodin. The patients obediently queued up for their pills: the alternative to a pill was a painful injection. Whatever their alleged illness (the doctors, trained in practice to act as stooges for the police, established whatever diagnosis they fancied) the treatment was the same. Neurotics, schizophrenics, paranoiacs, the manic and the depressed, all were principally treated with aminodin, a remedy as universal as the castor oil in Chekhov's *Ward 6*.

After the aminodin, it was time for the doctors' rounds and the patients went back to their wards. The maids dusted and scrubbed floors. The patients in their striped pyjamas lay on their beds, waiting, talking, cursing the food, the staff, their life and the world.

It was autumn. Crimson and yellow leaves were spinning in the gold-blue air outside, and somewhere far away, beyond the sunset, people were living: living and not only existing. But here you could only fill your belly, talk of life in which you had no share, and at the end of the day take a double dose of sedative and hope to sleep.

Ward 7 was a Noah's Ark in which every variety of creature was represented. Very roughly, they fell into three main groups—firstly, the failed suicides, classified as lunatics because it was assumed (by doctors and politicians, writers and ideologists) that anyone dissatisfied with the socialist paradise must be a lunatic, and the doctors had conveniently produced the theory that only a lunatic was capable of making an attempt on his own life: not, therefore, the inhuman conditions but individual cases of mental disorder accounted for the suicide rate. They were treated with aminodin for months, sometimes for years. Some took to it and were unwilling to leave. "It might be a lot worse outside," they said darkly. Except for Samdelov, they were all under thirty: almost without exception, suicide was attempted by the young.

The next largest group were the "Americans": people who had tried to get in touch with a foreign embassy—usually the American, hence the nickname—or with tourists from the free world. The boldest had expressed the wish to emigrate.

Finally there was the less clearly defined category of young people who had failed to find their proper place in our society and who rejected all our standards. If they didn't always know what they wanted, they knew exactly what they didn't want: to begin with, to be in the army. They were disgusted by the very thought of military drill and of listening all day long to the official truths which they regarded as pious falsehoods. Discipline was odious to them. They refused to submit to authority in any form and were sickened by reminders of the motherland and of the social tasks which they were nevertheless forced to undertake as most of them were members of the Komsomol (admission to the University depended almost as much on a Komsomol ticket as on finishing school). A stay at the Kanatchikov Villa meant exemption from military service and, for those who wanted it, a chance to think, to look at things from outside and to take their time over the choice of a career, as well as a holiday from home and the detested authority of their parents. . . .

Like several of the older patients . . . these young people had fetched up in the asylum through the intrigues of their families and, since they were there against their will, they took their status as prisoners for granted.

Apparently this was also taken for granted by the doctors, for, poor though their training was, they knew enough to realise that they were not dealing with sick men. In fact, there were neither patients nor doctors but only jailers in charge of inconvenient citizens. Not only was this true of Section 39, but in varying degrees of the hospital as a whole, which incidentally had been built before the revolution for a maximum of a thousand inmates and now held a population six times as large. In Ward 7 and in others after it the doctors (vrachi) came to be known as the enemy (vragi), and the day began with a hymn sung to the tune of the "International":

> Arise ye starvelings from your slumbers,
> Arise ye psychic slaves of woe,
> For reason in revolt now thunders
> Against the psychiatric foe . . .

The doctor in charge of the Section, Lydia Kizyak, a woman of indeterminate age and appearance but of unmistakable police functions, felt sure that all such songs were composed by Almazov and accused him of spreading anti-Soviet propaganda. He looked in astonishment at her boot-button eyes and the overalls which seemed to conceal a papier mâché body faintly scented with eau-de-Cologne.

"Do you really imagine I would waste my time on such nonsense?"

"Nonsense or not, you do yourself no good by it."

"The Government's anti-Soviet propaganda for the past half-century has been so effective that I wouldn't dream of entering into competition with it."

Taken aback, she left the room and avoided visiting Ward 7 after this incident. In general, she was afraid of the patients, never saw them alone and pretended not to hear when they tried to speak to her as she hurried through the corridor.

A similar functionary, though more highly placed, was Professor Stein. As a good Marxist, he believed that all mental disorders were caused by a mysterious malfunctioning of the body and refused to have any truck with the soul: the very sound of the word had something anti-Soviet about it. Arrogant and ill-mannered, he was detested by the patients. Most of the staff conformed to the Stein-Kizyak pattern. Among the happy exceptions were Professor Andrew Nezhevsky, chief consultant to the Ministry of Health, and a youngish doctor, Zoya Makhova, who was deputy head of the Section.

V

Tall, well-built, with grey hair and shrewd intelligent eyes, energetic in spite of his seventy-four years, Nezhevsky had a world reputation as a psychiatrist and often attended scientific congresses abroad. The hospital only consulted him in difficult cases which the doctors were afraid of treating with the usual aminodin.

Nezhevsky knew the right treatment but he also knew that it was inapplicable in Soviet conditions. . . . He thought it absurd to call "persecution mania" the state of mind of people who had been persecuted for forty years and whose fathers had been shot or died in concentration camps. It was time to stop repressing those who were merely guilty of insufficiently admiring the régime, time to give people freedom—freedom of movement to start with, since their continued stay in the Soviet paradise threatened to drive many of them to insanity or suicide. There were rumours that nearly half the population of Moscow had at one time or another been through the hands of the psychiatrists. Seventeen thousand a year passed through the Kanatchikov Villa alone, and it was only one of many; the notorious Dubny on the outskirts of the city hospitalised twenty thousand at a time. It was also persistently rumoured that many thousands of political prisoners were held in a big asylum in Kazan. Nezhevsky knew, of course, that mental hospitals were being used as prisons, and he was deeply shocked by the hypocrisy of the device which enabled the authorities to claim that there were no political prisoners but only "lunatics" receiving "treatment." He was bitterly aware that there was nothing he could do about the system—opposition would only have meant dismissal, and he couldn't live without his work. He did what he could for individuals by seeing to it that their treatment was harmless and releasing them after a couple of months, allegedly "cured." His prestige was such that no one dared go against him or even question his motives. Besides—what would they say in Europe? It was one thing to disregard opinion at home but quite another to be branded as barbarians by the world.

When he spoke of the successes claimed by Soviet psychiatry, Nezhevsky smiled his delightfully good-natured and disarming smile. "We've advanced beyond Ward 6," he said once. "Ward 7 has better amenities."

"And is still more terrifying," he added to himself, reminded of the modern comforts provided at Sing-Sing. He felt that the judgment of Chekhov's doctor was still up-to-date: "After inspecting the hospital, he concluded that it was an immoral institution, highly damaging to the patients' health. The only sensible thing to do was to close it and to free the inmates. But this he knew to be beyond the power of his unaided will." Progress had been made, of course: everything in Ward 7 was outwardly clean and decent, but as an institution it was even more immoral, since its deliberate object was to damage and not to cure. . . .

VI

Ward 7 was getting out of hand. It talked all night, and the nurses could do nothing about it.

"Almazov is a bad influence," Lydia Kizyak complained to the chief medical officer. "I'd give half my pay to see the last of him."

"Uh-uh," Adrianov, a fat old man, always tired-looking and short of breath, grunted thoughtfully. "There's a lot of talk about him in the hospital . . . Well-known writer . . . nothing wrong with him . . . gets no treatment . . . I don't like it. What about you, Dr. Kizyak—do you consider him insane?"

This was the question she had been dreading. Like all careerists she was terrified of complications; they were nearly always damaging. Her temperament made her immune to pity; least of all did she feel compassion for Almazov, but she was afraid of him and had almost ceased to visit his ward. There was nothing wrong with his health —she was even astonished that months in a mental hospital had not affected it. But it was one thing to know it and another to say it to the chief medical officer. There were many things to take into account. The foreign press had got hold of Almazov's case. As the doctor in charge, it was she, Kizyak, who would be held responsible if anything went wrong. No one doubted that the K.G.B had ordered his arrest but no paper had been signed by the K.G.B. so nothing could be pinned on them. All that happened was that an anonymous K.G.B. colonel rang up the Ministry, and instructions from the Ministry went to Dr. Yanushkevich. In effect, the police had acted on police authority; but officially, the entire responsibility rested upon Kizyak. It was up to her to produce a diagnosis, a treatment, a history of the case . . . And what was she to do? To base her diagnosis upon fictitious data was too dangerous. What if there were a commission of inquiry? Who knows—perhaps even an international commission? . . . Anything was possible . . . Everyone would wash his hands of the whole nasty business—it was Kizyak who would go to prison, the others were in the clear. . . .

VII

The days were long but the weeks and months went in a flash. What astonished Almazov was that the inmates of Ward 7, at first seething with impatience, seemed now to have quietened down, as if they were in no particular hurry to get out.

"I don't know why people are so keen to go home," said Samdelov one evening. They were talking as usual, sitting in a close circle, three and four to a bed. "Personally I'm very happy. I'm fed, I'm clothed, nobody preaches communism at me. Do you realise? No propaganda, and you can say what you like! Where else can you do that? . . ."

"It won't do, you know," said Almazov. "We can't just give in. We can't escape from reality and turn ourselves into vegetables! What would be the point of living at all? Prison isn't life!"

"The whole of Russia is a prison," Tolya said softly. "And there's no escape . . . except . . ."

"I've told you before, Tolya," Morenny raised his voice. "Cutting your throat is no solution—what you have to do is cut theirs."

"That's easier said than done," said Zagogulin. "How do you fight a mountain of inertia? You can't slit its throat. And there are too many nasty little people about, such as my wife, who is a pillar of the regime! And the bureaucrats! And the policemen! And such doctors as our Ilse" (Lydia Kizyak was known as Ilse Koch). "Hundreds of thousands of them to a handful of us!"

"Not such a handful as that," said Volodya. "And haven't you noticed there are more and more of us? We are thousands to-day, we'll be millions to-morrow. We don't advertise our presence, but we are there. We'll get together and we'll light such a blaze that no policeman on earth can put it out."

"Hush. Don't talk so loud." Zhenya looked round nervously. "You'll have us all shot."

"There's a hero, a romantic artist for you!" Volodya lost his temper. "Don't you realize, you trade union louse, that they can't do anything to us? We are insane—didn't you know?—they can't even try us! All the same, we are right and we'll win in the end."

"That's the spirit," said Almazov. "Our whole trouble is that we so exaggerate our weakness that it saps our will. All we do is tighten the noose round our own necks."

"Will is power, Nietzsche said," said Volodya.

"The odd thing is that we are so used to the triumph of evil, of might over right, that the very consciousness of being right makes us feel doomed and we capitulate in advance. To me this explains nihilism. Clearly nihilism is gaining ground. But its victory is unthinkable. It would mean the destruction of mankind. Only imagine—no one left to read *The Brothers Karamazov*, to play the 'Appassionata,' to look at the 'David' or 'The Last Supper'! But it is equally clear to me that this is what will happen unless Sino-Soviet fascism is destroyed first."

"It's clear to all of us," said Golin. "We won't give in."

VIII

In the morning Almazov was sent for by Professor Stein.

The long narrow room was crowded with doctors and trainees, about forty of them. The professor leaned back on his plush-covered settee and inspected Valentine with the curiosity of a visitor at the zoo, looking at a rare Indian elephant. The others looked at him as well.

"Well, shall we get acquainted, Valentine Ivanovich," said Stein with smooth informality. "My name is Abram Grigoryevich. Tell us why you are here—what are your symptoms?"

Almazov glared at him with such contempt that Stein looked uncomfortable.

"I have not the slightest wish to get acquainted with you, but evidently I must. The reason I am here is that I was brought by the police. My health is excellent. It's your job to make me ill. But I warn you, you won't succeed."

"How you actually got here is irrelevant. The point you should keep in mind is that healthy people are not in hospitals."

"That's exactly what the Cheka interrogators used to say to their victims: 'Innocent people are not in prison. You say you are innocent, that means you are anti-Soviet, so prison is the place for you.' The only difference is that now it's the madhouse."

"I see . . . You don't sound exactly sane!"

"I've heard that before as well. My colleagues used to tell me it took a lunatic to stand up to the power of the Soviet junta."

"Quite right! You *are* a lunatic! You need treatment."

"You can twist my words as much as you like. I don't stoop to argue with people of your sort."

Stein smiled stiffly. "We don't take offence at what our patients say to us."

"Nor do I at what lackeys or policemen say to me."

"Which are we? Lackeys or policemen?"

"Both."

"Is Soviet society made up of nothing else?"

"Soviet society is the rubbish dump of mankind and its stink poisons the air for the whole civilised world. I've been holding my nose and keeping my distance for a long time, but admittedly it's getting more and more difficult."

"How can you say such a fearful thing? No sane person could bring himself to say it!"

"Lackeys are always afraid of the truth. Especially when they meet it face to face."

"Well, it's quite clear to me that you are ill. Let me propose a deal—we'll give you a short course of treatment, you'll go through with it and everything will be all right." He held out his hand. Almazov pretended not to see it and walked out. . . .

IX

Professor Nezhevsky was amazed—astounded—twice on the same day, on each occasion by the behavior of Zoya Makhova.

The shock was the greater because in the past forty years he had ceased to be surprised at anything. He observed events with the detachment of a chronicler and, convinced that the Soviet nightmare would outlast him, displayed that patient indifference toward life which is either the gift of a great man or the result of the abysmal stupidity of the anthropoid.

A pupil of the French school of psychiatry, he dismissed the current notion of "mental illness"—if only because no one could give a definition of mental health, so that there was no firm principle by which to define or classify pathological phenomena. Soviet psychiatry, with its denial of the soul and of God, of intuition and revelation, he regarded as pure quackery.

"How can they treat mental disease when they don't know the meaning of the word 'psyche'? It's absurd" he had said in his excellent French to his friend, the French psychiatrist, Rene Gillard.

"That was a slip of the tongue, my friend," said Gillard in his mild, singsong voice; he was a short, thickset, elderly man with a shock of greying hair. "You and I know only of mental states—we don't call them diseases—and in so far as they are undesirable, we try to modify them by modifying whatever factors in the patient's way of life partly, or even wholly, accounts for them."

"I know, I know," Nezhevsky nodded. "I've been telling them about your methods. No one at the Ministry will even listen. But in any case, they are inapplicable in our circumstances. To begin with, we have literally millions of cripples—casualties of the Terror under Stalin and his junta. You realise that almost the whole country lived in panic terror for decades? You could safely diagnose every Russian as suffering from persecution mania. I needn't tell you that, even at the best, the cure would take a very long time. Unfortunately, my dear colleague, the outlook is not too favourable. For one thing, our young people, who are bullied mercilessly, are showing more and more signs of the same trouble. Secondly, our whole national way of life is such as to aggravate the state of depression—everlasting want, anxiety to make ends meet, privations, insecurity. One step away from subservience, one public criticism of some petty local autocrat, and a man may lose his job, his house, his position in society. The worst of it is that the outlook is so hopeless. My son was telling me the other day—he graduated in the 'thirties—at their graduation ball their party secretary made a pompous speech: 'I envy you, my dear young men, because by the time we get to the mid-century you won't even be middle-aged, and by then our country will be rich and prosperous, everything will be in abundance, life will be happier than it has ever been on earth!' Well, we've got through twelve years of the second half of the century and where are we? Such is the abundance that in many places there's a shortage of bread. The prices are three or four times higher than in the 'thirties. With every decade life is getting greyer, drearier, more joyless. And I'm not talking about food for the mind—there's nothing except the same old Marxist cud. No films, no plays, nothing you can call a book. Oh well, I'm not telling you anything new . . . And yet people want to live . . . But to come back to your methods—I told them at the Ministry that you avoid drugs, you rely on modifying the patient's way of life, your staff are forbidden to talk about 'illness,' the patients arrange their own timetable and are free to come and go, and men and women are free to mix—you even regard love as therapeutic—whereas our own hospitals have a prison discipline and we doctors go about clanking our keys like jailers. Of course they didn't believe a word of it! And do you know what Babadjan said to me?—'Typical bourgeois idealism! The West has been trying to hook us with that bait for a long time, but we don't bite' . . ."

"So you stick to happiness pills?"

"Yes, exactly. Happiness pills. Andaxin, aminodin, and the rest of the muck—our doctors think the world of it."

"And yet the long-term effects are anything but happy! Damage to memory, to eyesight, reduced sexual potency, apathy and indifference. Can they possibly think these are the things that make for happiness?"

"Why not? It suits our masters that we should have no memory—the less of it we have, the sooner we'll forget what they did to us. The blinder we are the less unattractive we'll find our surroundings. Apathy suits them down to the ground—apathetic people don't fly into rages, they don't protest, they don't hatch conspiracies. And to reduce sexual potency is not such a bad thing either—we are short of food and housing as it is. The whole object of our society is to train robots. In our hospitals, abuse and even blows are part of the treatment! I know hundreds of psychiatrists who are neither doctors nor psychiatrists."

"What sad things you tell me, my friend. How hard it must be for you to work without a milieu, without the help of enthusiastic colleagues!"

"You mustn't forget that I am apathetic myself. If I weren't inoculated with the same disease, I couldn't have survived. Nor can I really say I work. Every now and again there's a chance of helping some wretched man who is stranded in one of our prisons and who is worth the trouble. Most of the time I look on."

"Yes . . . I am infinitely luckier! I am thankful to say I can be proud of my assistants."

"Tell me, do you ever treat suicides?"

"They are not the sort of patient who turns to us. And our police don't bring them in the way yours do. A hospital is not a prison, we don't force people to have treatment. We'd be fools if we thought we could."

"Or sadists . . ."

"Yes . . . In fact, if such a patient were brought to me, I would refuse to take him. If he can't or doesn't want to go on living, it's his own affair. It's for him to dispose of his own life, not for the authorities. I must say, the idea of compulsory treatment really revolts me. We'd never stand for it. Of course our life has its dark sides like everywhere else. But compulsion in every form is disgusting—especially mental, psychological compulsion. . . ."

"With us it's a principle!"

"Is there really no possibility of criticising the regime?"

"Officially—none. Not a word can be said freely on the radio or in the press or even at a meeting. But people do criticise indirectly by telling anecdotes—that's where you find the real expression of our Soviet ethos. There are thousands of them—clever, sharp, spiteful, to the point. New ones turn up every day . . ."

It was a year since this dialogue had been held in Paris, and no reporter had got wind of it; neither had the Moscow doctors who were often put out by the amused smile on their distinguished colleague's face.

5

"PATIENT LABOUR" IN THE BRITISH MENTAL HOSPITAL SYSTEM

J. A. R. Bickford

> British psychiatrists rarely criticize their own mental health system. The following article by the physician-superintendent of De La Pole Hospital, in Willerby, Hull, is a significant exception.*

The psychiatric patient who returns to the community usually feels quite friendly to the mental hospital he has just left, and he would be incredulous if someone were to tell him that within the National Health Service there was a national un-health service which opposed his treatment and cure; and indeed we would all agree in dismissing such a notion as absurd. Nevertheless I suggest that in fact the official, though unformulated, policy has always been that a considerable proportion of psychiatric patients should never be discharged.

The economy of a mental hospital is based on "patient-labour." Patients as patients are not thought of when this term is used (that would make the speaker uncomfortable), but only the commodity they provide—labour. That patients should do a little domestic work, to foster a feeling of community and to teach them how to care for their homes, is reasonable. What is unreasonable is the extent to which the hospital is dependent on their work. In fact, without it the hospital could not run and the mental-

* From "Economic Value of the Psychiatric Inpatient," *The Lancet*, 1:714–15 (30 March), 1963.

hospital service would collapse. There are perhaps 20,000 long-stay patients, whose work debars them, except casually, from treatment. This number must be known to those who plan the hospital service and must influence their policy.

Nobody pretends that most of the work patients do is to their advantage. It is dull, negative, and without therapeutic value. It has to be performed efficiently because the hospital demands it. To "train" a mentally ill person is not easy, and it would be uneconomic to break his routine every month or so to train him to do another unfamiliar job, for during each interim period a trained worker would be lost. As it is, patients are indispensable, whether they work in the laundry (clean or foul sections), as polishers in the front hall, as office-cleaners on the swill-gang or the coal-gang, as path-sweepers, or in the gardens, or with the cobbler, tailor, or joiner.

The effect of the system is seen most clearly in the printing departments which some hospitals have. The work is interesting, the patient becomes skilled. The atmosphere is happy. A lot of excellent work is done for the National Health Service. All the same, these departments should be forbidden. Once the patient has become useful, the hospital is reluctant to discharge him, and he is probably unwilling to go. It is a relief for the doctors and the nurses to have the patient placed in a job. He does not cause trouble and worry by reminding them that he is still in the ward, the problem of treatment and discharge need not be considered. The hospital works that little bit better, a good servant has been found for the next two decades.

In some mental hospitals the patients may prepare the vegetables, carry round the laundry and the food, scrub the corridors, polish the wards, make the beds, wash the dishes, clean the baths and w.c.'s, or do all the mending. If the patients do not do the bulk of this work it will not be done. There are few porters and ward domestics because they would have to be paid. There is no need to pay patients properly. A ward of 40 patients should have three domestics and a half share of a porter to cover the whole week together with holidays. This would cost £26 a week.

If there is no help available, will the money be divided among the patients? It would seem reasonable, but is it done? Even where patients are moderately fairly treated, their rewards are likely to be cut every time there is a call to save money. Admittedly a patient does not always work long hours, probably under 20–30 a week, but for this he will be paid, perhaps 10s.–15s. a week. He feels that he is getting something; the hospital knows that it is. As a result patients who are well enough to work outside the hospital may not be allowed to do so. They are kept on the hospital's labour force. This suggests that the money value of their work inside the hospital (with a few shillings a week in return), is greater than the lodging allowance they would pay if employed outside.

Reports of hospital expenditure support these views:

The cost of domestic services (cleaners or porters) in different types of hospital per patient for a week is:

	£	s.	d.
Acute general hospital	2	17	10
Long-stay general hospital	1	16	8
Mental hospital (dealing with acute and long-stay patients)		9	10
Hospital for the subnormal		7	3

These modest figures are achieved despite the difficulties of running mental hospitals with their scattered villas, lack of lifts, wards on two or three floors, awkward kitchens, day rooms, and patients constantly bringing in dirt on their boots.

The grounds of mental hospitals are usually pleasant, so are those of a sanatorium. Is there any difference in the cost of each per patient per week?

	s.	d.
Sanatorium	9	1
Mental hospital	2	3
Hospital for subnormal	3	2

The difference in cost reflects the value of work done by patients.

In De La Pole Hospital, a third of the patients are employed almost full-time on tasks which are not of value to them and which are demanded of them. This takes no account of the large numbers who work for 3–4 hours on ward-cleaning, and the even larger number who work for an hour or so daily. . . .

How much should patients be paid? One way would be to assess the number of cleaners, gardeners, labourers, porters, seamstresses who should be employed, calculate their wages, and distribute the money between the patients who work; but this will never happen. A patient who uses a motor-mower all day in the summer gets 8s. a week, a patient who works for thirty hours a week as a kitchen maid or ward-domestic the same or less. Perhaps a woman in her nineties who cleans all day gets nothing because she has a small pension and the hospital cannot afford to pay her. If patients are not paid, they should at least be well housed and fed. The hospital is, after all, their home. Its quality can be gauged from the cost of domestic repairs and renewals and the cost of provisions per patient per week:

	Domestic Repairs and Renewals		Catering		
	s.	d.	£	s.	d.
Acute general hospital	8	6	3	10	2
Long-stay general hospital	6	3	2	3	10
Sanatorium	9	9	3	12	8
Maternity hospital	11	6	4	4	5
Children's hospital	12	11	4	3	8
Mental hospital	4	7	1	14	1
Hospital for the subnormal	3	9	1	10	4

These figures are all the more impressive when it is remembered that many patients in mental hospitals work hard, while in general hospitals many patients may eat little food for several days.

But many patients, because of their illness, contribute nothing to the hospital service—they might say they receive nothing. They are unlikely to be fit for discharge. They receive no treatment and are accommodated in a "long-stay annexe" or "long-stay ward". Where this repository is has not mattered much up to the present for many of the mentally ill, because it has been in the mental hospital nearest their home. But times are changing and in at least two areas patients are now to be moved.

In the Leeds region, some hospitals have reduced considerably the number of inpatients. To facilitate the rebuilding of the larger hospitals and structural alterations, it is proposed to move patients from Huddersfield and Wakefield to this hospital. Huddersfield and Wakefield are separated from Willerby by more than 60 miles respectively and the return journey by public transport takes 3 hours and costs about 30s.

In the North East Metropolitan region long-stay patients from Runwell Hospital are to be moved to Severalls Hospital. Most of them have homes within a dozen miles of Runwell, from which Severalls at Colchester is over 40 miles away.

The administrators' explanations for expedients of this kind are logical; but are patients to be regarded simply as accommodation problems? . . .

To move patients so far is wicked because it destroys almost inevitably the possibility of their discharge. It destroys the morale of the staff of the receiving hospital at a time when they feel they are beginning to be able to treat their own patients, and reimposes in perpetuity the inferior living conditions which have already been tolerated too long in our mental hospitals.

6

ILLEGITIMACY AND INSANITY

From *The Guardian*

A constant feature of efforts at mental hospital reform is a horrified revulsion against the psychiatric incarceration of "sane" persons coupled with an unquestioning acceptance of the necessity of such incarceration for "insane" persons. This view is strikingly illustrated in the following excerpts,* which also provide some statistical information about current British mental hospital practices.

I

The release from a mental hospital in Yorkshire of two sane women who had spent 44 and 51 years there respectively exposes several disturbing elements in the administration of such hospitals. Fifty years from now the care at present provided for the mentally ill and handicapped will seem as barbarous as the manner in which our grandfathers treated unmarried mothers in the twenties. How far have we progressed when the authorities acknowledge that there are many people in mental institutions today who have no need to be there except that there is no alternative accommodation for them?

The discovery yesterday of another similar case in the same hospital suggests a pattern. In other mental hospitals

* From "Insane Hospital Policies," *The Guardian*, May 22, 1972, p. 12; "A Third Wasted Life," ibid., p. 1; "How Many Lost Lives?" ibid., May 23, 1972, p. 15.

up and down Britain there are likely to be other sane inmates who were buried by embarrassed parents in an earlier era. The second issue of concern is the appeals system. One of the women released is said to have written many letters in an unsuccessful attempt to leave the hospital in which she was wrongly confined. The third issue is the number of mentally ill and handicapped patients who may not originally have been wrongly confined, but would now be better cared for in a residential home or hostel than in a mental hospital. The administrator of the Doncaster hospital which released the women estimated at the weekend that he could discharge 150 of his 420 patients if he could find alternative accommodation for them. Of the 60,000 adults in mentally handicapped hospitals, it has been estimated that 30,000 could be released. Of the 100,000 in mentally ill hospitals, about 10 per cent would be better off outside.

There are some obvious lessons that can be drawn from the Yorkshire case. The first is the need to improve the system of assessing patients. Under the Mental Health Act of 1959, long-term patients have to be assessed every two years. This is not the first case to suggest that the system is not working properly.

But it is no use being able to leave if there is no place to go. There needs to be much closer co-operation between local authorities and hospital authorities. Few local authorities are aware of how many patients could be released from their local mental hospitals. And there is a financial incentive for local authorities to keep the patients in the hospitals where they will not be a drain on the rates. Surveys by the National Association for Mental Health late last year showed the large variation in services between different local authorities and the widespread inadequacy of residential and day care facilities provided. To rectify this there needs to be, as the Association has recommended, a minimum level of standards which all councils must provide. For too long the mentally ill and handicapped have been the forgotten people in our National Health system.

II

A third patient who has been locked away for a lifetime because she had an illegitimate child has been discovered at St. Catherine's Hospital for the mentally handicapped, Doncaster.

The woman was committed as a "moral defective" under the Mental Deficiency Act of 1913. She was 19 and had just had a baby.

Last Friday, it was disclosed that two women who had been locked up for most of their lives because they had given birth to illegitimate children were released from the hospital in January and taken into an old people's home at Dewsbury. The hospital secretary, Mr. Ralph Blakeburn, said at the weekend that 120 of the 150 patients in the hospital could be released if there was anywhere for them to go.

The third patient is now 68 and has been in hospital since 1923. The woman told recent visitors that her father died when she was 11. When she was 19 she gave birth to a baby and her mother became ill soon afterwards. She lived near Huddersfield.

"I remember a woman came to our house and my mother was ill at the time," she said. "She got my mother to sign some papers and I was taken to a hospital at Rawcliffe, near Goole." She stayed at Rawcliffe until 1939 and was then transferred to St. Catherine's.

If she is released from the hospital she would like a "little job doing domestic work."

Mr. Blakeburn's policy is to encourage local authorities and relatives to take people away from the hospital's institutional life. But he said: "With some of the older people it is difficult. We feel it was wrong to commit them, but that was the law in the 1920s . . ."

III

However great the estimates of mental handicap patients capable of being discharged may be, the populations of long stay hospitals are not going to shrink dramatically overnight.

Yesterday, the Department of Health was in touch with St. Catherine's Hospital, Doncaster, where two ladies spent almost all their adult lives to ascertain details of their cases. It emerged that neither had been committed as "moral defectives" as had been claimed last week. The two women—one 74 and the other 66—have now been released. They have both been placed in a community home.

The women were committed under the Mental Deficiency Act of 1913 because they were considered "feeble minded"—they were living off the Poor Law, expecting illegitimate children and had been disowned by their families. The law puts it more delicately now: they would be said to be in need of care and protection. But one stigma is as bad as another. And so their lives went on, for a total of 96 years, growing more isolated from a world which they had scarcely time to know before being put away.

Would the chances of the women being released be as great if they had been voluntary patients in another part of the country? And are the efforts being made by the Health Service and the local authorities on a scale sufficient to make us confident that patients capable of leading either normal lives, or living in a non-institutional but sheltered environment, are able to do so?

The cases of mental handicap patients are reviewed at intervals of two years under the 1959 Mental Health Act. The latest available figures show that a total of 154,316 patients in three categories—mentally ill, psychiatric disorder and severe subnormality—were in hospitals in England and Wales as voluntary patients six months ago. In addition, 11,216 were being detained compulsorily.

It is impossible to get an overall estimate of the number who could be discharged. At St. Catherine's Hospital, officials say that 120 of the 520 inmates might be in this category. The Friern Hospital at New Southgate, London, has 1,700 patients and Dr. John Bradley, consultant psychiatrist, says that perhaps 150 of them could be discharged into some supportive care . . .

Nobody doubts that there are other similar examples of people who may years ago have been classified as mentally ill, and who since have languished in institutions because the community which put them there has no provision for receiving them back.

7

FACES IN THE WATER

Janet Frame

> Janet Frame (1924–) is a New Zealand novelist. *Faces in the Water*,* from which the following extracts are taken, is an autobiographical account of her experiences as a mental-hospital patient.

I

I was cold. I tried to find a pair of long woolen ward socks to keep my feet warm in order that I should not die under the new treatment, electric shock therapy, and have my body sneaked out the back way to the mortuary. Every morning I woke in dread, waiting for the day nurse to go on her rounds and announce from the list of names in her hand whether or not I was for shock treatment, the new and fashionable means of quieting people and of making them realize that orders are to be obeyed and floors are to be polished without anyone protesting and faces are made to be fixed into smiles and weeping is a crime. Waiting in the early morning, in the black-capped frosted hours, was like waiting for the pronouncement of a death sentence.

I tried to remember the incidents of the day before. Had I wept? Had I refused to obey an order from one of the nurses? Or, becoming upset at the sight of a very ill

---

* From *Faces in the Water* (New York: George Braziller, 1961), pp. 15–101.

patient, had I panicked, and tried to escape? Had a nurse threatened, "If you don't take care you'll be for treatment tomorrow." Day after day I spent the time scanning the faces of the staff as carefully as if they were radar screens which might reveal the approach of the fate that had been prepared for me. I was cunning. "Let me mop the office," I pleaded. "Let me mop the office in the evenings, for by evening the film of germs has settled on your office furniture and report books, and if the danger is not removed you might fall prey to disease which means disquietude and fingerprints and a sewn shroud of cheap cotton."

So I mopped the office, as a precaution, and sneaked across to the sister's desk and glanced quickly at the open report book and the list of names for treatment the next morning. One time I read my name there, Istina Mavet. What had I done? I hadn't cried or spoken out of turn or refused to work the bumper with the polishing rag under it or to help set the tables for tea, or to carry out the overflowing pig-tin to the side door. There was obviously a crime which was unknown to me, which I had not included in my list because I could not track it with the swinging spotlight of my mind to the dark hinterland of unconsciousness. I knew then that I would have to be careful. I would have to wear gloves, to leave no trace when I burgled the crammed house of feeling and took for my own use exuberance depression suspicion terror.

II

As we watched the day nurse moving from one patient to another with the list in her hand our sick dread became more intense.

"You're for treatment. No breakfast for you. Keep on your nightgown and dressing gown and take your teeth out."

We had to be careful, calm, controlled. If our forebodings were unwarranted we experienced a dizzy lightness and relief which, if carried too far, made us liable to be given emergency treatment. If our name appeared on the fateful list we had to try with all our might, at times unsuccessfully, to subdue the rising panic. For there was no escape. Once the names were known all doors were scrupulously locked; we had to stay in the observation dormitory where the treatment was being held.

It was a time of listening—to the other patients walking along the corridor for breakfast; the silence as Sister Honey, her head bowed, her eyes watchfully open, said grace.

"For what you are about to receive the Lord make you truly thankful."

And then we heard the sudden cheerful clatter of spoons on porridge plates, the scraping of chairs, the disconcerted murmur at the end of the meal when the inevitably missing knife was being searched for while the sister warned sternly, "Let no one leave the table until the knife is found." Then further scraping and rustling following the sister's orders. "Rise, Ladies." Side doors being unlocked as the patients were ordered to their separate places of work. Laundry, Ladies. Sewing room, Ladies. Nurses' Home, Ladies. Then the pegging footsteps as the massive Matron Glass on her tiny blackshod feet approached down the corridor, unlocked the observation dormitory and stood surveying us, with a query to the nurse, like a stockman appraising head of cattle waiting in the saleyards to go by truck to the slaughterhouse. "They're all here? Make sure they have nothing to eat." We stood in small groups, waiting; or crouched in a semi-circle around the great locked fireplace where a heap of dull coal smouldered sulkily; our hands on the blackened bars of the fireguard, to warm our nipped fingers.

For in spite of the snapdragons and the dusty millers and the cherry blossoms, it was always winter. And it was always our season of peril: Electricity, the peril the wind sings to in the wires on a gray day. Time after time I thought, What safety measures must I apply to protect myself against electricity? And I listed the emergencies—lightning, riots, earthquakes, and the measures provided for the world by man's Red Cross God Safety to whom we owe allegiance or die on the separated ice floe, in double loneliness. But it would not come to my mind what to do when I was threatened by electricity, except that I thought of my father's rubber hip boots that he used for fishing and that stood in the wash house where the moth-eaten coats hung behind the door, beside the pile of old Humor Magazines, the Finest Selections of the World's Wit, for reading in the lavatory. Where was the wash house and the old clothes with spiders' nests and wood lice in their folds? Lost in a foreign land, take your position from the creeks flowing towards the sea, and your time from the sun.

Yes, I was cunning. I remembered once a relationship between electricity and wetness, and on the excuse of going to the lavatory I filled the admission bath and climbed in, wearing my nightgown and dressing gown, and thinking, Now they will not give me treatment, and perhaps I may have a secret influence over the sleek cream-painted machine with its knobs and meters and lights.

Do you believe in a secret influence?

There had been occasions of delirious relief when the machine broke down and the doctor emerged, frustrated, from the treatment room, and Sister Honey made the welcome proclamation, "You can all get dressed. No treatment today."

But this day when I climbed in the bath the secret influence was absent, and I was given treatment, hurried into the room as the first patient, even before the noisy people from Ward Two, the disturbed ward, were brought in for "multiples," which means they were given two treatments and sometimes three, consecutively. These excited people in their red ward dressing gowns and long gray ward stockings and bunchy striped bloomers which some took care to display to us, were called by their Christian names or nicknames, Dizzy, Goldie, Dora. Sometimes they approached us and began to confide in us or touch our sleeves, reverently, as if we were indeed what we felt ourselves to be, a race apart from them. Were we not the "sensibly" ill who did not yet substitute animal noises for speech or fling our limbs in uncontrolled motion or dissolve into secret silent hilarity? And yet when the time of treatment came and they and we were ushered or dragged into the room at the end of the dormitory all of us whether from the disturbed ward or the "good" ward uttered the same kind of stifled choking scream when the electricity was turned on and we dropped into immediate lonely unconsciousness.

III

It was early in my dream. The tracks of time crossed and merged and with the head-on collision of hours a fire broke out blackening the vegetation that sprouts a green memory along the side of the track. I took a thimbleful of water distilled from the sea and tried to extinguish the fire. I waved a small green flag in the face of the oncoming hours and they passed through the scarred countryside to their destination and as the faces peered from the window at me I saw they were the faces of the people awaiting shock treatment. There was Miss Caddick, Caddie, they called her, bickering and suspicious, not knowing that she would soon die and her body be sneaked out the back way to the mortuary. And there was my own face staring from the carriageful of the nicknamed people in their ward clothes, striped smocks and gray woolen jerseys. What did it mean?

I was so afraid. When I first came to Cliffhaven and walked into the dayroom and saw the people sitting and staring, I thought, as a passerby in the street thinks when he sees someone staring into the sky, If I look up too, I will see it. And I looked but I did not see it. And the staring was not, as it is in the streets, an occasion for crowds who share the spectacle; it was an occasion of loneliness, of vision on a closed, private circuit.

And it is still winter. Why is it winter when the cherry blossom is in flower? I have been here in Cliffhaven for years now. How can I get to school by nine o'clock if I am trapped in the observation dormitory waiting for E.S.T.? It is such a long way to go to school, down Eden Street past Ribble Street and Dee Street past the doctor's house and their little girl's dollhouse standing on the lawn. I wish I had a dollhouse; I wish I could make myself small and live inside it, curled up in a matchbox with satin bed curtains and gold stars painted on the striking side, for good conduct.

There is no escape. Soon it will be time for E.S.T. Through the veranda windows I can see the nurses returning from second breakfast, and the sight of them walking in twos and threes past the border of snapdragons granny's bonnets and the cherry blossom tree brings a sick feeling of despair and finality. I feel like a child who has been forced to eat a strange food in a strange house and who must spend the night there in a strange room with a different smell in the bedclothes and different borders on the blankets, and waken in the morning to the sight of a different and terrifying landscape from the window.

The nurses enter the dormitory. They collect false teeth from the treatment patients, plunging them in water in old cracked cups and writing the names on the outside in pale blue ink from a ballpoint pen; the ink slips on the impenetrable china surface, and spreads, blurring from itself, with the edges of the letters appearing like the microfilm of flies' feet. A nurse brings two small chipped enamel bowls of methylated spirits and ethereal soap, to "rub up" our temples in order that the shock will "take."

I try to find a pair of gray woolen socks for if my feet are cold I know that I shall die. One patient is careful to put on her pants "in case I kick up my legs in front of the doctor." At the last minute, as the feel of nine o'clock surrounds us and we sit in the hard chairs, our heads tipped back, the soaked cotton wool being rubbed on our temples until the skin tears and stings and the dregs of the spirits run down into our ears making sudden blockages of sound, there is a final outbreak of screaming and panicking, attempts by some to grab leftover food from the bed patients, and as a nurse calls "Lavatory, Ladies," and the dormitory door is opened for a brief supervised visit to the doorless lavatories, with guards set in the corridor to prevent escape, there are bursts of fighting and kicking as some attempt to get past, yet realizing almost at once that there is nowhere to run to. The doors to the outside world are locked. You can only be followed and dragged back and if Matron Glass catches you she will speak angrily, "It's for your own good. Pull yourself together. You've been difficult long enough."

The matron herself does not offer to undergo shock treatment in the way that suspected persons to prove their innocence are sometimes willing to take the first slice of the cake that may contain arsenic.

Floral screens are drawn to conceal the end of the dormitory where the treatment beds have been prepared, the sheets rolled back and the pillows placed at an angle, ready to receive the unconscious patient. And now everybody wants to go again to the lavatory, and again, as the panic grows, and the nurse locks the door for the last time, and the lavatory is inaccessible. We yearn to go there, and sit on the cold china bowls and in the simplest way try to relieve ourselves of the mounting distress in our minds, as if a process of the body could change the distress and flush it away as burning drops of water.

And now there is the sound of an early morning catarrhal cough, the springing squeak of rubber-soled shoes on the polished corridor outside, syncopated with the hasty ping-pong steps of cuban-heeled duty shoes, and Dr. Howell and Matron Glass arrive, she unlocking the dormitory door and standing aside while he enters, and both passing in royal procession to join Sister Honey already waiting in the treatment room. At the last minute, because there are not enough nurses, the newly appointed Social Worker who has been asked to help with treatment comes leaping in (we call her Pavlova).

"Nurse, will you send up the first patient."

Many times I have offered to go first because I like to remind myself that by the time I am awake, so brief is the period of unconsciousness, most of the group will still be waiting in a daze of anxiety which sometimes confuses them into thinking that perhaps they have had treatment, perhaps it has been sneaked upon them without their being aware of it.

The people behind the screen begin to moan and cry. We are taken strictly according to "volts."

We wait while the Ward Two people are "done."

We know the rumors attached to E.S.T.—it is training for Sing Sing when we are at last convicted of murder and sentenced to death and sit strapped in the electric chair with the electrodes touching our skin through slits in our clothing; our hair is singed as we die and the last smell in our nostrils is the smell of ourselves burning. And the fear leads in some patients to more madness. And they say it is a session to get you to talk, that your secrets are filed and kept in the treatment room, and I have had proof of this, for I have passed through the treatment room with a basket of dirty linen, and seen my card. Impulsive and dangerous, it reads. Why? And how? How? What does it all mean?

It is nearly my turn. I walk down to the treatment room door to wait, for so many treatments have to be performed that the doctor becomes impatient at any delay. Production, as it were, is speeded up (like laundry economics— one set of clothes on, one set clean, one in the wash) if there is a patient waiting at the door, one on the treatment table, and another being given a final "rub-up" ready to take her place at the door.

Suddenly the inevitable cry or scream sounds from behind the closed doors which after a few minutes swing open and Molly or Goldie or Mrs. Gregg, convulsed and snorting, is wheeled out. I close my eyes tight as the bed passes me, yet I cannot escape seeing it, or the other beds where people are lying, perhaps heavily asleep, or whimperingly awake, their faces flushed, their eyes bloodshot. I can hear someone moaning and weeping; it is someone who has woken up in the wrong time and place, for I know that the treatment snatches these things from you leaves you alone and blind in a nothingness of being and you try to fumble your way like a newborn animal to the flowing of first comforts; then you wake, small and frightened, and the tears keep falling in a grief that you cannot name.

Beside me is the bed, sheets turned back pillow arranged

where I will lie after treatment. They will lift me into it and I shall not know. I look at the bed as if I must establish contact with it. Few people have advance glimpses of their coffin; if they did they might be tempted to charm it into preserving in the satin lining a few trinkets of their identity. In my mind, I slip under the pillow of my treatment bed a docket of time and place so that when and if I ever wake I shall not be wholly confused in a panic of scrabbling through the darkness of not knowing and of being nothing. I go into the room then. How brave I am! Everybody remarks on my bravery! I climb on to the treatment table. I try to breathe deeply and evenly as I have heard it is wise in moments of fear. I try not to mind when the matron whispers to one of the nurses, in a hoarse voice like an assassin, "Have you got the gag?"

And over and over inside myself I am saying a poem which I learned at school when I was eight. I say the poem, as I wear the gray woolen socks, to ward off Death. They are not relevant lines because very often the law of extremity demands an attention to irrelevancies; the dying man wonders what they will think when they cut his toenails; the man in grief counts the cups in a flower. I see the face of Miss Swap who taught us the poem. I see the mole on the side of her nose, its two mounds like a miniature cottage loaf and the sprout of ginger hair growing out the top. I see myself standing in the classroom reciting and feeling the worn varnished desk top jutting against my body against my bellybutton that has specks of grit in it when I put my finger in; I see from the corner of my left eye my neighbor's pencil case which I coveted because it was a triple decker with a rose design on the lid and a wonderful dent thumb-size for sliding the lid along the groove.

"Moonlit Apples," I say. "By John Drinkwater."

At the top of the house the apples are laid in rows
And the skylight lets the moonlight in and those
Apples are deep-sea apples of green.

I get no further than three lines. The doctor busily attending the knobs and switches of the machine which he respects because it is his ally in the struggle against overwork and the difficulties depressions obsessions manias of a thousand women, has time to smile a harassed Good Morning before he gives the signal to Matron Glass.

"Close your eyes," Matron says.

But I keep them open, observing the secretive signal and engulfed with helplessness while the matron and four nurses and Pavlova press upon my shoulders and my knees and I feel myself dropping as if a trap door had opened into darkness. I imagine as I fall my eyes turning inward to face and confound each other with a separate truth which they prove without my help. Then I rise disembodied from the dark to grasp and attach myself like a homeless parasite to the shape of my identity and its position in space and time. At first I cannot find my way, I cannot find myself where I left myself, someone has removed all trace of me. I am crying.

A cup of sweet tea is being poured down my throat. I grasp the nurse's arm.

"Have I had it? Have I had it?"

"You have had treatment," she answers. "Now go to sleep. You are awake too early."

But I am wide awake and the anxiety begins again to accumulate.

Will I be for treatment tomorrow? . . .

IV

In a few days I was up and dressed wandering around the ward and sitting in the garden under the willow tree and learning, as I tried to forget my still-growing disquiet and dread and the haunting smell of the other ward, as I became to all appearances one of the gentle contented patients of Ward Seven, that the E.S.T. which happened three times a week, and the succession of screams heard as the machine advanced along the corridor, were a nightmare that one suffered for one's own "good." "For your own good" is a persuasive argument that will eventually make man agree to his own destruction. I tried to reassure myself by remembering that in Ward Seven the "new" attitude ("mental patients are people like you and me") seemed to predominate the bright counterpanes, pastel-shaded walls supposed to soothe, a few abstract paintings hanging paint-in-cheek in the sitting room; tables for four in the dining room, gay with checked cloths; everything to keep up the pretense that Treecroft was a hotel, not a mental hospital, and anyway the words *mental hospital* were now frowned upon; the proper designation was now *psychiatric unit*. . . .

V

One day I was moved from the special table and became a member of the "rest" surging about in the dayroom. I was afraid. I sat on one of the long wooden forms and turned to face Betty who sat on the other end. I smiled at her. I hoped that my smile showed love and a desire to help her. Suddenly I received a heavy blow from her fist, right on my nose, and my eyes filled with tears that began as tears of pain but ended in tears of hopelessness and loneliness: how could I help them if they were going to hit me? A nurse came up to me.

"That's Betty's seat. Nobody sits on that form but Betty. She's homicidal."

"Why didn't you tell me?" I asked.

"Oh. I wanted to see what would happen," was the candid reply. "Don't take it badly. It's all in a day's fun. Here, join the lolly scramble."

The lolly scramble was a feature of some days and was held both for the amusement of the staff who often described themselves as "going dippy ourselves, stuck on duty here all day" and for the pleasure of the patients. The nurses, feeling bored because there hadn't been a recent fight, would fetch a bag of sweets from the tin which was bought every fortnight as part of the Social Security allowance for the patients. The paper lollies would be showered into the middle of the dayroom and it would be first come first served with fights developing, people being put in strait jackets, whistles blowing; and the tension which mounted and reached its peak at intervals—both in the patients and in the nurses who had long ago had to suppress any desire to "nurse" and were now overworked degraded, in many cases sadistic, custodians—found its release, for a time.

After a lolly scramble, when the fights had been dealt with, there was unusual quietness and dreaminess and sometimes laughter, and those who had been successful in the rush held tight to their sweet sticky booty. The toffees always had the same taste, of dark swampy syrup that made one feel sick and at the same time gave comfort. Although I longed to, I never joined the scramble, and viewing it from the outside, was filled with disgust that the staff had so far forgotten that the people in their charge were human beings, as to treat them like animals in a pen at the zoo.

My own taste for toffees came at night when, being hurried along the corridor to bed, I felt such pangs of hunger that I became skillful at darting unobserved into the open pantry, and sometimes snatching a handful of toffees from a newly opened tin. But that was a rare occasion. More often I seized in one hand a slice of bread from the bin and delved honey from a large tin, pasting it, ants and all, with my fingers across the bread, and thrusting the whole in the sweaty hairy hollow under my arm, and withdrawing it and eating it, salt and sweet and gritty, in the quiet of my room.

My room had no shutter. I could see the sky at night and down below a puddle-filled enclosure outside a brick building from which came the sound of an engine shunting and tides falling upon the beach, as if a private ferry were in operation with the bodies being taken from shore to shore. But my stay in my room, though not my secret gorgings of bread and honey was abruptly ended when, one evening as I lay in bed, I heard sinister whispering outside my door. I had been unusually difficult that day in obeying orders, had "talked back" to the nurses, had screamed out of hopelessness; and now I was apprehensive, wondering what my punishment would be. The voices continued their whispering.

"We'll give her shock treatment tomorrow," one said. "A worse shock than she's ever had; and she can't escape. You've locked the door securely?"

"Yes," replied the other. "She's down for shock. It will put her in her place I tell you. She needs to be taught a lesson. No breakfast for her tomorrow."

"No breakfast," the other voice repeated. "She's for shock."

My heart beat fast so that I found it hard to breathe; I was overcome by such a feeling of panic that although it seemed like breaking and distorting the only image of sky that was left to me, I smashed the window with my fist, to get out or to get at the glass and destroy myself to prevent the coming of tomorrow and the dreaded E.S.T.

For gone now were the old "brave" days at Cliffhaven when I had preserved enough calm to queue for treatment and to watch the beds with the unconscious patients in them, being wheeled from the treatment room. Ever since the morning in Four-Five-and-One when they had surprised me by giving me two consecutive treatments, although I had been given no more, and although, as I learned, I had been transferred to Lawn Lodge because they could "do nothing with me," I still lived in dread of the morning when the door would be unlocked and the nurse would greet me with, "No breakfast for you this morning. Keep on your nightgown and your dressing gown. You're for treatment."

Hearing the commotion of breaking glass the nurse hurried to the room and burst in, and I was put into the opposite room which was dark and shuttered, and I climbed shivering between the cold stiff sheets made colder by the mackintosh under them, and uncomfortable by the stalks of straw sticking through the mattress. I was given paraldehyde and slept.

The next morning my fear returned, yet I found out that I had been mistaken, that I was not "for treatment."

I could no longer control my fear; it persisted and grew stronger and day after day I made myself a nuisance by asking, asking, asking if they were planning to give me

E.S.T. or to do anything terrible to me, to bury me alive in a tunnel in the earth so that no matter how long I called for help no one would hear me, to remove part of my brain and turn me into a strange animal who had to be led about with a leather collar and chain and wearing a striped dress.

And now whenever I saw the Matron and Sister Wolf talking together I suffered agonies of suspense. I knew they were talking about me; they were planning to murder me with electricity, to send me to Mount Eden Prison where I would be hanged at daybreak. Sometimes I screamed at Matron and Sister to stop their conversation; sometimes now I attacked the nurses because I knew they were hiding the truth from me, refusing to tell me the fearful plans they were making. And I had to know. I had to know. How else could I make arrangements to protect myself, to gather all the devices for use in extreme emergency and take things calmly so that I would know which to use? If only there had been someone to tell me!

I would have asked the assurance of the doctor but where was he? It was well known that Lawn Lodge patients were "so far gone" that it was not much use the doctor devoting his valuable time to them, that it was wiser for him to be attending the others, the Ward Seven and the convalescent people who could be "saved." Only once I saw the doctor pass through the dayroom of Lawn Lodge. He limped quickly from door to door. On his face was an expression of horror and fear that changed to incredulity as if he were saying to himself, "It is not so. I am a young enthusiastic doctor, only a few years out of medical school. I live with my wife and child across the road in the house provided for me. My God what means the hospitality of the soul?"

PSYCHIATRIC JUSTICE IN CANADA

Harvey Currell, Peter Bruton, and Sidney Katz (from the Toronto *Daily Star* and the Toronto *Telegram*)

In all contemporary "civilized" societies, the judicial authorities often have a choice between prosecuting a person accused of a crime and committing him as mentally unfit to stand trial. When the prosecution's case is weak, or when the judicial authorities fear that the defendant will embarrass them in court—or when, for whatever reason, the law enforcement agencies of society wish to "dispose" of a "case" without the publicity of a trial—the accused may be declared mentally unfit to stand trial and imprisoned in a mental hospital.* One such case—that of Fred Fawcett—received considerable publicity in the Toronto press in the 1960s; indeed, the victim probably owes his freedom to the vigilance of the newspapers that did not accept the official verdict that he was crazy. The following story is a composite of excerpts from a series of newspaper articles on the Fawcett case.

I[1]

Fred Fawcett was born 50 years ago on the Euphrasia Township farm which his maternal great-grandfather ob-

* See Thomas S. Szasz, *Psychiatric Justice* (New York: Macmillan, 1965).
[1] Harvey Currell, "A Fresh Look at Fred Fawcett," the Toronto *Telegram*, April 12, 1965.

tained through a Crown grant in 1856. The farm is in rugged country just east of the Beaver Valley's rim, about 14 miles from Meaford, in Grey county.

Fred was an intelligent boy, went to local public schools and obtained his junior matriculation in three instead of the usual four years of high school. On the death of his father he and his younger brother Harold took over operation of the family's 20-acre home farm and a 100-acre outlying farm.

Crown authorities contend that during the 1950s, Fred Fawcett became involved in a series of disputes with authority over his family's land and rights stemming from their ownership of it. Eventually, from study of the Crown grant, Fred Fawcett decided that since the land had been granted by the Crown before Confederation in 1867, the Province of Ontario and its local municipalities had no legal right to tax it.

Provincial authorities contend that Fawcett went farther than this and concluded that the Crown deed meant that he was not subject to any Ontario laws.

II

The incident which led directly to Fawcett's arrest and subsequent confinement occurred on Aug. 28, 1961 when Grey county assessor Stuart R. Howey and Euphrasia Township assessor Henry G. Seabrook went to the Fawcett farm. Their purpose was to measure the buildings as part of a township-wide re-assessment program which had been carried out on all Euphrasia farms except Fawcett's.

Mr. Howey and Mr. Seabrook swore that they saw nobody but Fawcett on the farm, that Fawcett appeared with a pistol, ordered them to walk to the road.

When they turned to do so, the assessors testified, Fawcett fired a shot into the air or the ground, then hit Mr. Seabrook on the back of the neck with his fist or arm so that Seabrook fell to the ground.

The assessors swore that after Mr. Howey got into his

car, Fawcett banged on the front left window and then deliberately shot a hole through the left front tire. The assessors drove a mile, stopped and changed the tire, then went to Meaford where they met the Grey county Crown Attorney and Provincial Police Officer, reported the incident and handed over the damaged tire as evidence.

Three weeks later, after several attempts to serve summonses, a bench warrant was issued for Fawcett's arrest and five OPP officers and a Department of Transport inspector went to bring him in.

Roadblocks were set up. The Crown contends that Fawcett drove through one roadblock at which two shots were fired at his car by an OPP constable, went to his farm and with a loaded rifle refused for more than four hours to surrender. He finally did surrender without violence.

As a result of these and other incidents, the Crown argued successfully in court that Fawcett suffers from paranoia or a paranoid condition, that he has unshakeable delusions that his Crown grant makes him exempt from Provincial laws and that he is likely to use violence in defence of his mistaken and abnormal beliefs. . . .

As I mentioned earlier, the family acquired land in the 1850s through a deed or patent from the British Crown, made out in the name of Queen Victoria.

This is not at all unusual. In fact, every inch of privately-owned land southern Ontario has has at some time been granted or patented from the Crown and all the rights and privileges conveyed by such deeds are passed along to subsequent owners whether they get the land by inheritance or purchase.

Whether you own a farm in Parry Sound or a house lot in suburbia, you can trace your title back to a Crown deed at some time or other. Not too many families, however, still hold the land originally granted to them by the Crown and still have the original document.

The Fawcetts did have two such deeds, one for each of their farms and these began to assume more and more importance in Fred's thinking.

During his earlier years, Fred had taken a correspondence course in law from an institution in Illinois and he has always shown a keen interest in legal matters.

Fred began to examine carefully the wording of the Crown deed. He attached special importance to the fact that it was described as an "absolute" sale from the Crown and considered the following words of the deed vital:

> "To have and to hold the said parcel or tract of land, hereby granted, conveyed and assured unto the said William J. Marsh, his heirs and assigns, forever; saving, excepting and reserving, nevertheless, unto Us, Our Heirs and Successors, all mines of gold and silver, and the free uses, passage and enjoyment of, in, over and upon all navigable waters that shall or may be hereafter found on or under, or be flowing through or upon any part of the said parcel or tract of land hereby granted as aforesaid."

Fred Fawcett reasoned in this way about that paragraph: Queen Victoria had been very specific about what she wanted to retain on the land. She wanted any gold or silver found there and she wanted navigation rights on any present or future rivers.

If Queen Victoria had wanted taxation rights on the property, Fred Fawcett believed she would have said so. Since she had not said so, the Province of Ontario which wasn't even established in 1856, and its municipality, Euphrasia Township, had no basis to claim a right that Queen Victoria hadn't specifically reserved to the Crown.

Ontario Department of Health psychiatrists claim that these beliefs developed by Fawcett on the basis of the Crown deed wording have developed into a delusion and form the central core of Fred Fawcett's mental illness.

They further claim that from this central core, Fred Fawcett has developed a whole system of other false beliefs or delusions and has convinced himself that he is subject only to Federal Government jurisdiction and is not bound by any Ontario law since he doesn't recognize the existence of the Province of Ontario as far as he and his land are concerned.

III

Whether this is true or not, the fact remains that Fawcett stopped paying township taxes in 1952 and got away with it for a good number of years.

After taxes had been unpaid for four years, the County of Grey put the Fawcett farm up for tax sale in 1956. A Toronto man named Matsoko applied to buy it for unpaid taxes, as provided by Ontario law.

Before the would-be purchaser could obtain a title, one year and a day would have to elapse; during this time the Fawcetts would have the right to reclaim the land by paying the tax arrears and penalties.

Fred Fawcett waited until the redemption period was passed and until Mr. Matsoko applied in 1958 to Grey county court for a title and possession. He opposed the Matsoko application principally on grounds that the county hadn't advertised the tax sale the required number of times and had not complied to the letter with other legal requirements.

The action never came to courts. Mr. Matsoko abandoned his application, the land remained in the Fawcett name and the Fawcetts collected their court and lawyer's costs. It was a resounding victory for Fred.

The taxes remained unpaid. In the meantime, Fred Fawcett had scored another legal victory. During the mid-1950s, he and his brother had been in another wrangle with township authorities over the Warble Fly Act.

As a result of a petition from a majority of farmers, Euphrasia Township had declared the Act in force in the township. It provides that all cattle owners must spray their livestock to prevent spread of the Warble Fly infestation and provides that all cattle are to be inspected.

Two Warble Fly inspectors presented themselves one day at the Fawcett farm. Fred refused them admittance on the grounds that they had just come from other farms and might be carrying infectious cattle diseases on their boots or clothes.

He demanded that they return next morning before they'd been to any other properties. He also pointed out that it was unfair to expect him to bring cattle in from pasture in the middle of the day and that if the inspectors came early in the morning, the cattle would, as a matter of course, be at the barn.

One of the Fawcett brothers was charged with a violation of the Act, was convicted by a local magistrate, appealed and won his appeal with costs. Ontario had to rewrite the Warble Fly Act as a result. . . .

IV

Now let's review the circumstances surrounding Fred Fawcett's arrest on Sept. 18, 1961.

Seven charges were laid against Fawcett. Three concerned the incident of the assessors' visit. They were pointing a firearm, assault and property damage.

Four more charges arose out of the circumstances surrounding his arrest. These were two charges of pointing a firearm and two of obstructing police. . . .

On arrival in Owen Sound, Fawcett was not given bail. He was remanded to the county jail and later appeared before a magistrate. The magistrate remanded him to Penetang Mental Hospital for 30 days for a mental examination. While he was there, the Ontario Department of Health had him examined by psychiatrists, convened a board under the Ontario Mental Hospitals Act and certified him as mentally ill.

Fawcett was never returned to the magistrate's court. This fact led to an appeal to the Ontario Court of Appeal and later the Supreme Court of Canada by the Fawcett family. It was maintained that since Fawcett was remanded for mental examination under the Criminal Code, which is Federal law, that he should have been returned to the court which remanded him because Federal law takes precedence over the Provincial law under which Fawcett was certified. The Supreme Court of Canada dismissed the Fawcett appeal.

Three Ontario Department of Health psychiatrists testified at Fawcett's 1962 hearing that they were convinced he was in a paranoid state. Two independent psychiatrists testified that he was not.

In brief, the government's psychiatric testimony was that Fred had developed a persecution complex in his disputes with the township, that he had developed the delusion that the Crown grants rendered the Fawcett property exempt from taxation and upon this he had built the additional delusional argument that he is exempt from all Ontario laws.

On the other side, it was argued that Fred Fawcett is a friendly, reasonable man and that although his stand about the Crown deed may be a false belief, it is not a delusion. Fawcett's lawyers pointed out that he was given logical encouragement in his stand by a lawyer to whom he mentioned it. The lawyer told him: "you may have a point there."

Fawcett's lawyers also pointed emphatically to the fact that Fred has testified that he'd like to have his belief about the Crown deed tested in the courts and that his sister actually has issued a writ to institute such a suit but that it has been halted by Fred's hospitalization.

Fred Fawcett has stated that if the courts ruled against him in the matter of the Crown deed he would accept such a finding and would have to pay his taxes. This proves that Fawcett's beliefs are amenable to reason and are therefore not delusions, his lawyers argue.

On the other side, Crown lawyers say that the Crown grant theory is absurd, that if it is true for Fawcett it would be true for every other landowner in Ontario and then nobody would have to pay land taxes and the entire machine of government services would grind to a halt.

Mr. Justice Spence expressed the opinion that any first-year law student should be able to demolish the Fawcett argument. No reasonable or normal person could hold such a belief the Crown argues. Government lawyers have further maintained that Fawcett's statements that he would accept a verdict of the courts against him cannot be relied upon; that he might be merely stating this to get out of hospital and would revert to his old attitudes if he were returned to the old surroundings where they were developed in the first place. . . .

Having concluded that Fred Fawcett's belief about the Crown grants were a delusion, Mr. Justice Spence said he was convinced that the delusion had been expanded so that it caused Fred to believe he was immune from all Ontario laws and taxes.

The judge further found that Fawcett's belief was unshakeable and he refused to accept as proof to the contrary Fawcett's statement that he wanted the Crown grant theory tested in the courts and would accept the result. . . .

As to whether Fred Fawcett is dangerous to be at large, Mr. Justice Spence could not be quite so certain. He recalled that Fawcett could easily have shot one or both of the assessors instead of just a tire, and that he could just as easily have shot one or more of the police officers who came to arrest him.

He added however: "That presents a pretty convincing picture that the plaintiff, despite certain threats, is not a dangerous person, but it is asking the court to hazard a great deal on the plaintiff's failure to take dangerous action up to the present time. . . ."

In conclusion, the judge referred to a psychiatrist's statement:

"If the plaintiff could be allowed to stay on his farm without paying taxes or having any touch with any authorities, he would not be dangerous, but if anyone came into his area to enforce laws, he might be dangerous."

Said Mr. Justice Spence: "I think that is a sound analysis. I think that on the evidence which I have recited and other portions of the evidence which I accept, that is the true situation, and so then, the plaintiff may well be dangerous and it would be dangerous at the present time to order that he be released."

V[2]

More than 230 friends and neighbors of Fred Fawcett petitioned Premier John Robarts today to have Fawcett released from the Penetanguishene Hospital for the Criminally Insane where he has been held for the past 3½ years. . . .

The petition, presented at his Queen's Park office by Emerson Welsh, Maitland Purdy and Earl and Beverly Boyle—all farmers from Grey county, contained 180 names. An additional 50 names have been gathered but the impassable conditions of some of the country back-roads made it impossible to deliver them to the premier's office today.

The petition reads:

"We, the undersigned, are friends and neighbors of Frederick Fawcett who has lived among us all his life. We always found him to be an entirely honest and well-balanced human being. We strongly protest his continued detention at the Ontario Mental Hospital. We, his friends and neighbors, would like him back with us and he would be a threat to no one if he lived among us."

Reta Fawcett, Fred's sister, who accompanied the delegation, told the *Star*: "We had no difficulty in collecting the names. Many people voluntarily traveled many miles over difficult roads to sign it."

A previous petition, signed by 171 Grey county residents and delivered to the attorney-general's office in 1962, has mysteriously vanished. Attorney-General Arthur Wishart told the Legislature last Friday, "This is the first time I've heard of it. I didn't even know it existed." . . .

Premier John Robarts told a press conference today [Apr. 19, 1965] the three-man advisory board on the detention of patients will be asked to review Fawcett's case in about three months' time. . . .

[2] Sidney Katz, "Robarts Informed Testimony Against Fred Fawcett 'Unfair'," the Toronto *Daily Star*, April 13, 1965.

VI[3]

Fred Fawcett, the burly 50-year-old Owen Sound farmer who refused to pay the taxes on his land, is free.

At 5:04 p.m. yesterday [May 28, 1965], he walked out the front door of the Penetanguishene Hospital for the Criminally Insane where he had been incarcerated for almost four years.

As recently as a month ago, it was claimed that Fawcett suffered with delusions and was "too dangerous to be at large."

Smiling and neatly dressed in a blue serge suit, Fawcett said: "I feel exactly the same as I did three months ago or six months ago. I have never worried about my sanity nor have I had any doubts about it."

Fred Fawcett was released from Penetanguishene Hospital for the Criminally Insane after a "domestic decision" of the hospital superintendent and not as a result of government intervention, the *Star* was told today.

Barry B. Swadron, secretary of Ontario's advisory committee on the detention of patients, said his committee was "aware" of Fawcett's release but not responsible for it.

"It was a domestic decision on the part of Dr. B. A. Boyd, the hospital superintendent," he said.

"Neither our committee, nor anyone in the government made the decision. It was based solely on Dr. Boyd's medical judgment," he said.

Swadron avoided any firm reference to conditions of Fawcett's release. He called it "absent on probation."

He added: "We are fully aware of what is going on. Our committee, acting as a review board, will come down with the final decision as to Fawcett's future status.

"We expect to submit a report to Premier Robarts and the Minister of Health after reviewing the case," he said.

He refused to disclose when the review board would meet.

"I regret very much that this story has got out. It would

[3] Sidney Katz, "Fred Fawcett Goes Free," ibid., May 29, 1965.

have been better for Fawcett if he had been released without any fuss," he said.

Contacted at Penetanguishene, Boyd refused to discuss either conditions of Fawcett's release or comment on the reason for his decision.

"We have had a very rough time with your newspaper," he told the *Star*. "Therefore, I don't care to make any comment."

Minutes before Fawcett appeared at the hospital entrance with his lawyer, Bernard Kott of Toronto, fellow patients and attendants lined up to shake his hand and wish him well.

Dr. B. A. Boyd, the hospital superintendent, said to him: "I wish we could have met under other circumstances. I would have liked to have had you for a neighbor."

Dr. Boyd classified the Owen Sound farmer's release as "on probation." The usual procedure is to grant the patient permanent discharge after two or three months of freedom.

The dramatic and unexpected release brings to a triumphant climax Fawcett's four-year uphill campaign to prove his sanity and win his freedom.

It was a campaign in which a dozen psychiatrists gave conflicting evidence about Fawcett's sanity.

It included three unsuccessful bids through the courts: he was turned down by the Ontario Supreme Court in 1962 and 1965 and by the Supreme Court of Canada in 1964.

But Fawcett, aided by his family, his lawyer, the press and a handful of provincial legislators, continued the fight.

Finally, about six weeks ago, in response to the widespread concern that Fawcett was the victim of a miscarriage of justice, Premier John Robarts called a special news conference to announce that Fawcett's case would be reviewed by a special medical review board in July. . . .

Would Fred Fawcett be free today had it not been for the vast amount of newspaper publicity, and the continuing Opposition criticism of the Government's position in the Legislature?

Are there any other "Fred Fawcetts" in Ontario hospitals because their cases have not come to public attention?

Have authorities finally released Fawcett to avoid further embarrassment and controversy . . . or is it true that he has recovered in the last three months?

They remain questions, without answers.

Dr. Boyd said he reached his decision to release Fawcett independently and without regard to the public controversy surrounding the case. . . .

The fact of the matter remains, however, that as recently as last February it was claimed that Fred Fawcett was a paranoiac, possibly dangerous and should not be allowed home.

Dr. Boyd himself testified that Fawcett "suffers from a delusional structure and the core of that delusion is his farm. If he were returned to the farm there is no telling what might happen."

Yet when Fred Fawcett was released from Penetang last Friday evening he was allowed to return to his Owen Sound-area farm where all his troubles began.

What has happened to change the situation?

"Obviously," Dr. Boyd told me yesterday, "the circumstances have altered."

In what way?

"I'm not going to release any information about an individual patient," he said. . . .

Health Minister Dr. Matthew Dymond, a general practitioner, said he personally had seen patients with seemingly "hopeless" psychiatric disabilities make "miraculous" changes within days.

"It's difficult for the layman to understand—but it's a fact," he said. . . .

VII[4]

Fred Fawcett's long fight for release from an Ontario mental hospital is over at last. And the best evidence that he should never have been in such an institution lies in the circumstances of his release.

As most Toronto newspaper readers are now aware, Mr.

[4] "The Lesson of the Fred Fawcett Case," ibid.

Fawcett was committed to a mental hospital in 1961 as the result of an incident on his farm near Owen Sound, following a long dispute with township authorities over taxes. He was accused of threatening two assessors with a gun and subsequently resisting arrest. He denied these charges, and had eyewitness evidence to back his denials. But he never had an opportunity to establish his innocence in court. Instead he was committed to Penetanguishene Hospital for the Criminally Insane.

The theory behind the committal was that Fred Fawcett suffered from insane delusions, and was therefore both unfit to stand trial and too dangerous to be allowed at large. If this were true, one would think that it could be easily confirmed, both by the opinion of psychiatrists and by the behavior of the man himself.

Yet at a hearing before the Ontario Supreme Court, earlier this year, when Mr. Fawcett unsuccessfully attempted to obtain his freedom, three eminent psychiatrists testified that he was sane. Four others—three of them present or former government employees—testified that he was insane. Such a sharp disagreement between experts hardly suggests any clear and unmistakable indication of insanity.

But perhaps the surest sign that the original committal was wrong is the reaction of the government when public opinion became aroused—thanks in considerable measure to a series of articles by the *Star*'s Sidney Katz—and when questions were asked in the legislature. Premier Robarts announced last month that an advisory board consisting of a Supreme Court judge and two psychiatrists would review the case this summer. Now, without waiting for the board's investigation, the Penetanguishene Hospital has released Mr. Fawcett on parole.

This suggests irresistibly that Fred Fawcett was wrongly certified insane in the first place, and that once in custody he was kept there by bureaucratic stubbornness and inertia until public opinion forced the cabinet to look into the matter.

The affair has now ended more or less happily for Fred Fawcett. But the question arises—how many other Fred

Fawcetts are there? How many perfectly sane men and women are languishing in Ontario mental hospitals because of a mistaken diagnosis? And how many of them are doomed to spend their lives there because they lack the money and the friends to bring their cases to the attention of the courts, the legislature or the public?

9

POSITION STATEMENT ON THE MEDICAL TREATMENT OF THE MENTALLY ILL

The American Psychiatric Association and the National Association for Mental Health

> In March 1961, the Senate Subcommittee on Constitutional Rights conducted hearings on the "Constitutional Rights of the Mentally Ill." The American Psychiatric Association, represented by Francis J. Braceland, M.D., and Jack R. Ewalt, M.D., submitted a statement of its position to this Committee.* A slightly revised version of this statement was subsequently issued, as a "Special Information Bulletin," jointly by the American Psychiatric Association and the National Association for Mental Health.† With minor omissions, this latter version is reproduced below.

* "Excerpts from Testimony Presented on Behalf of the American Psychiatric Association, by Francis J. Braceland, M.D. and Jack R. Ewalt, M.D." in *Constitutional Rights of the Mentally Ill*, Hearings before the Subcommittee on Constitutional Rights of the Committee of the Judiciary, United States Senate, Eighty-seventh Congress, First Session, March 28, 29, and 30, 1961, Part 1—Civil Aspects (Washington, D.C.: United States Government Printing Office, 1961), pp. 79–84.

† Joint Information Service of the American Psychiatric Association and the National Association for Mental Health, "Psychiatric Points of View Regarding Laws and Procedures Governing Medical Treatment of the Mentally Ill." *Special Information Bulletin*, No. 1, September 1962, pp. 1–8.

I

Throughout their history, psychiatrists as physicians have taken issue with the laws and procedures which govern the admission, treatment, and discharge of patients to mental hospitals. From a medical point of view these procedures impede and delay treatment and since they often involve procedures similar in nature to criminal proceedings, they perpetuate the stigma attached to the mentally ill.

We, as doctors, want our psychiatric hospitals and our outpatient facilities to be looked upon as treatment centers for sick people in the same sense that general hospitals are so viewed. We want people in need of our services to come to them in the expectation of being benefited, not incarcerated. We want to be considered doctors, not jailers. We know that if our patients are committed, locked up, shorn of their civil liberties, that they will react with the same rage as would any citizen, and such rage is not an auspicious starting point for treatment. We look with envy at our colleagues in England where at least 70 per cent of all admissions to mental hospitals are voluntary as compared with our own country where certainly not more than 25 per cent are voluntary.

Since it is a feature of some mental illness that the victim does not admit to his illness, the problem arises of how to obtain treatment for such people. In short, treatment must be provided against the patient's will. This is the point at which the trouble starts. It is by no means entirely a legal problem. It is also a social and cultural problem. When one reviews the sorry history of standards of treatment and care of the mentally ill in American mental hospitals, it is little wonder that legal safeguards have been established to make it difficult for a citizen in need to be admitted to them. They have, until recent years, been viewed as places of custody rather than treatment, places for the custody of citizens who, albeit not criminal, were still troublesome enough to be put "out of sight, out of mind."

In recent decades, however, the new medical science of psychiatry, fighting an uphill battle, has sufficiently advanced that the public has become more sympathetic with the view that accepts mental illness as an illness which is correctable and modifiable if treated by modern therapies. It is in this context that psychiatry now seeks to revise legal procedures to facilitate and not hinder prompt access to treatment by all citizens who need it, and this without the embarrassment, the stigma, and the deprivation of civil rights all too often associated with obtaining treatment.

II

Psychiatrists are quite as much concerned as any citizen that no person shall be deprived of his life and liberty without due process of law; but they must, as physicians, also be concerned with a *citizen's right to medical treatment*. Admittedly, there is need of legal safeguards against what is commonly called the "railroading of people into mental hospitals"; but we would contend that this can be accomplished—and indeed has been in several states and foreign countries—without jeopardizing prompt and effective treatment of the mentally ill.

The problem is complicated by the fact that laws and procedures governing mental illness are formulated by some fifty state jurisdictions. They vary a great deal from one jurisdiction to another. Encouragingly, in recent years state laws governing the commitment and rights of the mentally ill have tended to become more flexible and more in accord with the medical point of view. But they are uneven in their development. It would be a great boon to the advancement of the treatment and care of the mentally ill of America if some national influence could be brought to bear that would encourage the states to adopt more uniform laws that more nearly reflected the medical view of a citizen's right to treatment.

There are a number of major principles that the medical profession, and psychiatry in particular, would like to see established in legal procedures.

Dr. Isaac Ray, one of the Founding Fathers of the American Psychiatric Association, said in 1869 what has never been better said, to wit, that any statute designed to regulate hospitalization should:

> "In the first place put no hindrance in the way to prompt use of those instrumentalities which are regarded as the most effectual in promoting the comfort and restoration of the patient. Secondly, it should spare all unnecessary exposure of private troubles and all unnecessary conflict with popular prejudices. Thirdly, it should protect individuals from wrongful imprisonment. It would be objection enough to any legal provision that it failed to secure these objects in the completest possible manner."

It is possible that our laws governing mental illness have contributed to protecting citizens from "wrongful imprisonment"; but they have certainly not, in general, met the other two of Dr. Ray's criteria. Some states, until very recently, actually required a jury trial with all its attendant embarrassment, indignity, publicity, and exposure of the patient's private affairs before he could be committed.

To illustrate how far astray the law can go from a medical point of view, Dr. Karl Bowman tells of a case with which he was acquainted involving a wife who decided that her husband was mentally sick. He was depressed and had delusions that persons were trying to kill him. Following the regular legal procedure, she swore out a warrant. The sheriff arrested the patient and he was taken to the county jail, there to await a hearing before the judge. That night he hanged himself in the jail. Sticklers for legal procedure, Dr. Bowman comments, may derive comfort from the fact that the sick man's legal rights were well preserved. He was arrested on a warrant by a sheriff. He was not sent to a hospital without due process of law and a chance to appear before a judge. Perhaps if he had, however, he might be alive today. In short, Dr. Bowman notes, the public has been so obsessed with the legal point of view and the alleged infallibility of legal procedures that they insist on protecting the so-called legal rights of the patient without thinking of what his medical rights are.

From a medical point of view, the worst features of the commitment laws and procedures of the past (and some of these features are still with us in some states) include these: Insistence that the patient appear personally in court with consequent exposure of his problems to the public; the frequent identification of mental illness with criminality as a result of court procedures; the acceptance of a lay judgment as to the degree of illness as occurs, for example, in a jury trial; frequent acceptance of commitment as tantamount to legal incompetence, thus depriving a mental patient of his civil rights; the use of archaic legal terminology such as "insane," "of unsound mind," "idiot," "feebleminded," etc.—all of them conveying a legal, rather than a medical, meaning; and embarrassing inquiries into the patient's financial status at the time of his commitment.

III

In general, psychiatrists favor a *simple commitment procedure* entailing an application to the hospital by a close relative or friend, and a certification by two qualified physicians that they have examined the subject and found him to be mentally ill. If judicial procedures must be brought into play at all, it is suggested that the court should have discretionary power to designate proper personnel to notify the patient that he is ill and in need of hospital care rather than require the patient to be present in person at a public hearing. The examination by court-appointed physicians may be properly conducted in a medical facility, or at the home of the patient, informally and in a manner that will have the least traumatic effect on him. In short, any procedures used should eliminate all public exposure and eschew any appearance of a criminal procedure.

It is of great importance that laws should provide for *emergency commitments* for limited periods of time without involving any court procedure. Over thirty states now have streamlined procedures for emergencies whereby a hearing may be waived, or a single physician instead of two physicians may commit a patient for a limited period of time. In such states there is a growing tendency to use emergency commitments for obvious reasons. They are speedier than regular commitment procedures and make it relatively easy for the doctors and the family concerned to take the patient directly to a hospital without going through the routine of a formal hearing. They allow for a temporary period of observing the patient in a medical setting during which formal commitment procedures may be instituted if deemed necessary. It is interesting that in Connecticut about 80 per cent of all admissions to mental hospitals are accomplished by emergency commitment.

All states but one now provide for *voluntary admissions* to mental hospitals. The provisions, sadly, have not been used to any great extent in this country, for whatever reasons. Some states require a medical certificate in support of a voluntary admission. In all cases a voluntary patient must be released upon his request, although there is often provision that such request need not be acted upon for several days during which time formal commitment procedures may be initiated, if deemed proper in the physician's judgment. Perhaps 20-25 per cent of admissions to U.S. mental hospitals are voluntary. That more are not so is probably due to such factors as lack of general public respect for the mental hospital as a treatment center; the fact that the hospitals are overcrowded and understaffed; and the lingering stigma associated with being a mental patient.

There can be no doubt, however, that the use of voluntary admission procedures is much to be encouraged—and the more so as the nation hopefully rallies behind a renewed effort to turn the public mental hospital into a genuine treatment center. Clearly, voluntary admissions encourage early treatment and a cooperative attitude towards the hospital by the patient. All of this is auspicious for more effective treatment and early recovery.

Here, again, there is a lack of legal clarity about the status of a voluntary patient—with regard to his exercise of various civil rights, for example—which serves to discourage voluntary admissions. These confusions need clarification.

It is clearly of the greatest importance that in protecting the rights of the patient who is hospitalized without his consent, some system of periodic re-examination of his case be instituted. Obviously, if a patient is well enough to be discharged, but no one examines him to determine the fact, then he is being deprived of his freedom illegally.

IV

It must be clearly understood that the establishment of a mental illness does not, *ipso facto*, warrant a finding of incompetency. Throughout the legal history of mental illness there has been considerable confusion about the two concepts, and in some states commitment can act as an automatic determination of incompetency. From a medical point of view there is not, necessarily, any connection between the two. In general, psychiatrists are much concerned that any mental patient within a hospital should exercise as many of his ordinary civil rights as he has the capacity to exercise, such capacity being determined by medical judgment. We have in mind such rights as signing checks, selling property, retaining an automobile license, making purchases, executing contracts, voting, making a will, and the like. He must also retain the right to communicate by sealed mail, to receive visitors, to the confidentiality of his case records, to habeas corpus, and the right to protest further hospitalization. . . .

This matter of being able to exercise civil rights is also of the greatest importance in rehabilitating the patient. After a patient has been medically adjudged as sufficiently recovered for return to society, one can imagine the effect upon him when he is not allowed to drive an automobile, or sign checks, make a contract, etc.

In general, all laws governing mental illness should recognize that many hospital patients are perfectly capable of handling their own affairs and that any automatic tie-up of incompetency and commitment is harmful. . . .

V

In 1951 the U.S. Public Health Service, at the instigation of the National Advisory Mental Health Council, issued a Draft Act Governing Hospitalization of the Mentally Ill as a guide for the states in revising their statutes. The provisions in the Draft Act are formulated in somewhat the same spirit as the new British Mental Health Bill. That is to say, the Draft Act, in general, provides maximum opportunity for prompt psychiatric and medical care; it protects the patient against emotionally traumatic or degrading treatment; and it contains safeguards against wrongful confinement and deprivation of rights. The major principles observed in formulating the Draft Act were these:

1. Provision for voluntary hospitalization—that is, easy access to a mental hospital in the same manner as a general hospital.
2. Maximum reliance on medical judgment in determining the need for hospitalization.
3. Provision for temporary involuntary hospitalization without court proceedings.
4. Provision for continuing review of the mental condition of a hospitalized patient and for his release or discharge.

To date only four states—Idaho, Missouri, South Carolina and Utah—have adopted the Draft Act almost in its entirety, although Florida and New Mexico have adopted much of it. And almost all the other states have adopted some features of the Act such as provision for voluntary admissions.

Although it appears that the Draft Act has by no means provided an answer to all of the legal problems involved, it seems to be generally agreed by both the psychiatric and legal professions to represent a real step forward.

In the long run, it will presumably be a fundamental change in public attitudes that will precipitate the kind of legal provisions governing the mentally ill that psychiatrists espouse. One cannot help but look wistfully, for example, at the general attitude that prevails in England and Holland where, it may be generally stated, patients are kept in mental hospitals only while their symptoms cause distress to themselves and others. The idea is to make hospital treatment as brief as possible and, at the same time, to make readmission a simple matter. Often a patient will be admitted for two weeks or a month so that the family may have a vacation, so to speak. This relieves the pressure on the family for a time and gives them the strength to continue caring for the sick relative later on.

Also, over the long haul, the surest way to rally public support behind laws that will facilitate rather than impede prompt and adequate medical care for the mentally ill lies in the development of far more adequate psychiatric services than anything our country has yet seen.

VI

We may well ask, why is a commitment procedure necessary anyway? Why would a delusional or hallucinating patient refuse to recognize these symptoms as those of an illness and seek treatment for them voluntarily? To be sure, there are often psychological reasons for resistance to treatment. Perhaps there will always be selected mentally sick people who will refuse to recognize their illness because of the distorted sense of satisfaction they derive from the symptoms of the illness. Still, we must recognize that the delusional patient conjures his delusions against a background of hundreds of years of intolerant prejudice against the very symptoms from which he suffers. The mentally sick patient may be disoriented but that does not make him foolish or insensitive. He is quite as aware as most of us of the public exposure that faces him if he goes to a hospital. He is alert to the tough time he will have getting a job when he gets out, if he does get out. He has read the newspapers about how overcrowded and understaffed the hospitals are. He knows that there lurks in the minds of his former friends the suspicion that he is a dangerous fellow. He is sensitive that a mother may recoil in fright if he stops to give her child a friendly pat on the head. What motivation has he to admit of a mental illness?

We are told by public opinion survey experts that the prevailing public image of the seriously mentally ill person continues to be an image of a violent, unstable, unreliable, dirty, disturbed, dangerous sort of a fellow and quite possibly one with criminal intent. One cannot help but hypothesize that our laws governing the mentally ill have developed in response to this public image in some measure. The general idea appears to have prevailed that if the seriously ill person is indeed such a risky fellow, then it becomes a terribly serious matter to accuse him of being sick, no matter how self-evident the symptoms may be. Thus all manner of legal safeguards must be established to insure that he shall not be so adjudged until the fact has been established beyond all possible doubt. In this spirit, legal procedures have taken on the atmosphere of a criminal trial, even though no crime has been committed. Similarly, once a sick person has been relegated to the custody of a mental hospital, the same spirit dictates that we shall not make it too easy for the patient to be discharged and returned to the community for rehabilitation with his civil rights intact.

To the extent that the hypothesis holds water, it is, from a physician's point of view, based on a distorted conception of what the typical mental patient really is like. It is not that the physician would plead that the typical mental patient is pleasant to deal with. He is a challenge from a social point of view, to be sure. That is why, at some stage in his illness, he may need to be protected from society, and society from him, in an inpatient facility. But, to put it mildly, this is something less than to charge him with being dangerous, criminally inclined, or habitually violent. Speaking of crime, there isn't a shred of evidence that the incidence of crime among ex-mental hospital patients is any higher than for the general population, and there is some evidence that it may be less. In a word, one of the great challenges of psychiatry today is to communicate convincingly to the public a more accurate clinical picture of what the typical mental patient really is like as the doctor sees him. This will ultimately foster greater confidence in the doctor's capacity to determine whether a patient can be retained in the community and a greater public acceptance of the mentally handicapped patient in the community.

10

OUT OF SIGHT, OUT OF MIND

Frank L. Wright, Jr.

Out of Sight, Out of Mind* is the official report of the National Mental Health Foundation of its investigation into the treatment of mental-hospital patients. According to Mr. Wright, the report is based on "the greatest wealth of factual material about conditions in mental hospitals that had ever been gathered in one place. . . . Each incident described is a short-story or character sketch unto itself, each undeniably true and accurate, each representing hundreds of similar incidents that are occurring all over this country today . . ."

I have selected a few representative vignettes from this volume.

I

"Bright morning, Mr. Pisky, isn't it?"

Mr. Pisky looked up from the bowl of unsweetened cereal he was eating, and blinked at the attendant standing there. A little smile broke on Pisky's face. "Yeah, bright! More cereal?" he asked.

"Sure enough. I'll bring it right over." And the attendant went away smiling, to try to scrape just a little more pasty oats out of the tin.

---

* *Out of Sight, Out of Mind* (Philadelphia: National Mental Health Foundation, Inc., 1947), pp. 27–28, 34–36, 49–51, 71–72, 73–74, 81–82, 99–100.

Those were the first words Pisky had spoken in two weeks. During most of that time he had been so depressed that he had to be told to eat every mouthful. This morning he had gotten out of bed by himself and had dressed himself. (That is, he had done everything but button his shirt—all its buttons were torn off, and he had let another patient tie it together with a string.) Now he was actually asking for food, and eating it as if he enjoyed it.

As soon as the attendant and his sixty-three patients were back on the ward, Pisky presented himself again. "Say, do you s'pose I could have my glasses and something to read?"

"Sure, you can have this magazine to read. But we'll have to ask the doctor for your glasses. The doc should be along before long, so you watch for him. Okay?"

"Hokay!" said Mr. Pisky.

Pisky had been around long enough—he had been in the hospital fifteen years—to know that the doctor didn't spend much time going through the ward. He took up his vigil right at the door of the ward and watched carefully for the doctor's appearance.

The attendant was down at the other end of the ward when Dr. Klemm swept in on his daily dash through the wards. One hour—ten wards—seven hundred patients—not much time.

Pisky stepped up timidly behind the doctor and touched his shoulder: "Please sir. . . ."

Dr. Klemm whirled around, pushed Pisky roughly onto a bench and cursed him roundly. "You——! Who do you think you are, putting your hand on me?"

Pisky quivered on the bench a moment, slid to the floor and ran for the toilet, where he crouched in a corner, crying.

Dr. Klemm strode out the door at the other end of the ward, muttering: "If I ever get fired or want to leave this hospital, I'll beat hell out of that patient before I go."

II

"Sure, I know how to treat these patients. I've had experience with them."

That was Anderson's reply to O'Toole, the charge attendant on Ward E. But O'Toole didn't think that experience was too valuable a recommendation. Baker and Landon, the last two men who had been sent to O'Toole, had been "experienced" too. But they had turned out to be dyed-in-the-wool "bughousers." "Floaters," some people called them, and O'Toole called them "drunken bums."

They came and went from one hospital to another; they never stayed at one place more than a few months. Their attitude seemed to be: "We'll run this bughouse like a bughouse ought to be run. If we happen to bang a patient up now and then, or if we let some of the 'nuts' die in their beds, who cares? We know the hospital will let us slip out quietly, and we can always get a job at some other hospital." And so they took out their own dissatisfactions on the patients, and got a kick out of cracking the whip over helpless inmates.

O'Toole looked at Anderson. The new man hardly looked like a "bughouser," but the hospital didn't get a chance to hire much else these days. So O'Toole asked, "How do you treat them?"

"Give 'em the old soft soap. That's the best thing I've ever found."

O'Toole thought that sounded pretty good. You could talk these old patients on Ward E into most anything, if you were patient enough and used the right approach. He had thought of his methods in higher terms than "soft-soaping," but he guessed the old slang expression covered the situation pretty well. So he said, "Okay, Anderson, I guess we'll get along." And then he started Anderson off into his job.

Everything went pretty well the first three days. Anderson wasn't much of a worker, but he seemed willing enough. O'Toole was sorry, but not particularly alarmed, when Anderson appeared on the fourth day with alcohol on his breath. After all, he thought, at least three-quarters of the attendants drank to excess. It was too much to hope that Anderson would fall into that other quarter.

That evening O'Toole noticed that Anderson was herding the patients into the bedrooms with some kind of weapon. He saw Anderson swing the weapon into a patient's bare back, and he called out, "Hey, what are you doing there, Anderson?"

"Giving these slow bastards the soft-soap treatment," Anderson replied.

"Well, cut it out. We don't go for rough stuff on this ward."

"You don't have to worry about this. See? I've got a square of soap in the toe of the sock. You can beat the hell out of these numbskulls with it, and it won't leave a mark anywhere. Watch." Anderson wound up and swung his soapsock directly into the abdomen of the unsuspecting patient nearest him.

But by then O'Toole was on hand. He took the sock away and told Anderson to get off the ward. Anderson looked at him, disbelieving for a moment. Then he scowled: "Why you stinkin' prissy-pants, you! You let these patients run the ward, and then you try to order me off it."

"I run this ward," said O'Toole, "and I run it for the patients—not for you. Now go down and turn in your keys while I call the supervisor."

Anderson sneered and walked off the ward. O'Toole reported the incident and went on putting the patients to bed.

Two days later, O'Toole was moved to another ward, where he worked entirely alone. Ward E was placed in charge of a man who was known throughout the hospital for his tough, brutal treatment of patients.

"Well," the supervisor explained, "we certainly couldn't have someone on that ward who couldn't get along with anyone else in the hospital!"

III

"Aren't you going to remove the gallbladder?" asked the young doctor assisting at the operation.

"We'll just wipe it out and leave a drain in it. That's best," replied the senior surgeon who performed most of the operations at the state hospital.

The young doctor—McMasters by name—showed his amazement even through his operating mask. He knew that for at least twenty years it had been standard procedure to remove inflamed gallbladders. He knew that removal was the only thing to do in this case. But he also knew that his suggestions held no weight against the clumsy confidence of Dr. Spellman, the senior surgeon.

Still, he could not hold his tongue when he saw that Dr. Spellman was going to close the incision with just one row of wire sutures—it needed to have at least three different closures if it was to heal. "The peritoneum is ready for closing," Dr. McMasters suggested.

But Dr. Spellman disregarded the suggestion and quickly closed all of the layers of the abdominal wall with the single row of stitches. "Finished," he announced.

That night, the inevitable happened. A few stitches broke through the tissue, and the wound reopened. At three a.m. the night nurse found the patient with his intestines spilled out of the abdominal wall and the wound wide open. Knowing that such a catastrophe required immediate restitching, she called Dr. Spellman at his apartment on the grounds, and reported what had happened. Dr. Spellman gave directions that a heavy dressing be drawn tight with adhesive tape to hold the intestines in. "I'll stop in to see the patient in the morning at eight-thirty," he concluded, and hung up.

When Dr. Spellman "stopped in" at eight-thirty, the patient was dead.

Dr. McMasters and Dr. Spellman met again over the patient's open abdomen at the autopsy. Signs of negligence were plainly evident.

"Well, after all, what could you expect?" Dr. Spellman commented. "He was just a poor dope."

Dr. McMasters turned on his heel and left the room. He had heard it said before, but now he believed it. Some doctors, instead of being in the Hippocratic tradition, were most certainly in the 'hypocritic' tradition.

IV

Patient Dubinsky, who usually walked up and down the ward from morning until night, lay on a bench in the toilet, moaning and groaning. His mental condition was such that he never spoke, so he could not describe the pains that assailed him. But Oliver, the attendant, investigated and found that Dubinsky had a continuous rectal discharge of blood and other matter. Obviously, Dubinsky was seriously ill.

Oliver took the patient to the infirmary that afternoon and was lucky to arrive just when Dr. Best was making his daily "rounds." Oliver explained the case. Dr. Best looked at the patient from across the hall and said, "Nurse, give that patient a rectal suppository when you get a chance." That afternoon, Dubinsky was returned to the ward, where he lay on a bench in the toilet, moaning, groaning, and discharging.

The following day, Oliver reported the condition to the building supervisor. He suggested that the discharge had such a terrible odor and was so abnormal that he wondered if it might not be the lining of the intestines. The supervisor didn't look at the patient at all, merely ordered: "Give him some mineral oil, and we'll put him on the list for a colonic irrigation later in the week."

On the third day, Oliver decided he would try once more to get something done. He took Dubinsky to the infirmary again. Again nothing positive was done, and the patient was sent back to the ward. That night, the night attendant supported Oliver's hand by writing in the report: "Patient Dubinsky breathing heavily and passing blood through bowels."

On the fourth day of Dubinsky's illness, Oliver finally got results—at least, he got permission to transfer Dubinsky to the infirmary for observation and treatment. It may be presumed that Dr. Best read the nurse's notes on Dubinsky each day thereafter. It is certain that the doctor never examined Dubinsky personally and never gave any orders for his treatment.

The nurse, who thought Dubinsky might have cancer or tuberculosis of the intestines, was not surprised. She had become accustomed to Dr. Best's methods of examination and prescription by guess—at a distance of ten feet. She had never seen him make a rectal examination, touch a festering sore, open the lids of a running eye, or even dress a wound.

Four weeks later, the whole unpleasantness came to an end when Dubinsky died. His illness was simply labeled "Diarrhea."

V

Cleaning up the music room was a tedious but interesting task. The hospital had been without any musical activity for several years, and a lot of junk had collected in the meantime: Miss Moran made all sorts of interesting discoveries among the piles of music and boxes.

She drew out one box labeled, "Property of James Doerr—Patient." Inside she found a large assortment of music, from Bach and Mendelssohn to Cohan and Berlin. But most interesting of all were several pieces of music written by James Doerr himself, as well as a number of original arrangements and orchestrations. Several printed programs and posters in the box showed that he had appeared with a troupe of entertainers in England and Scotland several years previously. Miss Moran made a mental note to look up James Doerr and to get him into her new music program if it was at all possible.

A week later, she had opportunity to refer to James Doerr's record. She found that the diagnosis of the investigating physician included this note: "Delusions of grandeur: believes he has written songs; believes he has been to Europe where he played before important personages."

VI

The blisters on Mr. Dunn's hands were so painful that he decided he'd better rest a day or two before going back to shoveling coal. He didn't want to give up his job on the coal pile—anything was better than just sitting on the ward all day long. But he had been an accountant before he entered the hospital, and shoveling coal was hard work for him.

When the powerhouse foreman came to collect his worker-patients, Mr. Dunn said, "I would like to be excused temporarily from outside work, Mr. Grace."

"Come on, you loafer. We've got coal to unload today."

"But, my hands—"

"Quit bellyaching," Mr. Grace ordered, as he pushed Dunn on through the door. Then he called to the ward attendant, "Okay, I've got my ten," and closed the door.

The rough handle of the shovel bit into Mr. Dunn's blistered hands. Tears of pain blurred his vision, but he kept working, slowly but constantly. This was occupational, he was sure—could it be therapy?

He didn't even wince when he heard Grace shout: "Dunn! Get a move on." He slowly urged his shovel under a pile of coal, gritted his teeth, gripped the handle, and lifted the shovelful into a wheelbarrow. He lowered the end of his shovel again, started to repeat the process. Then the flat of a shovel hit him heavily in the back, and he buckled under the blow.

Grace swung the shovel once more at Dunn's back and called for two other attendants to help him. The three of them drew Dunn to his feet, punched him a dozen times in the stomach and ribs, knocked him down again. Then they rushed him off to the violent ward.

The next day Dunn was sent to the medical ward and given an X-ray. Eighteen bruises were noted on the supervisor's report, and three ribs were listed as apparently broken.

Two days later, Mr. Dunn died. His post-mortem report reads: "Cause of death: Unknown."

11

THE MORAL CAREER OF THE MENTAL PATIENT

Erving Goffman

> Erving Goffman (1922–   ), is professor of anthropology at the University of Pennsylvania. The following is an abridged version of his now classic sociological analysis of the role of the mental-hospital patient.*

I

A relatively small group of prepatients come into the mental hospital willingly, because of their own idea of what will be good for them, or because of wholehearted agreement with the relevant members of their family. Presumably these recruits have found themselves acting in a way which is evidence to them that they are losing their minds or losing control of themselves. This view of oneself would seem to be one of the most pervasively threatening things that can happen to the self in our society, especially since it is likely to occur at a time when the person is in any case sufficiently troubled to exhibit the kind of symptoms which he himself can see. . . .

Coupled with the person's disintegrative re-evaluation of himself will be the new, almost equally pervasive circumstance of attempting to conceal from others what he takes to be the new fundamental facts about himself, and attempting to discover whether others too, have discovered

* From "The Moral Career of the Mental Patient," *Psychiatry*, 22:123–42 (May), 1959.

them. Here I want to stress that perception of losing one's mind is based on culturally derived and socially engrained stereotypes as the significance of symptoms such as hearing voices, losing temporal and spatial orientation, and sensing that one is being followed, and that many of the most spectacular and convincing of these symptoms in some instances psychiatrically signify merely a temporary emotional upset in a stressful situation, however terrifying to the person at the time. Similarly, the anxiety consequent upon this perception of oneself, and the strategies devised to reduce this anxiety, are not a product of abnormal psychology, but would be exhibited by any person socialized into our culture who came to conceive of himself as someone losing his mind. Interestingly, subcultures in American society apparently differ in the amount of ready imagery and encouragement they supply for such self-views, leading to differential rates of self-referral; the capacity to take this disintegrative view of oneself without psychiatric prompting seems to be one of the questionable cultural privileges of the upper class. . . .

Once the willing prepatient enters the hospital, he may go through the same routine of experiences as do those who enter unwillingly. In any case, it is the latter that I mainly want to consider, since in America at present these are by far the more numerous kind.[1] Their approach to the institution takes one of three classic forms: they come because they have been implored by their family or threatened with the abrogation of family ties unless they go "willingly"; they come by force under police escort; they come under misapprehension purposely induced by others, this last restricted mainly to youthful prepatients.

The prepatient's career may be seen in terms of an extrusory model; he starts out with relationships and rights,

[1] The distinction employed here between willing and unwilling patients cuts across the legal one of voluntary and committed, since some persons who are glad to come to mental hospitals may be legally committed, and of those who come only because of strong familial pressure, some may sign themselves in as voluntary patients.

and ends up, at the beginning of his hospital stay, with hardly any of either. The moral aspect of this career, then, typically begins with the experience of abandonment, disloyalty, and embitterment. This is the case even though to others it may be obvious that he was in need of treatment, and even though in the hospital he may soon come to agree.

The case histories of most mental patients document offenses against some arrangement for face-to-face living—a domestic establishment, a work place, a semi-public organization such as a church or store, a public region such as a street or park. Often there is also a record of some *complainant*, some figure who takes that action against the offender which eventually leads to his hospitalization. This may not be the person who makes the first move, but it is the person who makes what turns out to be the first effective move. Here is the *social* beginning of the patient's career, regardless of where one might locate the psychological beginning of his mental illness.

The kinds of offenses which lead to hospitalization are felt to differ in nature from those which lead to other extrusory consequences—to imprisonment, divorce, loss of job, disownment, regional exile, non-institutional psychiatric treatment, and so forth. But little seems known about these differentiating factors; and when one studies actual commitments, alternate outcomes frequently appear to have been possible. It seems true, moreover, that for every offense that leads to an effective complaint, there are many psychiatrically similar ones that never do. No action is taken; or action is taken which leads to other extrusory outcomes; or ineffective action is taken, leading to the mere pacifying or putting off of the person who complains. . . .

Separating those offenses which could have been used as grounds for hospitalizing the offender from those that are so used, one finds a vast number of what students of occupation call career contingencies. Some of these contingencies in the mental patient's career have been suggested, if not explored, such as socio-economic status, visibility of the offense, proximity to a mental hospital, amount of treatment facilities available, community regard for the type of treatment given in available hospitals and so on. For information about other contingencies one must rely on atrocity tales: a psychotic man is tolerated by his wife until she finds herself a boyfriend, or by his adult children until they move from a house to an apartment; an alcoholic is sent to a mental hospital because the jail is full, and a drug addict because he declines to avail himself of psychiatric treatment on the outside; a rebellious daughter can no longer be managed at home because she now threatens to have an affair with an unsuitable companion; and so on. Correspondingly there is an equally important set of contingencies causing the person to by-pass this fate. And should the person enter the hospital, still another set of contingencies will help determine when he is to obtain a discharge —such as the desire of his family for his return, the availability of a "manageable job", and so on. The society's official view is that inmates of mental hospitals are there primarily because they are suffering from mental illness. However, in the degree that the "mentally ill" outside hospitals numerically approach or surpass those inside hospitals, one could say that mental patients distinctively suffer not from mental illness, but from contingencies.

Career contingencies occur in conjunction with a second feature of the prepatient's career—the circuit of agents—and agencies—that participate fatefully in his passage from civilian to patient status. Here is an instance of that increasingly important class of social system whose elements are agents and agencies which are brought into systemic connection through having to take up and send on the same persons. Some of these agent roles will be cited now, with the understanding that in any concrete circuit a role may be filled more than once, and that the same person may fill more than one of them.

First is the *next-of-relation*—the person whom the prepatient sees as the most available of those upon whom he should be able to depend most in times of trouble, in this instance the last to doubt his sanity and the first to have done everything to save him from the fate which, it transpires, he has been approaching. The patient's next-of-relation is usually his next of kin; the special term is introduced because he need not be. Second is the *complainant*, the person who retrospectively appears to have started the person on his way to the hospital. Third are the *mediators*—the sequence of agents and agencies to which the prepatient is referred and through which he is relayed and processed on his way to the hospital. Here are included the police, clergy, general medical practitioners, office psychiatrists, personnel in public clinics, lawyers, social service workers, schoolteachers, and so on. One of these agents will have the legal mandate to sanction commitment and will exercise it, and so those agents who precede him in the process will be involved in something whose outcome is not yet settled. When the mediators retire from the scene, the prepatient has become an inpatient, and the significant agent has become the hospital administrator. . . .

An interesting feature of these roles is the functional effects of their interdigitation. For example, the feelings of the patient will be influenced by whether or not the person who fills the role of complainant also has the role of next-of-relation—an embarrassing combination more prevalent, apparently, in the higher classes than in the lower.

In the prepatient's progress from home to the hospital he may participate as a third person in what he may come to experience as a kind of alienative coalition. His next-of-relation presses him into coming to "talk things over" with a medical practitioner, an office psychiatrist, or some other counselor. Disinclination on his part may be met by threatening him with desertion, disownment, or other legal action, or by stressing the joint and exploratory nature of the interview. But typically the next-of-relation will have set the interview up, in the sense of selecting the professional, arranging for time, telling the professional something about the case, and so on. This move effectively tends to establish the next-of-relation as the responsible person to whom pertinent findings can be divulged, while effectively establishing the other as the patient. The prepatient often goes to the interview with the understanding that he is going as an equal of someone who is so bound together with him that a third person could not come between them in fundamental matters; this, after all, is one way in which close relationships are defined in our society. Upon arrival at the office the prepatient suddenly finds that he and his next-of-relation have not been accorded the same roles and apparently that a prior understanding between the professional and the next-of-relation has been put in operation against him. In the extreme but common case, the professional first sees the prepatient alone, in the role of the examiner and diagnostician, and then sees the next-of-relation alone, in the role of advisor, while carefully avoiding talking things over seriously with them both together. And even in those non-consultative cases where public officials must forcibly extract a person from a family that want to tolerate him, the next-of-relation is likely to be induced to "go along" with the official action, so that even here the prepatient may feel that an alienative coalition has been formed against him.

The moral experience of being third man in such a coalition is likely to embitter the prepatient, especially since his troubles have already probably led to some estrangement from his next-of-relation. After he enters the hospital, continued visits by his next-of-relation can give the patient the "insight" that his own best interests were being served. But the initial visits may temporarily strengthen his feeling of abandonment; he is likely to beg his visitor to get him out or at least to get him more privileges and to sympathize with the monstrousness of his plight—to which the visitor ordinarily can respond only by trying to maintain a hopeful note, by not "hearing" the requests, or by assuring the patient that the medical authorities know about these things and are doing what is medically best. The visitor then nonchalantly goes back into a world that the patient has learned is incredibly thick with freedom and privileges, causing the patient to feel that his next-of-relation is merely adding a pious gloss to a clear case of traitorous desertion.

The depth to which the patient may feel betrayed by his next-of-relation seems to be increased by the fact that another witnesses his betrayal—a factor which is apparently significant in many three-party situations. An offended person may well act forbearingly and accommodatingly toward an offender when the two are alone, choosing peace ahead of justice. The presence of a witness, however, seems to add something to the implications of the offense. For then it is beyond the power of the offended and offender to forget about, erase, or suppress what has happened; the offense has become a public social fact. When the witness is a mental health commission, as is sometimes the case, the witnessed betrayal can verge on a "degradation ceremony." In such circumstances, the offended patient may feel that some kind of extensive reparative action is required before witnesses, if his honor and social weight are to be restored.

Two other aspects of sensed betrayal should be mentioned. First, those who suggest the possibility of another's entering a mental hospital are not likely to provide a realistic picture of how in fact it may strike him when he arrives. Often he is told that he will get required medical treatment and a rest, and may well be out in a few months or so. In some cases they may thus be concealing what they know, but I think, in general, they will be telling what they see as the truth. For here there is quite relevant difference between patients and mediating professionals; mediators, more so than the public at large, may conceive of mental hospitals as short-term medical establishments where required rest and attention can be voluntarily obtained, and not as places of coerced exile. When the prepatient finally arrives he is likely to learn quite quickly, quite differently. He then finds that the information given him about life in the hospital has had the effect of his having put up less resistance to entering than he now sees he would have put up had he known the facts. Whatever the intentions of those who participated in his transition from person to patient, he may sense they have in effect "conned" him into his present predicament.

I am suggesting that the prepatient starts out with at least a portion of the rights, liberties, and satisfactions of the civilian and ends up on a psychiatric ward stripped of almost everything. The question here is how this stripping is managed. This is the second aspect of betrayal I want to consider.

As the prepatient may see it, the circuit of significant figures can function as a kind of betrayal funnel. Passage from person to patient may be effected through a series of linked stages, each managed by a different agent. While each stage tends to bring a sharp decrease in adult free status, each agent may try to maintain the fiction that no further decrease will occur. He may even manage to turn the prepatient over to the next agent while sustaining this note. Further, through words, cues, and gestures, the prepatient is implicitly asked by the current agent to join with him in sustaining a running line of polite small talk that tactfully avoids the administrative facts of the situation, becoming, with each stage, progressively more at odds with these facts. The spouse would rather not have to cry to get the prepatient to visit a psychiatrist; psychiatrists would rather not have a scene when the prepatient learns that he and his spouse are being seen separately and in different ways; the police infrequently bring a prepatient to the hospital in a strait jacket, finding it much easier all around to give him a cigarette, some kindly words, and freedom to relax in the back seat of the patrol car; and finally, the admitting psychiatrist finds he can do his work better in the relative quiet and luxury of the "admission suite" where, as an incidental consequence, the notion can survive that a mental hospital is indeed a comforting place. If the prepatient needs all of these implied requests and is reasonably decent about the whole thing, he can travel the whole circuit from home to hospital without forcing anyone to look directly at what is happening or to deal with the raw emotion that his situation might well cause him to express. His showing consideration for those who are moving him toward the hospital allows them to show consideration for him, with the joint result that these interactions can be sustained with some of the protective harmony characteristic of ordinary face-to-face dealings. But should the new patient cast his mind back over the sequence of steps leading to hospitalization, he may feel that everyone's current comfort was being busily sustained while his long-range welfare was being undermined. This realization may constitute a moral experience that further separates him for the time from the people on the outside. . . .

Inpatients commonly sense, at least for a time, that hospitalization is a massive unjust deprivation, and sometimes succeed in convincing a few persons on the outside that this is the case. It often turns out to be useful, then, for those identified with inflicting these deprivations, however justifiably, to be able to point to the co-operation and agreement of someone whose relationship to the patient places him above suspicion, firmly defining him as the person most likely to have the patient's personal interest at heart. If the guardian is satisfied with what is happening to the new inpatient, the world ought to be.

Now it would seem that the greater the legitimate personal stake one party has in another, the better he can take the role of guardian to the other. But the structural arrangements in society which lead to the acknowledged merging of two persons' interests lead to additional consequences. For the person to whom the patient turns for help—for protection against such threats as involuntary commitment—is just the person to whom the mediators and hospital administrators logically turn for authorization. It is understandable, then, that some patients will come to sense, at least for a time, that the closeness of a relationship tells nothing of its trustworthiness.

There are still other functional effects emerging from this complement of roles. If and when the next-of-relation appeals to mediators for help in the trouble he is having with the prepatient, hospitalization may not, in fact, be in his mind. He may not even perceive the prepatient as mentally sick, or, if he does he may not consistently hold to this view. It is the circuit of mediators, with their greater psychiatric sophistication and their belief in the medical character of mental hospitals, that will often define the situation for the next-of-relation, assuring him that hospitalization is a possible solution and a good one, that it involves no betrayal, but is rather a medical action taken in the best interests of the prepatient. Here the next-of-relation may learn that doing his duty to the prepatient may cause the prepatient to distrust and even hate him for the time. But the fact that this course of action may have had to be pointed out and prescribed by professionals, and be defined by them as a moral duty, relieves the next-of-relation of some of the guilt he may feel. It is a poignant fact that an adult son or daughter may be pressed into the role of mediator, so that the hostility that might otherwise be directed against the spouse is passed on to the child. . . .

The final point I want to consider about the prepatient's moral career is its peculiarly retroactive character. Until a person actually arrives at the hospital there usually seems no way of knowing for sure that he is destined to do so, given the determinative role of career contingencies. And until the point of hospitalization is reached, he or others may not conceive of him as a person who is becoming a mental patient. However, since he will be held against his will in the hospital, his next-of-relation and the hospital staff will be in great need of a rationale for the hardships they are sponsoring. The medical elements of the staff will also need evidence that they are still in the trade they were trained for. These problems are eased, no doubt unintentionally, by the case-history construction that is placed on the patient's past life, this having the effect of demonstrating that all along he had been becoming sick, that he finally became very sick, and that if he had not been hospitalized much worse things would have happened to him—all of which, of course, may be true. Incidentally, if the patient wants to make sense out of his stay in the hospital, and, as already suggested, keep alive the possibility of once again conceiving of his next-of-relation as a decent, well-meaning person, then he too will have reason to believe some of this psychiatric work-up of his past.

Here is a very ticklish point for the sociology of careers. An important aspect of every career is the view the person constructs when he looks backward over his progress; in a sense, however, the whole of the prepatient career derives from this reconstruction. The fact of having had a prepatient career, starting with an effective complaint, becomes an important part of the mental patient's orientation, but this part can begin to be played only after hospitalization proves that what he had been having, but no longer has, is a career as a prepatient.

II

The last step in the prepatient's career can involve his realization—justified or not—that he has been deserted by society and turned out of relationships by those closest to him. Interestingly enough, the patient, especially a first admission, may manage to keep himself from coming to the end of this trail, even though in fact he is now in a locked mental-hospital ward. On entering the hospital, he may very strongly feel the desire not to be known to anyone as a person who could possibly be reduced to these present circumstances, or as a person who conducted himself in the way he did prior to commitment. Consequently, he may avoid talking to anyone, may stay by himself when possible, and may even be "out of contact" or "manic" so as to avoid ratifying any interaction that presses a politely reciprocal role upon him and open him up to what he has become in the eyes of others. When the next-of-relation makes an effort to visit, he may be rejected by mutism, or by the patient's refusal to enter the visiting room, these strategies sometimes suggesting that the patient still clings to a remnant of relatedness to those who made up his past, and is protecting this remnant from the final destructiveness of dealing with the new people that they have become.

Usually the patient comes to give up this taxing effort of anonymity, of not-hereness, and begins to present himself for conventional social interaction to the hospital community. Thereafter he withdraws only in special ways—by always using his nickname, by signing his contribution to the patient weekly with his initial only, or by using the innocuous "cover address tactfully provided by some hospitals" or he withdraws only at special times when, say, a flock of nursing students makes a passing tour of the ward, or when, paroled to the hospital grounds, he suddenly sees he is about to cross the path of a civilian he happens to know from home. Sometimes this making of oneself available is called "settling down" by the attendants. It marks a new stand openly taken and supported by the patient, and resembles the "coming-out" process that occurs in other groupings.

Once the prepatient begins to settle down, the main outlines of his fate tend to follow those of a whole class of segregated establishments—jails, concentration camps, monasteries, work camps, and so on—in which the inmate spends his whole round of life on the grounds, and marches through his regimented day in the immediate company of a group of persons of his own institutional status.

Like the neophyte in many of these total institutions, the new patient finds himself cleanly stripped of many of his accustomed affirmations, satisfactions, and defenses, and is subjected to a rather full set of mortifying experiences: restriction of free movement, communal living, diffuse authority of a whole echelon of people, and so on. Here one begins to learn about the limited extent to which a conception of oneself can be sustained when the usual setting of supports for it are suddenly removed.

While undergoing these humbling moral experiences, the inpatient learns to orient himself in terms of the "ward system." In public mental hospitals this usually consists of a series of graded living arrangements built around wards, administrative units called services, and parole statuses. The "worst" level often involves nothing but wooden benches to sit on, some quite indifferent food, and a small piece of room to sleep in. The "best" level may involve a room of one's own, ground and town privileges, contacts with staff that are relatively undamaging, and what is seen as good food and ample recreational facilities. For disobeying the pervasive house rules, the inmate will receive stringent punishments expressed in terms of loss of privileges; for obedience he will eventually be allowed to reacquire some of the minor satisfactions he took for granted on the outside. . . .

The ward system, then, is an extreme instance of how the physical facts of an establishment can be explicitly employed to frame the conception a person takes of himself. In addition, the official psychiatric mandate of mental hospitals gives rise to even more direct, even more blatant attacks upon the inmate's view of himself. The more "medical" and the more progressive a mental hospital is— the more it attempts to be therapeutic and not merely custodial—the more he may be confronted by high-ranking staff arguing that his past has been a failure, that the cause of this has been within himself, that his attitudes to life are wrong, and that if he wants to be a person he will have to change his way of dealing with people and his conceptions of himself. Often the moral value of these verbal assaults will be brought home to him by requiring him to practice taking this psychiatric view of himself in arranging confessional periods, whether in private sessions or group psychotherapy. . . .

In the mental hospital, the setting and the house rules press home to the patient that he is, after all, a mental case who has suffered some kind of social collapse on the outside, having failed in some over-all way, and that here he is of little social weight, being hardly capable of acting like a full-fledged person at all. These humiliations are likely to be most keenly felt by middle-class patients, since their previous condition of life little immunizes them against such affronts, but all patients feel some downgrading. Just as any normal member of his outside subculture would do, the patient often responds to this situation by attempting to assert a sad tale proving that he is not "sick", that the "little trouble" he did get into was really somebody else's fault, that his past life course had some honor and rectitude, and that the hospital is therefore unjust in forcing the status of mental patient upon him. . . .

But the patient's apologia is called forth in a unique setting, for few settings could be so destructive of self-stories except, of course, those stories already constructed along psychiatric lines. And this destructiveness rests on more than the official sheet of paper which attests that the patient is of unsound mind, a danger to himself and others—an attestation incidentally which seems to cut deeply into the patient's pride and into the possibility of his having any. . . .

The mental-hospital setting, however, is more treacherous still. Staff have much to gain through discreditings of the patient's story—whatever the felt reason for such discreditings. If the custodial faction in the hospital is to succeed in managing his daily round without complaint or trouble from him, then it will prove useful to be able to point out to him that the claims about himself upon which he rationalizes his demands are false, that he is not what he is claiming to be, and that in fact he is a failure as a person. If the psychiatric faction is to impress upon him its views about his personal make-up, then they must be able to show in detail how their version of his past and their version of his character hold up much better than his own. If both the custodial and psychiatric factions are to get him to co-operate in the various psychiatric treatments, then it will prove useful to disabuse him of his view of their purposes, and cause him to appreciate that they know what they are doing, and are doing what is best for him. In brief, the difficulties caused by a patient are closely tied to his version of what has been happening to him, and if co-operation is to be secured, it helps if this version is discredited. The patient must "insightfully" come to take, or affect to take, the hospital's view of himself. . . .

In general, then, mental hospitals systematically provide for circulation about each patient the kind of information that the patient is likely to try to hide. And in various degrees of detail this information is used daily to puncture his claims. At the admissions and diagnostic conferences, he will be asked questions to which he must give wrong answers in order to maintain his self-respect, and then the true answer may be shot back at him. An attendant whom he tells a version of his past and his reason for being in the hospital may smile disbelievingly, or say, "That's not the way I hear it," in line with the practical psychiatry of bringing the patient down to reality. When he accosts a physician or nurse on the ward and presents his claims for more privileges or for discharge, this may be countered by a question which he cannot answer truthfully without calling up a time in his past when he acted disgracefully. When he gives his view of his situation during group psychotherapy, the therapist, taking the role of interrogator, may attempt to disabuse him of his face-saving interpretations and encourage an interpretation suggesting that it is he himself who is to blame and who must change. When he claims to staff or fellow patients that he is well and has never been really sick, someone may give him graphic details of how, only one month ago, he was prancing around like a girl, or claiming that he was God, or declining to talk or eat, or putting gum in his hair. . . .

In such contexts inmates can discover that deflations in moral status are not so bad as they had imagined. After all, infractions which lead to these demotions cannot be accompanied by legal sanctions or by reduction to the status of the mental patient, since these conditions already prevail. Further, no past or current delict seems to be horrendous enough in itself to excommunicate a patient from the community, and hence failures at right living lose some of their stigmatizing meaning. And finally, in accepting the hospital's version of his fall from grace, the patient can set himself up in the business of "straightening up," and make claims of sympathy, privileges, and indulgence from the staff in order to foster this.

Learning to live under conditions of imminent exposure and wide fluctuation in regard, with little control over the granting or withholding of this regard, is an important step in the socialization of the patient, a step that tells something important about what it is like to be an inmate in a mental hospital. Having one's past mistakes and present progress under constant moral view seem to make for a special adaptation consisting of a less than moral attitude to ego ideals. One's shortcomings and successes become too central and fluctuating an issue in life to allow the usual commitment of concern for other persons' views of them. It is not very practical to try to sustain solid claims about oneself. The inmate tends to learn that degradations and reconstructions of the self need not be given too much weight, at the same time learning that staff and inmates are ready to view an inflation or deflation of a self with some indifference. He learns that a defensible picture of self can be seen as something outside oneself that can be constructed, lost, and rebuilt, all with great speed and some equanimity. He learns about the viability of taking up a standpoint—and hence a self—that is outside the one which the hospital can give and take away from him.

The setting, then, seems to engender a kind of cosmopolitan sophistication, a kind of civic apathy. In this unserious yet oddly exaggerated moral context, building up a self or having it destroyed becomes something of a shameless game, and learning to view this process as a game seems to make for some demoralization, the game being such a fundamental one. In the hospital, then, the inmate can learn that the self is not a fortress, but rather a small open city; he can become weary of having to show pleasure when held by troops of his own, and weary of having to show displeasure when held by the enemy. Once he learns what it is like to be defined by society as not having a viable self, this threatening definition—the threat that helps attach people to the self society accords them—is weakened. The patient seems to gain a new plateau when he learns that he can survive while acting in a way that society sees as destructive of him.

12

ADJUSTMENT TO THE TOTAL INSTITUTION

Byron G. Wales

> Byron G. Wales (presumably a pseudonym) was identified in *Mental Hygiene*,* from where this piece is excerpted with minor omissions, as "a resident of Providence, R.I., [who] has experienced many years of intermittent hospitalization in neuropsychiatric institutions."

I

It is a recognized fact that when an individual has been in a neuropsychiatric institution for a long period of time, and has become so well-adjusted to the hospital milieu that he knows or cares to know of no other way of life, he is said to have become "institutionalized." The essence of the pattern involved occurs, if one lives long enough, with most human beings. Basically it is a degenerative process. It is resignation and apathy toward the conditions of their lives. It is surrender to the demands of a dispassionate "fate." Still, when this pattern is enacted in a man's youth, or in his prime, it is a tragic and premature epilogue to a life. . . .

Sooner or later many chronic mental patients in good contact are accused of or censured for being too dependent

* "Rewards of Illness: Observations on Institutionalization by a Former Neuropsychiatric Patient," *Mental Hygiene*, 44:55–63 (Jan.), 1960.

upon the protective environment of the hospital. When others speak of this dependency, it is almost implied that these attitudes are the patient's fault, that the patient really enjoys being taken care of by others, and that such attitudes are unnecessary and unnatural. Perhaps in the final analysis this is true. But it has been my experience that most professional personnel, like the majority of people in the community, seem loath to recognize the possibility that this dependency could be fostered and perpetuated in the artificial and highly structured social milieu of the hospital. . . .

In stressing real or fancied attitudes of dependency, little if any recognition appears to be given to the factors which tend to create passivity and reliance upon other people's decisions and resources. It should be fairly obvious that an institution, such as a neuropsychiatric hospital, is inherently notorious for inhibiting an individual's liberty and substituting security for freedom. Although a patient may be told that "everything is up to you," the mere fact that medical care, food, lodging and entertainment are provided automatically impresses the patient otherwise. He is told when to rise and when to go to bed, when to eat, when to work, when to be entertained. He is given, or not given, ground privileges and passes to leave the confines of the hospital at the discretion of authority figures whose power is, to all intents and purposes, absolute. And he is in most instances powerless over, and even unaware of, the criteria which influence these decisions.

A priori, he is a mental patient! And his daily interpersonal relationships with other patients, doctors, nurses, aides and ancillary personnel are fraught with the specter of mental illness. As it is usually in the nature of his illness that ego strength is diminished, surroundings replete with locked doors, rattling keys, refractory wards and men in white coats do little toward mitigating this situation. Thus, the mental patient is dealing primarily with a custodial rather than a therapeutic culture. And the degree of custodial emphasis proportionately influences dependent feeling over a period of time. . . .

II

How does a condition such as dependency and institutionalization evolve? It is a common feeling among patients that they have been unjustly deprived of their freedom. And in most instances, in one sense of the word, this is perfectly true. For very few individuals ever come to a mental hospital voluntarily. When someone becomes mentally ill, usually some other individual or agency has to step in and see to it that he receives proper treatment and care. Thus the mentally ill individual finds himself, in many instances, committed to an institution without having much to say about what is happening to him. Naturally these steps have been taken for the mentally ill person's protection or for the protection of society. But this does not alter the fact that in most places designed for the care and treatment of the mentally ill in our culture there are a great many locked doors—which heightens his sense of restriction and detention.

Because the mental patient is involved with a difficulty labeled "illness," almost any steps taken to mitigate his problems are considered justifiable. One does not usually delve deeply enough into the issues concerned to draw parallels. One is apt to forget the lessons of history regarding tyranny and injustice. It is not easy to bear in mind that the physician and other members of the staff in our mental institutions have a great deal of power in their relations with the committed patients. This is not to be construed as a statement that tyranny and injustice exist. But it is an attempt to point out that in any environment where there is dependency upon locks and keys to control the majority of its population, tyranny and injustice can flourish. At least this type of behavior can flourish far more easily than it could in an environment where physical restraints were absent. And tyranny and injustice can create dependency.

The acutely ill mental patient can, to some extent, counteract apathy and resignation in regard to his hospitalization by building up feelings of bitterness, resentment and even hate regarding actual or imagined oppression. In most cases though, it is otherwise with the chronic mental patient. Violent emotional responses and intellectual discord rooted in the sometimes faulty perception and evaluation of daily realities are eventually replaced by a gradual relinquishment of inward incentive, initiative, and resourcefulness. The colors, the forms and weathers of surrounding that seldom if ever change close in and weight down the spirit until there is apparently nothing to do from the patient's point of view but retreat inwardly. A repressive atmosphere of barren monotony dulls the senses until emotional spontaneity becomes atrophied and memories and dreams occupy the patient's mental life. Having, in the course of time, become conditioned and accustomed to this way of life, any sort of a change in routine becomes a painful experience. The patient has become dependent. . . .

Usually the staff of the mental hospital sets up the patient's goals and then therapeutically coerces the patient to strive toward these goals. Naturally, if the end results don't materialize the way the staff had planned, the patient is apt to be censured or punished.

It must be remembered that these remarks are not intended as an indictment, but as observations regarding one deplorable, and perhaps unavoidable, facet of institutional management. Moreover, they are pleas for recognition of the fact that daily all over our land there are a certain number of men and women who are sitting unhappily and unproductively on hospital wards designed for those who are actually acutely or chronically ill. Men and women who, if given the proper understanding and encouragement, hopefully might order and sustain their own lives in the community. . . .

The major part of the treatment program for the chronic mental patient, in most of our mental hospitals, appears to consist of prolonged milieu therapy. And milieu therapy in an institutional setting, in some cases, is woefully lacking in benign opportunities for individual growth. Milieu therapy appears to be aimed at resolving those facts of a patient's illness which are directly related to and affect the prevailing mores and customs of society. In short, the rights of society appear to be considered of more importance than the rights of the individual. It is not within the scope of this paper to delve into the merits of the various aspects of the question as to which is the more important. But it is assumed in this instance that as a hospital, according to most dictionaries, is "a place in which the sick and injured are cared for," the sick or injured individual is the more immediate concern. . . .

III

Mr. X, a geriatric patient, was a competent oral surgeon and a minor political figure in a southern community. He is married and has two grown children who are financially well off. He himself is comparatively well-to-do. For a number of years he has been hospitalized in a state hospital for mental diseases in New England. Although he is a World War I veteran with a service-connected disability, he prefers to stay where he is rather than go to a Veterans Administration hospital. He is an amiable gentleman in his early sixties possessing an alert intelligence. In the hospital he enjoys many privileges denied and even unknown to the average patient. His principal complaint is that he has a heart condition, although he will admit when pressed that the doctors have never been able to find anything organically wrong. . . .

Mr. Y, plagued by what appears to be a severe anxiety neurosis to the layman, was a professional photographer in his early twenties. While on pass some months ago he became intoxicated and fell asleep in a restaurant. Picked up by the police and charged with being drunk and disorderly he was brought into court where he was placed on probation. Upon his return to the hospital he was removed from a fully privileged ward and placed on a refractory ward where he spent several months in the company of very regressed psychotic patients. Upon regaining his status as a privileged patient residing on an open ward, he was given frequent passes in his own custody. At the same time the staff, not too diplomatically, impressed upon him that if he got into the least bit of trouble he would be summarily transferred to a correctional institution for an indefinite period of time. After starting out on a week-end pass he became apprehensive and hurriedly returned to the security of the hospital, vowing to forego passes in the future. . . .

Mr. Z, was hospitalized for a psychoneurotic condition complicated by a mild addiction to alcohol. A competent worker in his middle forties, he was soon satisfactorily fulfilling the duties connected with a work assignment in the dietary department of the state hospital where he had been committed. Transferred to a Veterans Administration hospital for further treatment, he became despondent and began brooding about the loss of his freedom. He then commenced drinking heavily while on pass. This soon resulted in a temporary loss of privileges, which added to his bitterness and resentment. Upon regaining his former status at the hospital he soon repeated the episode. This same pattern, with variations, was continued during approximately three years of hospitalization. Mr. Z then half-heartedly attempted suicide on two occasions. Transferred to another Veterans Administration hospital closer to his home he continued to display frequent gestures of rebellion. There were numerous elopements and two more suicidal attempts plus frequent alcoholic bouts within the confines of the hospital during nearly six years of continuous hospitalization. Within hours after he had been given a maximum hospital benefit discharge he was seeking readmittance to the hospital. This request was denied. When last heard from he was again in a state hospital, primarily for alcoholism.

On meeting Mr. X, Y, and Mr. Z, one would not be prone to think of them as mentally ill. Even after talking with them and observing them over long periods of time one would be hard put to discover any evidence of psychotic or discernible abnormal behavior as understood by the average individual. None of them was assaultive, destructive or hallucinating in his daily behavior. They were competent, conscientious workers who were liked and respected by others. None of them used an abnormal amount of obscene language; none was particularly irritable. Their movements were not manneristic; nor were they deluded; and certainly none of them was seclusive.

Still, all of them had been hospitalized for long periods of time. . . . Sooner or later, circumstances had forced them to adjust to the fact that a great deal of their time and energy must be spent in coping with confinement or in following a routine of unchanging rigidity. This, as with most patients, conflicted with the normal daily pattern of living which they had enjoyed before they became ill. This combination of circumstances—the fact that like most mentally ill individuals they were, except for the doctor, not in the hospital willingly, and once in the hospital they had been confined on closed wards—accounted for much bitterness and resentment regarding their hospital experience. And propaganda aimed toward the disavowal of those circumstances could serve no purpose other than to perpetuate the problem. . . .

IV

More than a hundred years ago Thomas Carlyle wrote that "The great law of culture is: Let each become all that he was created capable of being; expand, if possible, to his full growth; resisting all impediments, casting off all foreign, especially all noxious, adhesions; and show himself at length in his own shape and stature, be these what they may."

In practically all mental and emotional disorders, the ego, or the individual's conscious idea and understanding of himself and his relationships to the world in which he lives, is adversely affected. And a wounded, faltering ego is in no position to deal with life's everyday problems, least of all confinement and regimentation. Without our self-esteem or our self-respect none of us is of much use to ourselves or to others. Unwarranted restrictive measures are never conducive to growth.

Reliance upon the hospital for support at a time when an individual is mentally or physically unable to provide for himself is understandable. But it is illogical for hospital management to maneuver or allow itself to be maneuvered into a position in which it accepts responsibility for the welfare of an individual who does not need and does not consciously want this care and treatment. This is doing a disservice both to the patient and to society. Making "a good hospital adjustment" implies to the layman that, if the institution where an individual is hospitalized is therapeutically oriented, he should be considered well and ready for discharge. Unfortunately, where custodial care in a neuropsychiatric institution is the principal motivating factor, discharge of a patient when he has reached the peak of his capabilities and capacities for health seldom occurs. Thus a benign equinox in the patient's growth passes unheeded and his original emotional difficulties are eventually intensified. . . .

It would be superfluous to dwell here on the fact that mental illness in America has become a staggering problem. Conceivably, one day, any deviation from the mores and customs of the majority, by an individual, could lead to his being classed as mentally ill, thereby making him eligible for hospitalization. This is one of the reasons why it is felt that far too little attention is paid by professional personnel to those individuals confined in mental institutions who are not, medically speaking, psychotic. And who, being dangerous neither to themselves nor to society at the time, do not constitute a medical problem requiring hospitalization. Actually, of course, this is another facet of that larger problem known as "institutionalization."

Like any efficient business organization, the management of a hospital for mental disease is consciously interested in disseminating effective propaganda concerning the patient's hospital experience, to the patients themselves, to relatives, and to the public at large. As with all propaganda, much that is said is directed toward allaying doubts and overcoming what might be termed resistance regarding the methods of treatment and the goals of hospitalization. Little is heard, though, about the patient's real thoughts and feelings concerning hospitalization and the loss of his freedom. And time after time one sees men and women who have regained their health still in the institution.

It is like hospitalizing a man with a broken leg and then keeping him in the hospital for months and even years after the leg has healed—rationalizing the situation many times by saying that if the patient were discharged he or she might go right out and break the leg all over again. Ludicrous as that may sound, there would be many tragic facets to such a situation. Innumerable new problems would be created having nothing to do with the original broken leg. Foremost among them would be the problem of dependency as it is related to "Institutionalization." Bearing in mind that this is greatly simplifying an idea of dependency as an iatrogenic entity, and that generalizations are dangerous, one may attempt to visualize the various implications of such a situation. . . .

V

What are the rewards intrinsic in the institutional structure? What are the rewards of illness? Primarily, of course, as has already been pointed out, the patient has no concern about where his next meal is coming from, where he is going to sleep, or where he is going to find shelter from the elements. All of these things are taken care of for him by powerful authority figures who will brook little or no criticism in most instances. Many times the patient feels that he must inhibit any criticism of the staff or of the organization of the hospital, lest he be transferred to a refractory ward.

The chronic mental patient can usually make no decisions of his own except in the most trifling matters. True, ground privileges for good behavior and the occasional pass home (usually in someone else's custody) are matters that, on the surface, ultimately appear to depend upon the patient. But for the long-term patient who has had months or even years of hospitalization behind him the incentive and inclination to leave the refuge of the ward or of the hospital has all but vanished. He has usually tried too many times to surmount the barriers that separate him from the extramural community. Perhaps friends or family are no longer waiting for him. Or perhaps their philosophies are so imbued with the fact that he is considered a chronic case that he no longer has the desire to make an attempt to meet them on an adult basis of equality. And perhaps he has been made to feel that he is somehow different and has finally come to prefer the society of his own kind —other mental patients. Abnormality, for this type of patient, has become normality over a period of time. . . .

To function properly, both physiologically and psychologically, each of us must possess some measure of freedom. . . . The artificial barriers so prevalent in the institutional environment must therefore obviously be inherently antitherapeutic in their effect upon the patient. Even the most regressed patients perceive this and express their longing and hunger for freedom, in acts of aggression and in apathetic behavior. Propaganda to the effect that all behavior of this type is entirely dependent on inward factors and on the patient's illness are thus a distortion of the truth. Conversely, elopements and other management problems cannot always be explained on a strictly medical basis. It is not necessarily a symptom of mental illness to think it expedient to abandon or seek escape from an unbearable position.

For most of us freedom means being at liberty to make our own decisions. Simple decisions like where and when and what to eat. To be able to work and to play, and to rest, in accord with the demands of our natures. To be able to choose and pursue, unhampered by another man's moral judgments and autocratic controls, those avenues of expression most in keeping with our individuality. To be in a position to expend our energies in harmony with the rhythm of growth unique with each of us alone. To be free to acquire the wisdom and knowledge most in keeping with our inclinations and tastes—regardless of the social level of this pursuit of happiness. To be in a position to combat the coercion and ill-considered advice and opinions of others. And to be free to shun the well-intentioned

ADJUSTMENT TO THE TOTAL INSTITUTION

tyrannies thoughtlessly imposed upon us by others, which tend to make us hypocrites. When we are abundantly in possession of these intangibles most of us function fairly adequately—if we have our health also—both in our relations with ourselves and in our relations with our fellows.

The mental patient has lost the ability and the opportunity in many instances to enjoy most of these things.

It is a paradox that when a long-term patient is released from a mental hospital, the reaction from the accumulated emotional tension and intellectual conflict—prevalent in an environment where, to a greater or lesser extent, one is dependent upon the decisions and resources of others—may for some time lead to more rather than less difficulty in the man's readjustment to the accepted normality of society at large. Hospitalization may have eradicated the overt symptoms of his illness at the expense of his character, personality, and individuality as a human being.

13

THE UNICORN IN THE GARDEN

James Thurber

> James Thurber (1894–1961) was a highly successful writer, journalist, and cartoonist; from 1926 till his death, he was a regular contributor to *The New Yorker* magazine, where the following piece first appeared.*

Once upon a sunny morning a man who sat in a breakfast nook looked up from his scrambled eggs to see a white unicorn with a gold horn quietly cropping the roses in the garden. The man went up to the bedroom where his wife was still asleep and woke her. "There's a unicorn in the garden," he said. "Eating roses." She opened one unfriendly eye and looked at him. "The unicorn is a mythical beast," she said, and turned her back on him. The man walked slowly downstairs and out into the garden. The unicorn was still there; he was now browsing among the tulips. "Here, unicorn," said the man, and pulled up a lily and gave it to him. The unicorn ate it gravely. With a high heart, because there was a unicorn in his garden, the man went upstairs and roused his wife again. "The unicorn," he said, "ate a lily." His wife sat up in bed and looked at him, coldly. "You are a booby," she said, "and I am going to have you put in the booby-hatch." The man, who had never liked the words "booby" and "booby-hatch," and who liked

---

* "The Unicorn in the Garden," in *The Thurber Carnival* (New York: Harper & Brothers, 1945), pp. 268–69.

them even less on a shining morning when there was a unicorn in the garden, thought for a moment. "We'll see about that," he said. He walked over to the door. "He has a golden horn in the middle of his forehead," he told her. Then he went back to the garden to watch the unicorn; but the unicorn had gone away. The man sat down among the roses and went to sleep.

As soon as the husband had gone out of the house, the wife got up and dressed as fast as she could. She was very excited and there was a gloat in her eye. She telephoned the police and she telephoned a psychiatrist; she told them to hurry to her house and bring a strait-jacket. When the police and the psychiatrist arrived they sat down in chairs and looked at her, with great interest. "My husband," she said, "saw a unicorn this morning." The police looked at the psychiatrist and the psychiatrist looked at the police. "He told me it ate a lily," she said. The psychiatrist looked at the police and the police looked at the psychiatrist. "He told me it had a golden horn in the middle of its forehead," she said. At a solemn signal from the psychiatrist, the police leaped from their chairs and seized the wife. They had a hard time subduing her, for she put up a terrific struggle, but they finally subdued her. Just as they got her into the strait-jacket, the husband came back into the house.

"Did you tell your wife you saw a unicorn?" asked the police. "Of course not," said the husband. "The unicorn is a mythical beast." "That's all I wanted to know," said the psychiatrist. "Take her away. I'm sorry, sir, but your wife is as crazy as a jay bird." So they took her away, cursing and screaming, and shut her up in an institution. The husband lived happily ever after.

MORAL: DON'T COUNT YOUR BOOBIES UNTIL THEY ARE HATCHED.

14

THE INSANITY BIT

Seymour Krim

Seymour Krim (1922–) is considered one of the elder statesmen of the literary movement known as the "Beats." He received the Longview Award for Literature in 1960. "The Insanity Bit,"* here reprinted, is based on his experiences as a mental-hospital patient in 1955.

I

Until this time of complete blast-off in seemingly every department of human life, the idea of insanity was thought of as the most dreadful thing that could happen to a person. Little was actually known about it and the mind conjured up pictures of Bedlam, ninnies walking around in a stupor, a living death that lasted until the poor damned soul's body expired and peace tucked him or her away for eternal keeps. But in this era of monumental need to rethink and re-define almost every former presumption about existence—which has inspired a bombing way of looking at what once were considered the most unbudgeable rocks of reality—the locked door of insanity has been shaken loose and shall yet be hurled wide open. Until one day the prisoners of this definition will walk beside us sharing only the insane plight of mortality itself, which makes quiet madmen of us all.

* "The Insanity Bit," from *Views of a Nearsighted Cannoneer* (New York: Excelsior Press, 1961), pp. 59–75.

THE INSANITY BIT

Every American family has its "psychotic" cousin or uncle; every friend has wept, prayed, hoped (and finally slid into indifference) for another friend sweating it out in insulin or electric-shock behind the grey walls (public institution) or beyond the clipped roses (private sanitarium). Although my brother, Herbert J. Krim, was institutionalized when I was barely in my 20's—and I co-signed the certificate for a prefrontal lobotomy which ended with his death by hemorrhage on the operating table at Rockland State Hospital—I still had the conventional ideas about insanity that are shared by all "responsible" readers of *The New York Times*. It is true that as a serious writer I had inherited a great tradition of complete independence and honesty to my actual experience, regardless of what I was supposed to feel; but this was sabotaged by my youth, my ignorance, and an inability to separate my own personal life from a responsibility to question the cliches of experience to their ultimate depth. Like most American writers, from would-be's to celebrities, I was intensely preoccupied by my acutely painful and highly exaggerated subjective image—the Jewish cross, looks, sex, masculinity, a swarm of fears and devices for concealment that were secondary to my decent abilities and serious obligations as a writer intent on telling the truth. In other words: I was too narcissistically and masturbatorially stuck on myself to appreciate the horrible waste of my brother Herbert's death; and with the snotty sense of superiority usually felt by the young American writer, I thought *I* would be forever immune to the judgments of a society which I loftily ignored, or nose-thumbed, without ever coming to grips with on the actual mat of life. Like every creative type of my generation whom I met in my 20's, I was positive I was sanctified, protected by my "genius," my flair, my overwhelming ambition.

I was as wrong as you can be and still live to tell about it. In the summer of 1955, when I was 33, the thousand unacknowledged human (not literary) pressures in my being exploded. I ran barefooted in the streets, spat at members of my family, exposed myself, was almost bodily thrown out of the house of a Nobel Prize-winning author, and believed God had ordained me to act out every conceivable human impulse without an ounce of hypocritical caution. I know today that my instinct was sound, but my reasoning was self-deceptive. It was not God who ordained me, but I who ordained God for my own understandable human purposes. I needed an excuse to force some sort of balance between my bulging inner life and my timid outer behavior, and I chose the greatest and most comforting symbol of them all. He was my lance and my shield as I tore through the New York streets acting out the bitter rot of a world-full of frustrations that my human nature could no longer lock up. I was finally cornered on the 14th floor of the St. Regis Hotel by two frightened friends and another brother; and with the aid of handcuffs seriously-humorously clipped on by a couple of bobbies I was led off to Bellevue, convinced all along that I was right. I tolerated those who took me away with the kindly condescension of a fake Jesus.

From Bellevue I was soon transferred to a private laughing academy in Westchester and given insulin-shock treatments. No deep attempt was made to diagnose my "case"—except the superficial and inaccurate judgment that I had "hallucinated." Factually, this was not true; I did not have visual images of people or objects which were not there; I merely believed, with the beautiful relief of absolute justice which the soul of man finds when life becomes unbearable, that God had given me the right and the duty to do everything openly that I had secretly fantasied for years. But this distinction was not gone into by my judges and indifferent captors. They did not have the time, the patience, or even the interest because work in a flip-factory is determined by mathematics: you must find a common denominator of categorization and treatment in order to handle the battalions of miscellaneous humanity that are marched past your desk with high trumpets blowing in their minds.

Like all the other patients, I was considered beyond reasoning with and was treated like a child; not brutally, but efficiently, firmly and patronizingly. In the eyes of this enclosed world I had relinquished my rights as an adult human being. The causes for my explosion were not even superficially examined, nor was the cheek-pinching house psychiatrist—with a fresh flower in the button hole of his fresh daily suit—truly equipped to cope with it even if he had tried, which he did not. Private sanitariums and state institutions, I realized much later, were isolation chambers rather than hospitals in the usual sense; mechanical "cures" such as the one I underwent in a setup of unchallenged authority, like the Army or a humanitarian prison, slowly brought 75 per cent of the inmates down to a more temporarily modest view of reality. Within nine or ten weeks I too came down, humbled, ashamed, willing to stand up before the class and repeat the middle-class credo of limited expressiveness and the meaning of a dollar in order to get my discharge.

In three months' time I was out, shaken, completely alone, living in a cheap Broadway hotel-room (having been ashamed to go back to Greenwich Village) and going to a conventional Ph.D. psychologist (I had been to three medically-trained therapists in the preceding decade) as a sop to both my conscience and family. I had broken beyond the bounds of "reality"—a shorthand word which is used by the average psychiatrist for want of the more truthfully complex approach that must eventually accommodate our beings' increasing flights into higher altitudes—and come back to the position I was in before. But once again the causes that had flung me into my own sky continued to eat me up. Sexually unconfident, I went to whores, ate my meals alone, and forced myself to write a few pieces in that loneliest of places, a tiny blank hotel-room in the middle of nowhere. For the first time in my life the incentive to live, the isolation and frustration of my existence, grew dim; while the psychologist smiled and smoked his pipe—and did the well-adjusted, tweedy, urbane act behind his tastefully battered desk as he ladled out platitudes—I was saving up the sleeping bombs, and when I had enough to do the trick I burned the letters I had received through the years from the several men and women I had loved, destroyed my journal of 15 years' standing, and one carefully chosen night went to a hotel in Newark, N.J.

My plan was to take the pills and slowly conk out in the full bathtub, ultimately drowning like Thomas Heggen; if one missed the other would work. I splurged on a beautiful death-room in a modernistic hotel, one that included a bathroom with the biggest tub in the house. But it was too small to fit my long body. The idea of not being able to drown and of surviving the pills afterwards, perhaps to become a burden or an invalid, began to scar what seemed like a paradise of suicide. I went instead to a Polish bar in downtown Newark, vaguely seeking the eternal anodynes of snatch and booze while I mentally played with my fate.

I found the booze and saw a coarse, ignorant Polish girl do such a life-giving, saucy, raucous folk-dance (on the small dance-floor to the right of the bar) that I broke into loving sobs like prayers over my drink. The sun of life blazed from her into my grateful heart. I went back to the beautiful hotel-room, poured the pills down the toilet, and went to sleep. The next morning I returned to Manhattan a chastened man, shaking my head at how close I had come to non-being.

When I told my tale to Mr. Pipe, my psychologist, he speedily hustled me off to a legitimate head-doctor who doped me until a private ambulance came. Very much in my right and one and only mind but too paralyzed by drugs to move, I was once again taken on the long ride—this time to another hedge-trimmed bin in Long Island. I was helpless to protest, mainly because of the shame and guilt I felt for even contemplating suicide. Obviously I was not crazy, mad, psychotic, out of my mind, schizophrenic, paranoiac. I was simply a tormented man-kid who had never steeled himself to face the facts of life—who didn't know what it meant to have principles and live by them come grief or joy—and who thought that human worth and true independence comes as easily as it does in the movies we were all emotionally faked on. As a sputtering fiction-writer and fairly active literary critic, I had had occasional peaks of maturity and illumination; but as a man I was self-deceptive, self-indulgent, crying inwardly for the pleasures of a college-boy even while in my imagination I saw myself as another Ibsen or Dreiser. Ah, the extraordinary mismating of thoughts in the mind of the modern American literary romantic, as fantastic and truly unbelievable a stew of unrelated dreams as have ever been dreamt, believe me!

Once again I was on the human assembly-line: electric shock clubbed my good brain into needless unconsciousness (and I walked to my several executions like a brave little chappie instead of questioning them) and unquestioned Old Testament authority ruled our little club. Good-natured, but mostly cowlike and uneducated male orderlies carried out the orders from above; and apart from the mechanical treatment and the unimaginative grind of occupational therapy, each patient was left completely on his or her bewildered own, a sad and farcical sight when one considered the $125 per week that their frightened families were paying.

I saw now that nine-tenths of the people I was quartered with were not "insane" by any of the standards a normally intelligent person would use: the majority had lost confidence in their own ability to survive in the world outside, or their families were *afraid* of them and had palmed them off on "experts," but positively no serious effort was being made to equip them to become free and independent adults. This was their birthright—beyond country and society, indeed an almost religious obligation—but they were palliated with pills or jolted with shock, their often honest rage echoed back to them as a sign of their "illness." Some of them must have been "sick," you say. I answer: Who can not be conceived as such in a world so complex ("The truth is there is a truth on every side"—Richard Eberhart) that each group has its own method for judging manners, behavior, ideas, and finally the worth of human values? What was more important was that I, a person from a hip milieu and with a completely opposite set of values, could see their so-called sickness with the human sensibility that an immersion in literature and experience had given me—rather than as a clinical manifestation. When I later recognized the objective provinciality of many psychiatrists in precisely the humanistic areas that could cover the actions of the majority of the inmates without finding it "psychotic," I realized that the independent thinker and artist today must learn to be resolute towards a subtle, socially powerful godfather who often drips paternalism: namely, the newly-enthroned psychiatric minority that has elevated itself to a dangerous position of "authority" in the crucial issues of mind, personality, and sanity.

I now began to fight persistently—but still with shakiness—for my release; my life was my own: it did not belong to the cliches of the salesman-aggressive, well-barbered, Jewish-refugee (my brother, my enemy!) house psychiatrist or to my smiling, betweeded nonentity of a psychologist, who paid me diplomatically inscrutable visits like a Japanese ambassador. Even if I had been or if there were such a reality as a "raving maniac"—which, perhaps childishly, I implore the over-imaginative, zeitgeist-vulnerable reader to believe is an impossible conception today—I would and should have fought for my release. What the institution-spared layman does not realize is that a sensitive and multiple-reacting human being remains the same everywhere, including a sanitarium, and such an environment can duplicate the injustice or vulgarity which drove your person there in the first place. By this I mean that a mental hospital is not an asylum or a sanctuary in the old-fashioned sense: it is just a roped-off side-street of modern existence, rife with as many contradictions, half-truths and lousy architecture as life itself.

Both of the sanitariums I was in were comparable to Grossinger's, in that they took in only financially comfortable, conventionally middle-class, non-intellectual people. By every human standard my being there was life's sarcastic answer to whatever romantic ideas I had about justice. Since the age of 19 I had deliberately led an existence of experimentation, pursuit of truth, bohemianism, and non-commercialism: fate's punishment for my green naivete was for me to recover my supposed mental health in this atmosphere of uncriticizable authority, air-conditioned by just the whiffs of truth that are perfumed and bland, and based on a pillar of middle-class propriety with the cut-throat reality of money underneath. Could I accept my former life, which had produced some good work, as a lie to myself—which the house-psychiatrist wanted me to do (in effect) in his one psychotherapeutic pass at me (he left me alone after this)? I could not and never would: not only for myself but for the great principles and accomplishments of others, both living and dead, which had been my guide throughout my adult life. I might fail—but why go on having an identity at all if in a crisis you will throw away not only your past years, but the moral achievements of rare souls who have shared in your emotional and intellectual experience and whose own contributions to existence are also at stake?

When I heard this second house-psychiatrist literally equate sanity with the current cliches of adjustment and describe Greenwich Village as a "psychotic community," I saw with sudden clarity that *insanity* and *psychosis* can no longer be respected as meaningful definitions—but are used by limited individuals in positions of social power to describe ways of behaving and thinking that are alien, threatening, and *obscure* to them. (A year later when I took a psychiatrist friend of mine to the San Remo, she told me with a straight face that it reminded her of the "admission ward in Bellevue," where she had interned. This was her analogy on the basis of accurate but limited experience, that increasing chasm which separates intelligent people from understanding each other. I realized with a sense of almost incommunicable hopelessness that the gap between her and the well-known poet with whom I had had a beer at the Remo two weeks before was tremendous, and that between these two poles of intelligence the neutral person —who could see the logic of each—was being mashed up with doubt and conflict. The poet was at home, or at least the heat was off, there; while the psychiatrist felt alien and had made a contemptuous psycho-sociological generalization. There was little bond of shared values and therefore genuine communication between both of these intelligent and honest human beings, each of whom contributed to my life.)

To finish with my four months in the sanitarium: I argued and reasoned for the basic right to the insecurity of freedom, and finally a good friend did the dirty infighting of getting me out. Had I to do it over again, I believe I would now have the guts to threaten such an institution or psychologist with a law suit, ugly as such a procedure can be to a person already vulnerable with the hash-marks of one legally defined "psychotic episode" and the contemplation of the criminal act of suicide. But I had been—as so many of Jack Kerouac's subterraneans are when faced with the machinery of official society—milk and sawdust when, in such situations, you must be iron and stone in spite of your own frailty. It is not that the present-day authorities of mental life want to railroad anyone, as in your Grade C horror movie; it is merely that as one grows older it becomes clear that there are almost irremediable differences between people in the total outlook towards life.

Mine had hardened as a result of my experiences, and I realized it was better to die out in the world if need be than be deprived of the necessity to confront existence because of the cheap authority of a lock and key. The majority of people who stay in mental institutions for any length of time do not want to return to the uncertain conditions outside the walls: which in our time spells out to emotionally anarchic, multi-dimensional, brain-trying, anxiety-loaded, and—O hear me mortality, from the Year One!—ultimate and divine life.

II

I returned downtown—to the very Village that I heard the psychiatrist place deep in Freudian Hell, with that pious over-extension of terminology which reveals a limited private morality behind the use of so-called scientific language—and tried to tenderly pick up the threads of my former social life. I saw that my closest and most brilliant friends did not really understand, or were afraid to understand, the contemporary insanity bit. Almost all of them had been soul-whirled by psychotherapy at some time, and each had the particularly contemporary fear of insanity which has become the psychological H-bomb of city life; in theory they may have granted that insanity was no longer the uniform horror it seems to the inexperienced imagination—like a spook in the night—but centuries of inherited fear, plus the daily crises of 1950's living, made them emotionally cautious about seeing my experience as merely an *extension* of their own.

One, a poet-philosopher whom I admire, clapped me on the back and said with some literary awe that I had "returned from the dead, like Lazarus." This struck me as greatly melodramatic, untruthful, and saddening because intellectuals and especially artists should be the very people to understand that insanity today is a matter of definition, not fact; that there can no longer be a fixed criterion, just as there is no longer a reality like that described by Allen Ginsberg in "Howl" (an exciting achievement), where he sees "the best minds of my generation destroyed by madness."

I believe this is lurid sentimentality. Ginsberg may have seen the most gifted people of his generation destroyed by an *interpretation* of madness, which is a much more real threat in a time of such infinite, moon-voyaging extension to experience that the validly felt act is often fearfully jailed in a windowless cell of definition by hard-pressed authorities, whose very moral axis is in danger of toppling. Madness today is a literary word; insanity is a dated legal conception as rigid as an Ibsen play; and "psychosis," the antiseptic modern word that sends chills down the ravines of my friends' minds, has become so weakened (despite its impressive white-jacketed look) by narrow-minded, square, and fast-slipping ideological preconceptions that it must be held at arm's length, like a dead rat, for any cool understanding. When this is done, I believe you will see that the word and the state of mind it tries to fix are subject to the gravest questioning; much of which centers around the amount of freedom either permitted to human expression or, more important, what it must take for itself to live in this time when such *unfamiliar* demands are made on the being. Norms crack when they can no longer fight back the content that spills over cookie-mold conceptions of "sane" behavior—and they must be elasticized to stretch around the new bundle of life.

Two weeks before I was back walking down 8th Street a gratefully free neurotic, I had been thought of in the minds of compassionate but uninformed friends as a fairly wild-eyed psychotic. The mere fact that I had been in a sanitarium had pulled a curtain of emotional blindness down over my friends' vision; and yet I was the same person I had been when I entered the happy-house. The unexamined fear of an "insanity" which no longer exists as a framed picture conventionalizes the very people who should view this now only *symbolic* word with clear, unafraid, and severely skeptical eyes. I had not been among "the dead"—unless killing time looking at "Gunsmoke" and Jackie Gleason on TV, playing bridge, and reading Tolstoy and Nathanael West is considered death. I had not been "destroyed by madness," Mr. Ginsberg!—in fact, the act of incarceration made me realize how significant (indeed indelible) individual freedom is, and thus helped brick-and-mortar my point of view rather than destroy it. When I was once again semi-knit into a way of life in my new Village home, I discovered that other writers and intellectuals whom I knew had also undergone the sanitarium or mental-hospital holiday, but had kept mum because of indecision as to how frankly one should confess such a stigma.

I understood their practical caution, but discovered that they lived in a sewer-light of guilt, fear and throat-gagging anxiety, instead of openly and articulately coping with the monster of doubt. "Do you think I'm sane?" is the question I ultimately began to hear from these brilliant people (one scarred tribesman to another!) who had been intimidated into denying the worth of their most pregnant ideas, the very ones that create *new concrete standards of sanity* or *sense* in a time that has emotionally, if not yet officially, out-lived the abstractions of the past. For myself—although uncertain as to how expressive I should be, even with the very intellectuals I had always considered my brothers in a completely free inquiry into every nook and cranny of life—the problem was suddenly answered when a gifted young writer told a charming hostess I had just met that I had been in "two insane asylums."

I was pierced and hurt, not because I actually considered my supposed nuttiness a yellow badge of dishonor, but because the writer in question had ducked out from under his own experience (which I instinctively knew included some of the crises which had launched me upon the streets like a human missile) and pretended such melodrama was foreign to him. I was appalled because I thought that of all people my fellow highbrow writers should be the first to understand and concede the universal nature of the blows that had felled me in the eyes of official society. But I was wrong. There are spikes on the truth which are so close to the slashed heart of contemporary morality that men and women will lie and refuse acknowledgments, even when it is necessary to the survival of others, they forfeit their humanhood and final worth to life by doing this, but even in the small band of the avant-garde the pursuit of the truth is given up with that weak excuse: "a practical sense of reality."

After this turncoat put-down by a member of my own club, so to speak, there was no longer any issue for myself. I could not live with the squirming burden of secretiveness because my personal history had become public gossip in the small Village group I traveled with. After snake-bitten laughter at my own romantically cultivated simple-mindedness in thinking my fall would be taken with the hip sophistication I had truly expected, I was glad I had become a stooge or victim; because I basically knew that I had played a juicy part in a contemporary American morality play that is going to do standing-room nightly until its implications are understood. We live in what for the imaginative person are truly hallucinated times, because there is more life on every side—and the possibility of conceiving this surplus in a dizzying multitude of ways—than our inheritance and equipment enables us to deal with. My type and perhaps your type of person only *acted out* what other less passionate people feel, but do not express. A "breakdown" such as mine can therefore be learned from:

The first thing one can see is that the isolating of a person saves his or her friends and family from being embarrassed (trivial as this seems, it is a nasty factor in institutionalization), perhaps hurt, and theoretically stops the "sick" person from doing something irreparable while in the grip of the furies. Seen this way, the enforced shackling of an individual seems sad but reasonable. But contemporary adults, however disturbed (often with justice!), are not children; there is doubt in my mind whether we have any right, other than blunt self-interest, to impose our so-called humanitarian wishes on another to the degree where we jail them in order to save them. I must illustrate this with my own case. When I was considered out of my mind during my original upward thrust into the sheer ecstasy of 100 per cent uninhibitedness, I was aware of the "daringness" of my every move; it represented at heart an existential *choice* rather than a mindless discharge. It could not be tolerated by society, and I was punished for it, but my "cure" was ultimately a chastisement, *not a medical healing process*. In my own exhibitionistic and self-dramatizing way, when I flipped, I was nevertheless instinctively rebelling against a fact which I think is objectively true in our society and time: and that is the lack of alignment between an immense inner world and an outer one which has not yet legalized, or officially recognized, the forms that can tolerate the flood of communication from the mind to the stage of action.

Traditionally, it was always taught that the artistic person could work out his or her intense private life by expressing it on the easel or typewriter. In faded theory this seems reasonable, but with the billionaire's wealth of potential human experience both fore, aft and sideways in the world today, it is abnormal not to want to participate more Elizabethanly in this over-abundant life. The hunchbacked joy the artist once may have had in poring over the objects of his interest, and then putting the extract into his work, can no longer be honestly sufficient to the most human hearts today. There has arisen an overwhelming need for the highly imaginative spirit (based on the recognition that the mere mind of man can no longer lock up the volume of its experience) to forge a bridge so that the bursting galaxy of this inner world can be received in actual public life. But there is such a time-lag between our literally amazing subjective life—which has conceptions of a powerful altitude equal to the heaven-exploring freedom of privacy—and the mummery of outer behavior, that when the contemporary imaginator expresses his genuine thoughts in public he often feels that he has exposed himself beyond redemption. Room has not yet been made by those who dominate social power for the natural outward show of the acrobatic thinking that ceaselessly swings in the surrealistic minds of our most acute contemporaries. Put crudely but simply, a bookish notion of what constitutes "normality" in this supremely a-normal age drives the liveliest American sensibilities back into the dungeon of self—creating pressures which must maim the soul one way or another—rather than understanding that the great need today is for imagination to come gloriously out in the open and shrink the light-years that separate the mind from external life. (Trying to fill this need is, hands-down, one of the significant accomplishments of the beats—in my opinion—no matter what defensive moralists say; the raw junk that they have peddled occasionally under a Kotex flag of liberation is a different matter, which doesn't rightly fit in here.)

It was trying to close this distance between Me and Thou, between the mind and externality, that I was instinctively attempting when I cut loose with my natural suffocating self in 1955 upon the taboo grounds of outer life. I could stand unfulfilled desire no longer. Thus it is my conviction today that ideals of social behavior must squat down and broaden to the point where they can both absorb and see the necessity for "aberrations" that were once, squarely and Teddy Rooseveltianly, regarded as pathological. The imagination of living human beings, not dead gods, must be openly embodied if there is to be some rational connection between what people actually are and what they are permitted to show. But as with every significant change in meaning, such acts of expressiveness will cost blood before they will be tolerated and understood by psychiatrists, sociologists, the law, police, and all other instruments of social force. Ironically, it is the very "psychotics" in institutions who have unwittingly done the most to initiate a bigger and more imaginative conception of what constitutes *meaningful* behavior. By dealing with people imprisoned in this category, the most perceptive laymen and psychiatrists are beginning to see symbolic meanings where before they saw flat irrationality, because their approach was literal (as if anyone who had the imagination to go "mad" would be stuffy enough to act in prose!). It is then borne in upon them, out of common sense and humility, that a much more expanded conception of what is "sane" is a prerequisite to doing justice to the real emotional state of human beings today; not the abstract theorems of a clean Euclidian conception, but the real, harsh, multiple, often twisted, on-again, off-again mishmash of the so-called normal mind. One can say without pretense that the pioneering "psychotic" is the human poet of the future; and the most imaginative, least tradition-bound psychiatrists are now playing the role of New Critics, learning to closely read the difficult and unexpected meanings of what formerly were thought of as obscure—in fact, off-limits—warpings of humanity.

III

In my own case I was brought face-to-face because of my trial by shock (both electric and the human aftermath) with a crucial reality which I had long dodged. It can be put approximately this way: A serious artist-type must in the present environment, as always—cliches have a way of becoming profundities when you have to live them!—literally fight for survival if he or she is going to embody the high traditions that originally made the hot pursuit of truth through art the greatest kick in their lives. But to follow this ideal today is tougher than perhaps it has ever been before; and there are specific reasons why. Foremost is the increasing loss of position for the poet (the artist incarnate) as "the unacknowledged legislator of the race" in a period when the terrifying bigness of society makes the average person resort to more immediate and practical oracles (psychiatrists, sociologists, chemists) than to the kind of imaginative truth that the artist can give. Secondly, the artist-type in our mass society is no longer "privileged" in any way, if indeed he ever was; by this I mean that the laws and shibboleths of the huge democratic tribe judge him as severely as they do the shoemaker next door. Whatever pampering the serious artist once received has become a laugh in our time, when everyone is hustling on approximately the same level for success, lovers, status, money, headlines, thrills, security—for everything.

The emergence of an emotionally mutinous democracy has upset the old categories and cast us all into the boiling sea of naked existence, without the props of class, or profession, or the certainty about one's worth as judged by the seemingly clear-cut hierarchies of the past. While, in my opinion, this should be sizzlingly beautiful to every true artist-type, because it is adventurous in the highest conceivable and most mortally dangerous sense, it is also full of the most sinking fears and doubts. For example: can the intelligent writer, painter or composer—the individual with a view of life all his own, which he believes to be true—be indifferent to the prevailing social climate and risk everything by sticking to a viewpoint which will bring him into conflict with the most *normal* (shared by the most people) human emotions in a mass society? (Tag him with the label of "insanity," estrangement from the tempting pie of regular-guy and regular-gal American experience, bring him the isolating fate of being misunderstood even by the "enlightened," and regarded as a personal challenge by others who have made an uneasy truce.)

This is a very serious problem and entails a bigger threat than in the past. Since the artist-type can no longer be realistically considered as being "outside" our definition of society or human nature—and must in this country above all others be seen within the circle of a mass-democratic humanity, for that is where his final strength probably lies —his defections will be judged by those in positions of social power as fluky aberrations *no different from anyone else's*. He will be judged and penalized by the same standards; and in a majority of cases, from what I have seen, his will and stamina are broken (or rationalized into loose harness) and his point of view changed. Frankly, for the artist-type in our environment there is no longer any solid ground whatever under his feet—anything solid he possesses must be won from air and shaped by fanatical resoluteness. For all is open to question today, is a gamble, and has none of the "official" security of the acknowledged professions or even any semblance of unity within his own field. It is for such reasons that the genuine artist-thinker is in such an unenviable and peculiar position in America right now. He is of society and yet, by instinct and inheritance, apart from it: therefore he has to clarify his position in his own mind to a menthol-sharp degree if he wants to survive with intactness, because, as I've tried to show, he will be crushed subtly or conclusively unless he separates his eternal role in society from the onrush of personal doubt that every human being worth the name lives with today.

I learned as a result of my far-out public exhibition, and the manhandling that followed, to distrust the definitions of crude social authority as they pertained to myself and my friends, who share a generally akin point of view and are all either professionals or semi-professionals in the arts and intellectual life. We can not be skimmed off the top and bracketed as thinly as I had been diagnosed at Bellevue;

and the psychiatrists who impatiently felt for the bumps within my head, while presumably competent at a human-machine level, are not as a group sensitive, informed or sympathetic enough with my purposes in life to be of help. In fact, in a basic way they must be my defining opposition in history (daily life) while my friends beyond time (the ideal)—if that doesn't read too pretentiously. It was a sharp revelation for me to learn this as a result of my on-your-hands-and-knees, boy! defeat with authority. As I confessed before, like so many confused young Americans puttering around in the arts, I had phonily pumped into my serious intentions the gassiest dreams of what the struggle for ideas truly is, of false and sentimentalized views of authority (both bowing before it and blowhard defiance), and in general acted more like a Hollywood caricature of a "genius" than a person with the ballbreaking desire to uphold the immortal flame of art in his smallish hand.

I found after I had been handcuffed, ambulanced, doped, needled, marched in formation and given a leather belt to make as if I were in my dotage rather than the prime of life, that I *had to* disagree basically and deliberately with the cowardly normal notion of what constitutes insanity because it is only by *the assertion of the individual spirit that we can change definitions of reality that are already insecure and losing their hold on the conceptual imagination*. In other words, if a majority of people agree that what was once confidently called insanity no longer exists in its traditional sense, can not truthfully be a determining measurement in a time like this where each good person in the reaches of his mind is often an amateur lunatic by older slogans of "rationality," then the enslavement of the word and meaning are broken. Not only was I forced to this simple attitude because my human spirit refused the reduction of my total self to only one exaggerated aspect of it—namely the pathological label—I saw in both sanitariums no consistency in what was thought of as "sick."

In short, I could no longer afford to think of contemporary insanity as an exact objective phenomenon, like thunder or cancer, but rather as an interpretation of human thought and behavior conditioned by inherited prejudices, fear, questionable middle-class assumptions of the purpose of life, a policeman's narrow idea of freedom, and dollar-hard AMA notions of responsibility and *expediency* ("1. Apt and suitable to the end in view; as, an expedient solution; hence, advantageous. 2. Conducive to special advantage rather than to what is universally right."—Web. New Colleg. Dict.). No longer could I see any true authority or finality in a conception that could be too conveniently tailored to fit the situation. I knew then that anyone who dares the intellectual conventions of this local time must be prepared to have "psychotic" or any of its variants—paranoid, schizophrenic, even the mild psychopathic!—thrown at them. The pathological interpretation of human nature has become a style in our period (overemphasized by the junior science of psychiatry) and has come to mirror the fears, anxieties and values of those currently in positions of social authority more often than the person who is being gutted. Within the iron maiden of this fashion—which undeniably hurts, right down to the roots of the soul—the independent person and the artist-type have no choice but to trust implicitly what they see with their intellect and imagination; for when the climate changes, only the individual vision will stand secure upon its God-given legs of having had faith in actual experience.

I therefore believe that the fear and even the actual living through of much that used to be called "insanity" is almost an emotional necessity for every truly feeling, reacting, totally human person in America at this time—*until* he or she passes through the soul-crippling (not healing) judgment of such language and comes out of the fire at the point where other words and hence different conceptions are created from the wounds. The psychiatric vocabulary and definitions, which once seemed such a liberating instrument for modern man, have unwittingly woven a tight and ironically strangling noose around the neck of the brain; contemporary men and women—especially intellectuals—tremblingly judge themselves and others in the black light of psychopathology and shrink human nature to the size of their own fears instead of giving it the liberty of their greatest dreams. But we can be grateful that the human soul is so constructed that it ultimately bursts concepts once held as true out of its terrible need to live and creates the world anew just in order to breathe in it. One final thought: should any readers see this article as an effort at self-justification they are right, as far as they go; but they should remember that it is only out of the self and its experience (even if I have failed here) that new light has ever been cast on the perpetual burden of making life ever more *possible* at its most crucial level.

15

JOHNNY PANIC AND THE BIBLE OF DREAMS

Sylvia Plath

> Sylvia Plath (1932–63), writer and poet, waged an unsuccessful war against the constraints of the feminine role, was labeled mentally ill, hospitalized, and treated with electroshock. She died by suicide. The following selection is a thinly veiled account of her experiences as a mental-hospital patient.*

Every day from nine to five I sit at my desk facing the door of the office and type up other people's dreams. Not just dreams. That wouldn't be practical enough for my bosses. I type up also people's daytime complaints: trouble with mother, trouble with father, trouble with the bottle, the bed, the headache that bangs home and blacks out the sweet world for no known reason. Nobody comes to our office unless they have troubles. Troubles that can't be pinpointed by Wassermanns or Wechsler-Bellevues alone.

Maybe a mouse gets to thinking pretty early on how the whole world is run by these enormous feet. Well, from where I sit I figure the world is run by one thing and this one thing only. Panic with a dog-face, devil-face, hag-face, whore-face, panic in capital letters with no face at all—it's the same Johnny Panic, awake or asleep.

When people ask me where I work, I tell them I'm assistant to the secretary in one of the outpatient departments of the Clinics Building of the City Hospital. This

* "Johnny Panic and the Bible of Dreams," *The Atlantic Monthly*, September 1968, pp. 54–60.

sounds so be-all, end-all they seldom get around to asking me more than what I do, and what I do is mainly type up records. On my own hook though, and completely under cover, I am pursuing a vocation that would set these doctors on their ears. In the privacy of my one-room apartment I call myself secretary to none other than Johnny Panic himself.

Dream by dream I am educating myself to become that rare character, rarer, in truth, than any member of the Psychoanalytic Institute: a dream connoisseur. Not a dream-stopper, a dream-explainer, an exploiter of dreams for the crass practical ends of health and happiness, but an unsordid collector of dreams for themselves alone. A lover of dreams for Johnny Panic's sake, the Maker of them all.

There isn't a dream I've typed up in our record books that I don't know by heart. There isn't a dream I haven't copied out at home into Johnny Panic's Bible of Dreams.

This is my real calling.

Some nights I take the elevator up to the roof of my apartment building. Some nights, about 3 a.m. Over the trees at the far side of the Common the United Fund torch flare flattens and recovers under some witchy invisible push, and here and there in the hunks of stone and brick I see a light. Most of all, though, I feel the city sleeping. Sleeping from the river on the west to the ocean on the east, like some rootless island rockabying itself on nothing at all.

I can be tight and nervy as the top string on a violin, and yet by the time the sky begins to blue I'm ready for sleep. It's the thought of all those dreamers and what they're dreaming wears me down till I sleep the sleep of fever. Monday to Friday what do I do but type up those same dreams. Sure, I don't touch a fraction of them the city over, but page by page, dream by dream, my Intake books fatten and weigh down the bookshelves of the cabinet in the narrow passage running parallel to the main hall, off which passage the doors to all the doctors' little interviewing cubicles open.

I've got a funny habit of identifying the people who come in by their dreams. As far as I'm concerned, the dreams single them out more than any Christian name. This one guy, for example, who works for a ball-bearing company in town, dreams every night how he's lying on his back with a grain of sand on his chest. Bit by bit this grain of sand grows bigger and bigger till it's big as a fair-sized house and he can't draw breath. Another fellow I know of has had a certain dream ever since they gave him ether and cut out his tonsils and adenoids when he was a kid. In this dream he's caught in the rollers of a cotton mill, fighting for his life. Oh, he's not alone, although he thinks he is. A lot of people these days dream they're being run over or eaten by machines. They're the cagey ones who won't go on the subway or the elevators. Coming back from my lunch hour in the hospital cafeteria I often pass them, puffing up the unswept stone stairs to our office on the fourth floor. I wonder, now and then, what dreams people had before ball bearings and cotton mills were invented.

I've got a dream of my own. My one dream. A dream of dreams.

In this dream there's a great half-transparent lake stretching away in every direction, too big for me to see the shores of it, if there are any shores, and I'm hanging over it looking down from the glass belly of some helicopter. At the bottom of the lake—so deep I can only guess at the dark masses moving and heaving—are the real dragons. The ones that were around before men started living in caves and cooking meat over fires and figuring out the wheel and the alphabet. Enormous isn't the word for them; they've got more wrinkles than Johnny Panic himself. Dream about these long enough, and your feet and hands shrivel away when you look at them too closely; the sun shrinks to the size of an orange, only chillier, and you've been living in Roxbury since the last Ice Age. No place for you but a room padded soft as the first room you knew of, where you can dream and float, float and dream, till at last you actually are back among those great originals and there's no point in any dreams at all.

It's into this lake people's minds run at night, brooks and gutter-trickles to one borderless common reservoir. It bears no resemblance to those pure sparkling blue sources of drinking water the suburbs guard more jealously than the Hope diamond in the middle of pinewoods and barbed fences.

It's the sewage farm of the ages, transparence aside.

Now the water in this lake naturally stinks and smokes from what dreams have been left sogging around in it over the centuries. When you think how much room one night of dream props would take up for one person in one city, and that city a mere pinprick on a map of the world, and when you start multiplying this space by the population of the world, and that space by the number of nights there have been since the apes took to chipping axes out of stone and losing their hair, you have some idea what I mean. I'm not the mathematical type: my head starts splitting when I get only as far as the number of dreams going on during one night in the state of Massachusetts.

By this time, I already see the surface of the lake swarming with snakes, dead bodies puffed as blow-fish, human embryos bobbing around in laboratory bottles like so many unfinished messages from the great I Am. I see whole storehouses of hardware: knives, paper cutters, pistons and cogs and nutcrackers; the shiny fronts of cars looming up, glass-eyed and evil-toothed. Then there's the spider-man and the web-footed man from Mars, and the simple, lugubrious vision of a human face turning aside forever, in spite of rings and vows, to the last lover of all.

One of the most frequent shapes in this large stew is so commonplace it seems silly to mention it. It's a grain of dirt. The water is thick with these grains. They seep in among everything else and revolve under some queer power of their own, opaque, ubiquitous. Call the water what you will, Lake Nightmare, Bog of Madness, it's here the sleeping people lie and toss together among the props of their worst dreams, one great brotherhood, though each of them, waking, thinks himself singular, utterly apart.

This is my dream. You won't find it written up in any casebook.

Now the routine in our office is very different from the

routine in Skin Clinic, for example, or in Tumor. The other clinics have strong similarities to each other; none are like ours. In our clinic, treatment doesn't get prescribed. It is invisible. It goes right on in those little cubicles, each with its desk, its two chairs, its window, and its door with the opaque glass rectangle set in the wood. There is a certain spiritual purity about this kind of doctoring. I can't help feeling the special privilege of my position as assistant secretary in the Adult Psychiatric Clinic. My sense of pride is borne out by the rude invasions of other clinics into our cubicles on certain days of the week for lack of space elsewhere: our building is a very old one, and the facilities have not expanded with the expanding needs of the time. On these days of overlap the contrast between us and the other clinics is marked.

On Tuesdays and Thursdays, for instance, we have lumbar punctures in one of our offices in the morning. If the practical nurse chances to leave the door of the cubicle open, as she usually does, I can glimpse the end of the white cot and the dirty yellow-soled bare feet of the patient sticking out from under the sheet. In spite of my distaste at this sight, I can't keep my eyes away from the bare feet, and I find myself glancing back from my typing every few minutes to see if they are still there, if they have changed their position at all. You can understand what a distraction this is in the middle of my work. I often have to reread what I have typed several times, under the pretense of careful proofreading, in order to memorize the dreams I have copied down from the doctor's voice over the audiograph.

Nerve Clinic next door, which tends to the grosser, more unimaginative end of our business, also disturbs us in the mornings. We use their offices for therapy in the afternoon, as they are only a morning clinic, but to have their people crying, or singing, or chattering loudly in Italian or Chinese, as they often do, without break for four hours at a stretch every morning is distracting to say the least. The patients down there are often referred to us if their troubles have no ostensible basis in the body.

In spite of such interruptions by other clinics, my own

work is advancing at a great rate. By now I am far beyond copying only what comes after the patient's saying: "I have this dream, Doctor." I am at the point of re-creating dreams that are not even written down at all. Dreams that shadow themselves forth in the vaguest way, but are themselves hid, like a statue under red velvet before the grand unveiling.

To illustrate. This woman came in with her tongue swollen and stuck out so far she had to leave a party she was giving for twenty friends of her French-Canadian mother-in-law and be rushed to our emergency ward. She thought she didn't want her tongue to stick out, and to tell the truth, it was an exceedingly embarrassing affair for her, but she hated that French-Canadian mother-in-law worse than pigs, and her tongue was true to her opinion, even if the rest of her wasn't. Now she didn't lay claim to any dreams. I have only the bare facts above to begin with, yet behind them I detect the bulge and promise of a dream.

So I set myself to uprooting this dream from its comfortable purchase under her tongue.

Whatever the dream I unearth, by work, taxing work, and even by a kind of prayer, I am sure to find a thumbprint in the corner, a bodiless midair Cheshire cat grin, which shows the whole work to be gotten up by the genius of Johnny Panic, and him alone. He's sly, he's subtle, he's sudden as thunder, but he gives himself away only too often. He simply can't resist melodrama. Melodrama of the oldest, most obvious variety.

I remember one guy, a stocky fellow in a nail-studded black leather jacket, running straight into us from a boxing match at Mechanics Hall, Johnny Panic hot at his heels. This guy, good Catholic though he was, young and upright and all, had one mean fear of death. He was actually scared blue he'd go to hell. He was a pieceworker at a fluorescent light plant. I remember this detail because I thought it funny he should work there, him being so afraid of the dark as it turned out. Johnny Panic injects a poetic element in this business you don't often find elsewhere. And for that he has my eternal gratitude.

I also remember quite clearly the scenario of the dream I had worked out for this guy: a Gothic interior in some monastery cellar, going on and on as far as you could see, one of those endless perspectives between two mirrors, and the pillars and walls were made of nothing but human skulls and bones, and in every niche there was a body laid out, and it was the Hall of Time, with the bodies in the foreground still warm, discoloring and starting to rot in the middle distance, and the bones emerging, clean as a whistle, in a kind of white futuristic glow at the end of the line. As I recall, I had the whole scene lighted, for the sake of accuracy, not with candles, but with the ice-bright fluorescence that makes the skin look green and all the pink and red flushes dead black-purple.

You ask, how do I know this was the dream of the guy in the black leather jacket. I don't know. I only believe this was his dream, and I work at belief with more energy and tears and entreaties than I work at re-creating the dream itself.

My office, of course, has its limitations. The lady with her tongue stuck out, the guy from Mechanics Hall—these are our wildest ones. The people who have really gone floating down toward the bottom of that boggy lake come in only once, and are then referred to a place more permanent than our office, which receives the public from nine to five, five days a week only. Even those people who are barely able to walk about the streets and keep working, who aren't yet halfway down in the lake, get sent to the outpatient department at another hospital specializing in severer cases. Or they may stay a month or so in our own observation ward in the central hospital, which I've never seen.

I've seen the secretary of that ward, though. Something about her merely smoking and drinking her coffee in the cafeteria at the ten o'clock break put me off so I never went to sit next to her again. She has a funny name I don't ever quite remember correctly, something really odd, like Miss Milleravage. One of those names that seem more like a pun mixing up Milltown and Ravage than anything in the city phone directory. But not so odd a name, after all, if you've ever read through the phone directory, with its Hyman Diddlebockers and Sasparilla Greenleafs. I read through the phone book, once, never mind when, and it satisfied a deep need in me to realize how many people aren't called Smith.

Anyhow, this Miss Milleravage is a large woman, not fat, but all sturdy muscle and tall on top of it. She wears a gray suit over her hard bulk that reminds me vaguely of some kind of uniform, without the details of cut having anything strikingly military about them. Her face, hefty as a bullock's, is covered with a remarkable number of tiny maculae, as if she'd been lying under water for some time and little algae had latched onto her skin, smutching it over with tobacco-browns and greens. These moles are noticeable mainly because the skin around them is so pallid. I sometimes wonder if Miss Milleravage has ever seen the wholesome light of day. I wouldn't be a bit surprised if she'd been brought up from the cradle with the sole benefit of artificial lighting.

Byrna, the secretary in Alcoholic Clinic just across the hall from us, introduced me to Miss Milleravage with the gambit that I'd "been in England too."

Miss Milleravage, it turned out, had spent the best years of her life in London hospitals.

"Had a friend," she boomed in her queer, doggish basso, not favoring me with a direct look, "a nurse at St. Bart's. Tried to get in touch with her after the war, but the head of the nurses had changed, everybody'd changed, nobody'd heard of her. She must've gone down with the old head nurse, rubbish and all, in the bombings." She followed this with a large grin.

Now I've seen medical students cutting up cadavers, four stiffs to a classroom about as recognizably human as Moby Dick, and the students playing catch with the dead men's livers. I've heard guys joke about sewing a woman up wrong after a delivery at the charity ward of the Lying-In. But I wouldn't want to see what Miss Milleravage would write off as the biggest laugh of all time. No thanks and then some. You could scratch her eyes with a pin and swear you'd struck solid quartz.

My boss has a sense of humor too, only it's gentle. Generous as Santa on Christmas Eve.

I work for a middle-aged lady named Miss Taylor who is the head secretary of the clinic and has been since the clinic started thirty-three years ago—the year of my birth, oddly enough. Miss Taylor knows every doctor, every patient, every outmoded appointment slip, referral slip, and billing procedure the hospital has ever used or thought of using. She plans to stick with the clinic until she's farmed out in the green pastures of social security checks. A woman more dedicated to her work I never saw. She's the same way about statistics as I am about dreams: if the building caught fire she would throw every last one of those books of statistics to the firemen below at the serious risk of her own skin.

I get along extremely well with Miss Taylor. The one thing I never let her catch me doing is reading the old record books. I have actually very little time for this. Our office is busier than the stock exchange with the staff of twenty-five doctors in and out, medical students in training, patients, patients' relatives, and visiting officials from other clinics referring patients to us, so even when I'm covering the office alone, during Miss Taylor's coffee break and lunch hour, I seldom get to dash down more than a note or two.

This kind of catch-as-catch-can is nerve-racking, to say the least. A lot of the best dreamers are in the old books, the dreamers that come in to us only once or twice for evaluation before they're sent elsewhere. For copying out these dreams I need time, a lot of time. My circumstances are hardly ideal for the unhurried pursuit of my art. There is, of course, a certain derring-do in working under such hazards, but I long for the rich leisure of the true connoisseur who indulges his nostrils above the brandy snifter for an hour before his tongue reaches out for the first taste.

I find myself all too often lately imagining what a relief

it would be to bring a briefcase into work, big enough to hold one of those thick, blue, cloth-bound record books full of dreams. At Miss Taylor's lunchtime, in the lull before the doctors and students crowd in to take their afternoon patients, I could simply slip one of the books, dated ten or fifteen years back, into my briefcase, and leave the briefcase under my desk till five o'clock struck. Of course, odd-looking bundles are inspected by the doorman of the Clinics Building, and the hospital has its own staff of flatfeet to check up on the multiple varieties of thievery that go on, but for heaven's sake, I'm not thinking of making off with typewriters or heroin. I'd only borrow the book overnight and slip it back on the shelf first thing the next day before anybody else came in. Still, being caught taking a book out of the hospital would probably mean losing my job and all my source material with it.

This idea of mulling over a record book in the privacy and comfort of my own apartment, even if I have to stay up night after night for this purpose, attracts me so much I become more and more impatient with my usual method of snatching minutes to look up dreams in Miss Taylor's half hours out of the office.

The trouble is, I can never tell exactly when Miss Taylor will come back to the office. She is so conscientious about her job she'd be likely to cut her half hour at lunch short and her twenty minutes at coffee shorter if it weren't for her lame left leg. The distinct sound of this lame leg in the corridor warns me of her approach in time for me to whip the record book I'm reading into my drawer out of sight and pretend to be putting down the final flourishes on a phone message, or some such alibi. The only catch, as far as my nerves are concerned, is the Amputee Clinic is around the corner from us in the opposite direction from Nerve Clinic, and I've gotten really jumpy due to a lot of false alarms where I've mistaken some pegleg's hitching step for the step of Miss Taylor herself returning early to the office.

On the blackest days when I've scarcely time to squeeze one dream out of the old books and my copy work is nothing but weepy college sophomores who can't get a lead in *Camino Real*, I feel Johnny Panic turn his back, stony as Everest, higher than Orion, and the motto of the great Bible of Dreams, "Perfect fear casteth out all else," is ash and lemon water on my lips. I'm a wormy hermit in a country of prize pigs so corn-happy they can't see the slaughterhouse at the end of the track. I'm Jeremiah vision-bitten in the Land of Cockaigne.

What's worse: day by day I see these psyche-doctors studying to win Johnny Panic's converts from him by hook, crook, and talk, talk, talk. These deep-eyed, bush-bearded dream-collectors who preceded me in history, and their contemporary inheritors with their white jackets and knotty-pine-paneled offices and leather couches, practiced and still practice their dream-gathering for worldly ends: health and money, money and health. To be a true member of Johnny Panic's congregation one must forget the dreamer and remember the dream: the dreamer is merely a flimsy vehicle for the great Dream-Maker himself. This they will not do. Johnny Panic is gold in the bowels, and they try to root him out by spiritual stomach pumps.

Take what happened to Harry Bilbo. Mr. Bilbo came into our office with the hand of Johnny Panic heavy as a lead coffin on his shoulder. He had an interesting notion about the filth in this world. I figured him for a prominent part in Johnny Panic's Bible of Dreams, Third Book of Fear, Chapter Nine on Dirt, Disease, and General Decay. A friend of Harry's blew a trumpet in the Boy Scout band when they were kids. Harry Bilbo'd also blown on this friend's trumpet. Years later the friend got cancer and died. Then, one day not so long ago, a cancer doctor came into Harry's house, sat down in a chair, passed the top of the morning with Harry's mother, and on leaving, shook her hand and opened the door for himself. Suddenly Harry Bilbo wouldn't blow trumpets or sit down on chairs or shake hands if all the cardinals of Rome took to blessing him twenty-four hours around the clock for fear of catching cancer. His mother had to go turning the TV knobs and water faucets on and off and opening doors for him. Pretty soon Harry stopped going to work because of the spit and dog droppings in the street. First that stuff gets on your shoes, and then when you take your shoes off it gets on your hands, and then at dinner it's a quick trip into your mouth and not a hundred Hail Mary's can keep you from the chain reaction. The last straw was, Harry quit weight lifting at the public gym when he saw this cripple exercising with the dumbbells. You can never tell what germs cripples carry behind their ears and under their fingernails. Day and night Harry Bilbo lived in holy worship of Johnny Panic, devout as any priest among censers and sacraments. He had a beauty all his own.

Well, these white-coated tinkerers managed, the lot of them, to talk Harry into turning on the TV himself, and the water faucets, and to opening closet doors, front doors, bar doors. Before they were through with him, he was sitting down on movie-house chairs, and benches all over the Public Garden, and weight lifting every day of the week at the gym in spite of the fact another cripple took to using the rowing machine. At the end of his treatment he came in to shake hands with the clinic director. In Harry Bilbo's own words, he was "a changed man." The pure Panic-light had left his face; he went out of the office doomed to the crass fate these doctors call health and happiness.

About the time of Harry Bilbo's cure a new idea starts nudging at the bottom of my brain. I find it as hard to ignore as those bare feet sticking out of the lumbar puncture room. If I don't want to risk carrying a record book out of the hospital in case I get discovered and fired and have to end my research forever, I can really speed up work by staying in the Clinics Building overnight. I am nowhere near exhausting the clinic's resources, and the piddling amount of cases I am able to read in Miss Taylor's brief absences during the day are nothing to what I could get through in a few nights of steady copying. I need to accelerate my work if only to counteract those doctors.

Before I know it I am putting on my coat at five and saying good-night to Miss Taylor, who usually stays a few minutes overtime to clear up the day's statistics, and sneaking around the corner into the ladies' room. It is empty. I slip into the patient's john, lock the door from the inside, and wait. For all I know, one of the clinic cleaning ladies may try to knock the door down, thinking some patient's passed out on the seat. My fingers are crossed. About twenty minutes later the door of the lavatory opens and someone limps over the threshold like a chicken favoring a bad leg. It is Miss Taylor, I can tell by the resigned sigh as she meets the jaundiced eye of the lavatory mirror. I hear the click-cluck of various touch-up equipment on the bowl, water sloshing, the scritch of a comb in frizzed hair, and then the door is closing with a slow-hinged wheeze behind her.

I am lucky. When I come out of the ladies' room at six o'clock the corridor lights are off and the fourth floor hall is empty as church on Monday. I have my own key to our office; I come in first every morning, so that's no trouble. The typewriters are folded back into the desks, the locks are on the dial phones, all's right with the world.

Outside the window the last of the winter light is fading. Yet I do not forget myself and turn on the overhead bulb. I don't want to be spotted by any hawk-eyed doctor or janitor in the hospital buildings across the little courtyard. The cabinet with the record books is in the windowless passage opening onto the doctor's cubicles, which have windows overlooking the courtyard. I make sure the doors to all the cubicles are shut. Then I switch on the passage light, a sallow twenty-five-watt affair blackening at the top. Better than an altarful of candles to me at this point, though. I didn't think to bring a sandwich. There is an apple in my desk drawer left over from lunch, so I reserve that for whatever pangs I may feel about one o'clock in the morning, and get out my pocket notebook. At home every evening it is my habit to tear out the notebook pages I've written on at the office during the day and pile them up to be copied in my manuscript. In this way I cover my tracks so no one idly picking up my notebook at the office could ever guess the type or scope of my work.

I begin systematically by opening the oldest book on the

bottom shelf. The once-blue cover is no-color now, the pages are thumbed and blurry carbons, but I'm humming from foot to topknot: this dream book was spanking new the day I was born. When I really get organized I'll have hot soup in a thermos for the dead-of-winter nights, turkey pies, and chocolate eclairs. I'll bring hair curlers and four changes of blouse to work in my biggest handbag Monday mornings so no one will notice me going downhill in looks and start suspecting unhappy love affairs or pink affiliations or my working on dream books in the clinic four nights a week.

Eleven hours later. I am down to apple core and seeds and in the month of May, nineteen thirty-four, with a private nurse who has just opened a laundry bag in her patient's closet and found five severed heads in it, including her mother's.

A chill air touches the nape of my neck. From where I am sitting cross-legged on the floor in front of the cabinet, the record book heavy on my lap, I notice out of the corner of my eye that the door of the cubicle beside me is letting in a little crack of blue light. Not only along the floor, but up the side of the door too. This is odd since I made sure from the first that all the doors were shut tight. The crack of blue light is widening and my eyes are fastened to two motionless shoes in the doorway, toes pointing toward me.

They are brown leather shoes of a foreign make, with thick elevator soles. Above the shoes are black silk socks through which shows a pallor of flesh. I get as far as the gray pinstripe trouser cuffs.

"Tch, tch," chides an infinitely gentle voice from the cloudy regions above my head. "Such an uncomfortable position! Your legs must be asleep by now. Let me help you up. The sun will be rising shortly."

Two hands slip under my arms from behind, and I am raised, wobbly as an unset custard, to my feet, which I cannot feel because my legs are, in fact, asleep. The record book slumps to the floor, pages splayed.

"Stand still a minute." The clinic director's voice fans the lobe of my right ear. "Then the circulation will revive."

The blood in my not-there legs starts pinging under a million sewing machine needles, and a vision of the clinic director acid-etches itself on my brain. I don't even need to look around: the fat potbelly buttoned into his gray pinstripe waistcoat, woodchuck teeth yellow and buck, every-color eyes behind the thick-lensed glasses quick as minnows.

I clutch my notebook. The last floating timber of the *Titanic*.

What does he know, what does he know?

Everything.

"I know where there is a nice hot bowl of chicken noodle soup." His voice rustles, dust under the bed, mice in the straw. His hand welds onto my left upper arm in fatherly love. The record book of all the dreams going on in the city of my birth at my first yawp in this world's air he nudges under the bookcase with a polished toe.

We meet nobody in the dawn-dark hall. Nobody on the chill stone stair down to the basement corridors where Jerry the Record Room boy cracked his head skipping steps one night on a rush errand.

I begin to double-quickstep so he won't think it's me he's hustling. "You can't fire me," I say calmly. "I quit."

The clinic director's laugh wheezes up from his accordion-pleated bottom gut. "We mustn't lose you so soon." His whisper snakes off down the whitewashed basement passages, echoing among the elbow pipes, the wheelchairs and stretchers beached for the night along the steam-stained walls. "Why, we need you more than you know."

We wind and double, and my legs keep time with his until we come, somewhere in those barren rat tunnels, to an all-night elevator run by a one-armed Negro. We get on and the door grinds shut like the door on a cattle car and we go up and up. It is a freight elevator, crude and clanky, a far cry from the plush one in the Clinics Building.

We get off at an indeterminate floor. The clinic director leads me down a bare corridor lit at intervals by socketed bulbs in little wire cages on the ceiling. Locked doors set with screened windows line the hall on either hand. I plan to part company with the clinic director at the first red exit sign, but on our journey there are none. I am in alien territory, coat on the hanger in the office, handbag and money in my top desk drawer, notebook in my hand, and only Johnny Panic to warm me against the Ice Age outside.

Ahead a light gathers, brightens. The clinic director, puffing slightly at the walk, brisk and long, to which he is obviously unaccustomed, propels me around a bend and into a square, brilliantly lit room.

"Here she is."

"The little witch!"

Miss Milleravage hoists her tonnage up from behind the steel desk facing the door.

The walls and the ceiling of the room are riveted metal battleship plates. There are no windows.

From small, barred cells lining the sides and back of the room I see Johnny Panic's top priests staring out at me, arms swaddled behind their backs in the white ward nightshirts, eyes redder than coals and hungry-hot.

They welcome me with queer croaks and grunts as if their tongues were locked in their jaws. They have no doubt heard of my work by way of Johnny Panic's grapevine and want to know how his apostles thrive in the world.

I lift my hands to reassure them, holding up my notebook, my voice loud as Johnny Panic's organ with all stops out.

"Peace! I bring to you . . ."

The Book.

"None of that old stuff, sweetie," Miss Milleravage is dancing out at me from behind her desk like a trick elephant.

The clinic director closes the door to the room.

The minute Miss Milleravage moves I notice what her hulk has been hiding from view behind the desk—a white cot high as a man's waist with a single sheet stretched over the mattress, spotless and drumskin tight. At the head of the cot is a table on which sits a metal box covered with dials and gauges. The box seems to be eyeing me, copperhead-ugly, from its coil of electric wires, the latest model in Johnny-Panic-Killers.

I get ready to dodge to one side. When Miss Milleravage grabs, her fat hand comes away a fist full of nothing. She starts for me again, her smile heavy as dogdays in August.

"None of that. None of that. I'll have that little black book."

Fast as I run around the high white cot, Miss Milleravage is so fast you'd think she wore roller skates. She grabs and gets. Against her great bulk I beat my fists, and against her whopping milkless breasts, until her hands on my wrists are iron hoops and her breath hushabys me with a lovestink fouler than Undertaker's Basement.

"My Baby, my own baby's come back to me . . ."

"She," the clinic director says, sad and stern, "has been making time with Johnny Panic again."

"Naughty naughty."

The white cot is ready. With a terrible gentleness Miss Milleravage takes the watch from my wrist, the rings from my fingers, the hairpins from my hair. She begins to undress me. When I am bare, I am anointed on the temples and robed in sheets virginal as the first snow. Then, from the four corners of the room and from the door behind me come five false priests in white surgical gowns and masks whose one lifework is to unseat Johnny Panic from his own throne. They extend me full-length on my back on the cot. The crown of wire is placed on my head, the wafer of forgetfulness on my tongue. The masked priests move to their posts and take hold: one of my left leg, one of my right, one of my right arm, one of my left. One behind my head at the metal box where I can't see.

From their cramped niches along the wall, the votaries raise their voices in protest. They begin the devotional chant:

> The only thing to love is Fear itself.
> Love of Fear is the beginning of wisdom.
> The only thing to love is Fear itself.
> May Fear and Fear and Fear be everywhere.

There is no time for Miss Milleravage or the clinic director or the priests to muzzle them.

The signal is given.

The machine betrays them.

At the moment when I think I am most lost the face of Johnny Panic appears in a nimbus of arc lights on the ceiling overhead. I am shaken like a leaf in the teeth of glory. His beard is lightning. Lightning is in his eye. His Word charges and illumes the universe.

The air crackles with the blue-tongued, lightning-haloed angels.

His love is the twenty-story leap, the rope at the throat, the knife at the heart.

He forgets not his own.

16

CITY PSYCHIATRIC

Frank Leonard

Frank Leonard is a welfare investigator and supervisor in New York's Harlem as well as a writer. The excerpts that follow are from the documentary novel *City Psychiatric*,* based on Mr. Leonard's experiences as an attendant at several mental hospitals, including a large metropolitan receiving hospital.

I

In his basement office, Franklin Ross had just crumpled up the sandwich wrappers and wax paper cup from his lunch, and thrown them into the wastebasket beside his desk, when the phone rang. He picked up the receiver. "Franklin Ross," he said. There was silence at the other end of the line, and then, just before the click of the receiver, a voice mumbled a word—"Shit!"—and the phone was dead.

Ross replaced the receiver. Someone had apparently been trying to get an outside line on one of the ward phones but had forgotten to dial 9 first. It happened every so often. Ross's number was 744. By coincidence, the phone number of a free-delivery liquor store a few blocks away was SI 4-2232. If someone using a hospital phone forgot to dial 9 first to get an outside line, the first three

* *City Psychiatric*. With a Foreword by John Bartlow Martin (New York: Ballantine Books, 1965), pp. 41-47, 52-56, 99-104.

digits were the same. Someone dialing the liquor store would get Ross instead. Of course, there were many other phone numbers that began the same way. Still, Ross knew that a large amount of alcohol came into the hospital and that this particular liquor store was a favorite with employees. The bottles were always turning up on the occasional inspections, either by himself or by the engineers surveying holes in the walls or ceilings for possible repair. Out of one hole in the ceiling of the laundry room on Ward A6 the engineers had taken fifty-four empty pint rum bottles.

The consumption of alcohol worried Ross. First, he was afraid some of the liquor might be finding its way to the patients, though there was no evidence of it. Second, since he was in charge of accident control, the effect of the liquor on the attendants and the nurses concerned him. It could make them less alert, so that they themselves might be hurt, say on the disturbed men's ward or it might affect their judgment so that a patient was harmed or not prevented from harming himself.

Still, Ross thought, he should be the last one to judge others for their use of alcohol. He didn't drink at work, but that was simply self-preservation. Work was where he came to forget alcohol.

Ross dismissed the phone call from his mind and turned back to his desk. In his "In" basket was a pile of papers that had been put there just before lunch by the messenger. Ross picked up the first sheet. It was a letter, handwritten on lined paper, and the envelope was stapled to it.

> Dear Sir,
> My son George was sent to Valley State Hospital by your Doctor Schwartzrock. Doctor Schwartzrock treated him and me without even common Decency and he wouldn't explain nothing to us. He said my son is Crazy. I hate to bother you but does he have to treat us like a dog just because were in trouble? Even a mental person is supposed to be a man, even so, isint he?

Ross shook his head. Still another letter complaining about Schwartzrock. The hospital got one or two every six months. And for every one that was actually written and received, Ross wondered how many other cases there were of injured or outraged feelings and sensibilities, of people unwilling or unable to write. Ross could remember parts of some letters by heart.

"My brother was a professor of history for ten years and this doctor of yours shouts at him that he's a bum." That was Schwartzrock. He called a spade a spade, a cripple a cripple, a weakling a weakling, and a bum a bum. "Why not?" Schwartzrock had demanded once when Ross was new at the hospital and had brought one of the complaining letters to him. "My business is reality," Schwartzrock told him. "I have no time for euphemism and no time for hurt feelings." Schwartzrock's cool blue eyes, behind severe, old-fashioned, wire-rimmed lenses, had narrowed just the tiniest bit and instinctively, professionally scrutinized for a moment Ross's flushed face and reddened nose, which even then showed the unmistakable signs of alcohol consumption. Then Schwartzrock told him, "Now, if you'll get out, I can get back to work."

Ross could never think of that encounter without a small inward tremor. Schwartzrock, by his very existence, because of the type of man he was, intimidated Ross and made him acutely aware of his own shortcomings. Though small in stature, Schwartzrock was an active, energetic man. He had been a psychiatrist at the hospital for fifteen years. In that time he had probably diagnosed twenty thousand people. Schwartzrock not only diagnosed. He decided whether a person were well enough to have a chance of getting along on the outside even if he was mentally ill, or whether, for the protection of himself or of society, he ought to go to a state hospital. Another sort of man might have trembled at each decision, with the shape of someone's life thus held—to some small degree—in his own hands. But Schwartzrock's make-up was such that he did not tremble. He decided calmly, quickly, almost instinctively, and with skill probably matched by no other psychiatrist at the hospital.

Schwartzrock was also the patriarch of a large and very successful family. One daughter was a doctor, one son a lawyer, another son was still at Harvard, and another daughter was in England on a Fulbright. In addition to his other accomplishments, Schwartzrock was also a scholar of the Jews in Italy during the Renaissance. Finally—God only knew where he found the time—Schwartzrock had a small private practice of his own.

On the other hand, Ross conceded that, by any objective standards he himself must be judged a failure. As a young medical student, full of youthful reverence for life, he had an affair with another medical student—a pretty, slim, and unstable Japanese girl. When she told him she was pregnant, he reacted with confusion, disbelief, and obvious displeasure. Late that day Ross was appalled to find the girl dead in his small apartment, an empty container of rat poison beside her. Ross proceeded to drink his way out of medical school and then fled to Mexico City in a search for something he could not name. He did not find it. He developed rheumatic fever, however, and finally came back to the United States with a slightly weakened heart, to see what he could piece together out of the ruins of his medical school career. He took up hospital administration as a poor second and got a degree in two years.

He found a good job at an expensive private midwestern psychiatric hospital and married an attractive, intelligent, aggressive, and ambitious girl. But before the marriage was two years old, Ross's world had begun to turn sour. Toward the end of the first year, the same patients he had seen in his first few months began to return with their original illnesses and begin again that expensive and torturous series of electric-shock treatments that had "cured" them only a few months earlier at a cost of several thousand dollars. Some came back more and more frequently, first every eight months, then every five, and then, when their savings were finally gone, their families would be told that Oakside could not admit them this time. They would end up in the overcrowded state hospital, whose name, appropriately, since it was the final home for most, was St. Peter's. . . .

II

One scene was still fresh in Ross's mind and seemed to catch, like a rare candid photo, the very spirit of Oakside. One day Ross had watched as one of the hospital's psychiatrists took a woman who was still confused from a shock treatment and coaxed her into signing a check, after which he filled in the amount of his fee.

By the end of his second year Ross had begun to drink more and work less, and before the third year was half over, he was fired. His wife left him then, thinking this was the end of him. Ross stopped drinking only after he found himself in a hospital with his left wrist cut open by a broken whisky bottle. Hospital officials reported it to the police as a suicide attempt. Ross could not believe it. He could not remember anything about the incident but he did not believe he could really have been trying to kill himself.

At this point, a mediocre best-selling novel about a mental hospital gave Ross the idea of trying to write a better one of his own, about Oakside. Halfway through, he realized that his book was worse, not better, and he gave it up. He got a job at the big state hospital in Chicago, which was just then beginning its famous lobotomy experiments.

For a year and a half at the hospital Ross watched the progress of those experiments with growing disbelief and revulsion. The doctors were deadly serious. From one failure after another they drew what they thought were clues pointing toward the secret of eventual success. Lobotomy was tried as a cure for everything from psychosis to juvenile delinquency to promiscuity to alcoholism.

Finally Ross watched with horror as plans were made to cut into the brain of Susan de Angelus, a frail, beautiful woman with golden curls and deep brown eyes. At thirty-six she had already tried five times to kill herself. Usually, someone so determined to die would have succeeded, but through a series of coincidences each of the suicide attempts had failed.

The woman's case history was filled with violence and death. Not only had she been raped by an uncle and conceived a child by that union, but when the child—a little girl—was two years old, the uncle, in a drunken rage, had beaten her to death. Later, as a teacher in a school for deaf mutes, Susan de Angelus had watched helplessly as a dormitory fire killed seven of her pupils. When her fiance was killed in an auto accident, she finally decided that she could not bear any more.

But the doctors at Chicago Psychiatric thought they knew better. They were going to reconcile her to the world by cutting into certain nerve centers in her brain. The girl's uncle, rotting away in a Chicago penitentiary, willingly signed the necessary papers.

A week before the operation, Ross talked to the woman. She was numb with terror. They talked a few minutes, and Ross was appalled by her helpless fear and also by her gentleness and beauty. Before he knew it, he was telling her, "I'm going to get you out of here."

The amazement and gratitude in her eyes were too much for Ross, and he left abruptly, fighting back tears. Susan de Angelus agreed to go to a private hospital, and Ross got her out of Chicago Psychiatric on a writ of habeas corpus. Her freedom cost him his job, as he had known it would. At the new hospital Ross visited her every day, trying to win her back to life. The day before she was to leave the hospital for a trial weekend outside, she finally succeeded in killing herself, by knotting a piece of cord around her neck and hanging herself in her room during the night.

Ross drank his way to the West Coast, spent time on the alcoholic wards of two California hospitals, had his nose broken in a California jail, and finally ended up on a medical ward, near death from loss of blood with a severed artery in his left wrist. The wound had been caused by a broken bottle. Again, the hospital authorities called it an attempted suicide. Again, Ross could remember nothing about it.

During his convalescence he began a book about lobotomies. The book was turned down by every publisher to whom he sent it, sixteen in all. Finally, at the end of his rope, he used some of his deceased father's friends as a lever to get himself into City Psychiatric as an administrative assistant.

Compared to Schwartzrock's, his life seemed a miserable, wasted thing. Another encounter with Schwartzrock—or any other doctor, for that matter—was certainly to be avoided. The other doctors were worse than Schwartzrock. Schwartzrock had absolutely no malice in him; he didn't have the time. But the other, younger doctors were often eager to test out their status. The doctors were the true elite at City, if such a shabby institution could be said to have an elite. Ross had, literally, no status. He was, in a sense, part of City's occupational rehabilitation plan, since those in charge knew he had been a jobless alcoholic before they hired him. Ross's tenure at City Psychiatric was a sort of gift from those above, which could be withdrawn any time he aroused the displeasure of his superiors—or even of his equals, the other administrative assistants. He could not afford to involve himself in disagreements. On any issue, a showdown could end in only one way. He would lose. . . .

III

Maxim Schwartzrock was in a hurry now to get to his private office. He had had enough of the hospital for one day. He had only two more patients to see before he left. Both were waiting in his outer office. He had their charts before him in his "In" basket. On top of the charts was a green memo slip with Schwartzrock's name on it, and attached to the slip was a handwritten letter which began:

My son George was sent to Valley State Hospital by your Doctor Schwartzrock . . .

Schwartzrock scanned the letter briefly and dropped it into his wastebasket. Then he picked up the first of the two charts and barked out the man's name: "Hyman Shapiro!"

He had seen Shapiro once already and diagnosed him as schizophrenic, but he wanted to see him again briefly before he had the final commitment paper made out. A fat, shapeless, triple-chinned, smooth-skinned, and rosy-cheeked boy of twenty-eight waddled in the door, came over to the desk, and asked, "Why am I here?"

"Let me ask the questions, Shapiro."

"Why am I here?" said the boy, placidly, as if he hadn't heard.

"You're here because your mother's had a belly full of you, that's why. She's tired of cleaning up your messes. And I don't blame her. She's tired of the way you act, Hyman. Understand?"

The boy was silent.

"Your mother's had a *belly full!* She doesn't want any more of it. So you know what I'm going to do for her?"

"No," said Hyman Shapiro sullenly.

"I'm going to give her a vacation. I'm going to send you away for two months. If you learn how to act in two months, you might get out. But don't count on it. Because I don't think you'll *ever* learn how to act."

"My mother wants me home."

"That's not what she told the cops, is it?"

"She already apologized to me for that," said Hyman Shapiro, "she wants me home again. She's sorry."

"If she wants you home she better let me know about it."

"She will."

"O.K., get out."

"You won't send me away to that nasty place?"

"If your mother wants you back she can have you. God knows no one else wants you."

"Thank you, doctor."

"Don't thank me. I can't stand the sight of you. Get out."

Hyman Shapiro reached into the pocket of his yellow

hospital bathrobe and pulled out a small square business card and handed it to Schwartzrock. "What's this?" said Schwartzrock irritably. He took the card and turned it right side up.

"My mother fixes suits. I notice you got a hole in the elbow. She'll fix it for you for nothin'."

Schwartzrock smiled sourly and shook his head. "Your mother should do me a favor for turning you loose on her again? She'd probably cut up my suit for rags." Schwartzrock crumpled up the card and threw it in his wastebasket. "Get out, Hyman, get out, get out."

He shook his head as Shapiro went out the door. He picked up the last chart and called out the name: "Al Payne."

In walked a short, sporty little man in blue hospital pajamas with the sleeves rolled up past his biceps. A blue Marine Corps emblem was tattooed on his right biceps.

"Hello, doc," said the man.

"Been here before, Payne?"

"Yes, doc."

"I thought I recognized you. Had a gastrectomy, didn't you?"

"Yeah."

"You better stop drinking or they'll be taking the rest of your insides out, Payne."

"I can't, doc."

"Well, I'm sending you away for two months to dry out and think about it."

"Doc, I fought on Guadalcanal."

"I don't give out medals, Payne. I'm a doctor. Besides, that was twenty years ago."

"I don't want a medal, doc. I got one. Two, in fact."

"Yeah, yeah, so what's the point?"

"Can't I get into the VA Hospital?"

"Nope."

"Why not?"

"Because you didn't become a drunk on Guadalcanal."

"I seen my brother get his head smashed off there, doc.

I seen his own brains on the ground with one eye lookin' up at me. That's what started me."

"The VA is full, Payne."

"O.K., doc."

The phone rang. Schwartzrock picked it up. "Schwartzrock. Yeah, this is Dr. Schwartzrock. Yeah, I know the case. Yeah. Yeah." As he listened, Schwartzrock put his hand over the mouthpiece and spoke to Payne. "O.K., Payne."

"Doc," said Payne. "Can I go back to Valley State?"

Schwartzrock checked the address on the chart. "You're in Metropolitan territory."

"How 'bout puttin' down my mother's address?"

"Where's that?"

"Five oh three East Twenty-sixth Street."

"O.K.," said Schwartzrock. He crossed out Payne's address and wrote in his mother's instead.

"Thanks, doc."

"Yeah, yeah," said Schwartzrock, speaking into the telephone and waving Payne out of the room with his free hand. As he listened on the phone he finished writing his notes on Payne's chart, tossed it into his "Out" basket, and then broke into the conversation.

"Yes, your brother has got to go to a state hospital. Am I sure? Lady, I'm the doctor. Of course I'm sure. . . . So he gets worse. He probably will. . . . I said he probably will get worse at a state hospital. . . . That's right, lady. Most people do . . . Because he'd get worse if he stayed at home, too . . . That's right. Half get worse, period. Home, state hospital, it's all the same. Half get worse. Better he should be in a state hospital where they can handle him than home choking you . . . Yeah, yeah, I think it's best, that's right."

Schwartzrock slammed down the phone, looked at his watch, and got up from his desk. "Joe!" he barked to the ward clerk. Joe, a little, potbellied Negro, came to the door.

"Joe, make up commitment papers on Al Payne. I'll be in for a while in the morning."

"Got time to see Eli Ferth for a minute?" the clerk asked. "He's been asking all afternoon to see you."

"Nope, I'm through for today."

Schwartzrock opened the side door to his office and stepped out. . . .

IV

A tall, middle-aged man with a little brown mustache entered hesitantly. It was the truck driver who had cried all night in the park. He sat down in the chair next to Schwartzrock's desk. Schwartzrock flipped the pages of the man's chart. Voluntary admission. "*Complains of nervousness and loneliness,*" the admitting doctor had scrawled on the chart.

"O.K., Jennings, what's the trouble?"

Jennings searched a moment for the right word.

"I . . . I feel I have a . . . a problem, doctor," he began with great difficulty. He felt extremely self-conscious.

Schwartzrock gave a short, mirthless laugh.

"Don't we all, Jennings, don't we all."

Jennings' face reddened with embarrassment. At that moment, another patient—an old man with white hair—came into the office, and Jennings' self-consciousness lessened for a moment.

"Is this the way out?" the old man asked. He had a glass eye in the left socket, and the socket was ringed with a crust of dry mucus. When he was at home, either his son or his daughter-in-law would clean the eye with boric acid, but no one had done it today.

"What's your name, Pop?" said Schwartzrock.

"Frank Anderson. I'm trying to find the way out."

Schwartzrock had the man's chart on his desk. He picked it up and perused the notes of the admitting psychiatrist. "*Son and daughter-in-law unable to keep this eighty-two-year-old male at home any longer. Set fire to some papers in the house last week and they are afraid he might do it again when they are not around. Wanders away from the house and becomes lost.*"

"I'll talk to you in a minute, Frank," said Schwartzrock.

"Who are you?" said Anderson.

"I'm the doctor."

"What doctor?"

"You're in the hospital."

"Well, I feel fine and I want to go home. I don't belong here. My son is keeping lunch for me."

"Wait outside, Pop," said Schwartzrock. "I'll talk to you in a minute."

"I don't want to talk to you, I just want to go home."

"Brooks!" called Schwartzrock. A slim Negro attendant, wearing sneakers and dark glasses, came to the door.

"Brooks, have him wait until I'm through here."

"Come on, Pop," said Brooks, pulling Anderson by the arm.

"I want to go home," he protested. What he really wanted was to find a toilet. He had to go to the bathroom, and he didn't know where the bathroom was. At home, he knew exactly where it was.

When Anderson had gone, Schwartzrock turned back to Jennings. "O.K., Jennings, so you have a problem."

Jennings did not know why Schwartzrock seemed to be making it difficult for him. But he could not back down now. The decision to come to City Psychiatric had taken him too long to make and had cost him too much effort. So he had to go through with it. All the posters in the subway and the ads on television said that mental illness was a disease and could be cured. He knew he was ill. He was miserable most of the time. He didn't want to live that way any longer. He had lived that way for fifteen years, and each year he had become more miserable and alone. Now he had to do something about it.

"Well?" said Schwartzrock impatiently.

Jennings swallowed. "I . . . I feel . . . well, I have difficulty driving my truck, especially at night. This very great anxiety, this fear—I had a small accident about a month ago. Since then I've had a morbid fear that I might have another accident and be hurt. And I feel. . . ."

Jennings groped for a word. "Lonely. Alone in the world. Sometimes I feel—what's the use, why not end it?"

"Why not, indeed?" asked Schwartzrock, peering intently at the man through his wire-rimmed glasses.

Jennings looked at him questioningly.

"Yes," said Schwartzrock, nodding. "Why not end it? Why not?" he repeated with a note of anger in his voice.

Jennings did not understand him. He stared at Schwartzrock speechlessly.

Schwartzrock was angry. He had heard so many idle threats of suicide; he had heard that threat made so often for the effect it would produce—for sympathy or shock—that he had contempt for anyone who alluded superficially to suicide. He always tried to call their bluff, as he had done with Jennings.

"Look, Jennings, lots of people are lonely, and I'm a very busy man, so why don't you just tell me what you want?"

"I don't *know*, doctor," said Jennings helplessly. "I need help. I thought this was the place to come."

"We're busy, Jennings; we don't have time to pass out sympathy. If we did we'd never get anything done. You have two choices. You can either go home again or you can go to a state hospital. You came voluntarily, so it's up to you. Make up your mind."

"Can't you explain anything to me?"

"What do you want to know?"

"What would they do for me at a state hospital?"

"They'd give you tranquilizers and they'd probably give you some shock treatments."

"What are they?"

"They take two electrodes, see?" said Schwartzrock, doubling up his fists and holding them out in front of him, a foot apart. "And then they put one on each side of your head." Schwartzrock held his fists at his temples. "And then they turn on the juice. *Zzzzzzz!*"

Jennings was appalled at Schwartzrock's parody.

"You want that, Jennings?"

Schwartzrock long ago had become hardened to even

the most desperate and pitiful cases he encountered. It had been a necessity. No man could have done his job for fifteen years—for even one year, seeing a thousand patients a year—and not become hardened. If he had no personal feelings for even the most pathetic and terrible cases, then for those like Jennings—the emotional weaklings, he called them—Schwartzrock's impatience approached contempt. They tried to lean on him, he felt, but he forced them to face what was, for them as for everyone else, a very harsh reality.

Jennings had stood up. He was confused, and he was afraid. There was a touch of unreality to what he was experiencing. He had come here for help, and now the experience he was going through had some of the characteristics of a bad dream. In some ways, the fear he felt now—fear of the hospital and fear of what was ahead for him now that he had come here—was worse than what he had felt outside.

"When you make up your mind," Schwartzrock said, "let me know. I'll see you again Monday. Anderson!"

As Jennings left the room, Schwartzrock filled in his diagnosis on the chart: "*Dependent personality. Borderline schizophrenic.*"

Frank Anderson entered the room and approached the desk. By now he had soiled his pajamas, and the strong, bitter smell of excrement followed him into the room.

"Shame on you, Frank," said Schwartzrock. "You're too old to do a thing like that."

Frank Anderson had never soiled himself like this before; he was filled with confusion and embarrassment.

"I did *nothing!*" he said angrily. "All I want is to go home. My son will be worried."

"Your son brought you here."

"No!"

"How old are you, Frank?"

"Forty-eight. How old are you?"

"What year is it?"

Anderson flushed uncomfortably. He realized he did not know for sure. "Nineteen twenty-eight," he said decisively, so that the man would not know he was unsure.

"And where are you now?" asked Schwartzrock.

"Where am I?"

"Yes," said Schwartzrock. "What place is this?"

"It's a jail. I don't know which one. No one told me anything."

"O.K., Frank," said Schwartzrock, beginning to write on the chart.

"I want to go *home!*" said Anderson. "I've done nothing. How can you keep me?"

"You'll go home, Frank, you'll go home," said Schwartzrock mildly. Schwartzrock had some sympathy for the very old; age was one disease that would eventually take everyone. On the chart he wrote: *"Senile psychosis. Transfer to A8 for commitment."*

Schwartzrock looked at the mucus crusted around Anderson's eye. "What's wrong with that eye?" he asked.

"Nothing!" said Anderson.

Schwartzrock shrugged. Whatever it was, it was a medical problem. They had doctors and nurses for that sort of thing. "O.K.," said Schwartzrock, "you go outside now, Frank. It's almost lunch time."

"I don't want lunch here. I have a lunch at home."

"Brooks!" called Schwartzrock. Brooks came in. "Take him outside," said Schwartzrock. "Make sure he gets some lunch."

"Come on, Pop," said Brooks, pulling Anderson by the arm.

Schwartzrock put on a white straw hat and a thin white cord jacket. Then he went out the back door of his office, which permitted him to leave without going through the ward. He was in a hurry now. He had a long schedule of appointments with his private patients during the afternoon and then a long evening of research on his new book.

THE MACHINE IN WARD ELEVEN

Charles Willeford

Charles Willeford is a recognized writer of short stories. "The Machine in Ward Eleven"* was hailed by the *Science Fiction Quarterly* as "The weirdest tale that has been published in America since Edgar Allan Poe." This essay is here reprinted in slightly abbreviated form.

I

I like Ruben. He is a nice guy. He doesn't lock my door at night. He closes it, naturally, so that none of the doctors nor any of the other nurses will notice that it isn't locked when they're just walking past, but he doesn't lock it. (An unlocked door gives me a delicately delightful sense of insecurity.) And this is the kind of thing a man appreciates in a place like this.

A little thing here is a big thing; the differences between this place and the private hospital are much greater than fifty dollars a day.

Ruben also lights my cigarettes and, what's more, he doesn't mind lighting them. The day nurse, Fred, always appears to be exasperated when I call out to him for a light. I don't blame Fred, of course. The day nurse has many things to do compared to Ruben's duties. He has to get the hallway and latrines cleaned, the privileged pa-

* From *The Machine in Ward Eleven* (New York: Belmont Books, 1963), pp. 7–35.

tients off to O.T. And all of the meals are eaten during the day, too. Fred is responsible for the cart, the collection of the trays and spoons afterward, and so on. I've never had a chance to talk much to Fred, but at night, I talk to Ruben quite a little. Which means I listen, and that's what I need to do.

The American Red Cross furnishes each patient with a carton of cigarettes every week, although there isn't any limitation—at least I don't think there is—on how many cigarettes we can smoke in a week. A carton a week is plenty for me. But we aren't allowed to have matches or a lighter. The male nurse is supposed to open the cell door and light them for us when we call him. If the nurse is busy, a man has to wait, that's all. There have been times when I've had to wait so long that when Fred or one of the loose patients (there are quite a few of these loose ones who are allowed to carry matches, and they do little odd jobs around the hospital, only their work details are called "therapy") came around to light my cigarette, I actually forgot what I called out for in the first place.

But at night it is different. The men in the other eleven (that number always makes my stomach feel queasy) cells in this locked ward are all good sleepers. Except for Old Man Reddington. Right after the supper meal, or within an hour or so, most of them are asleep. Old Man Reddington, in Number Four, has nightmares that are truly terrible. If I had nightmares like his I'd never go to sleep. But when I've mentioned his nightmares to him, he denied having any, so I guess he doesn't remember them. I wonder if I have nightmares? That's something I'll have to pump Ruben about some time. The reason I don't go to sleep early is because of my long, peaceful afternoon nap every day. I'm not allowed to go to Occupational Therapy, so when the older patients leave the ward for O.T. after lunch I'm locked in my cell. It's quiet then, and I sleep. I have nothing to think about; my memory is almost all gone, except for isolated, unsatisfactory, and unresolved little incidents. Trying to remember things, however, is a fascinating little game. . . .

II

"I don't really care, Ruben," I said to him the other night (I know it wasn't tonight), "but every week when the Gray Lady comes around with the cigarettes I get a different brand. And even though I'm satisfied with whatever brand I'm given, I don't think it's right. I realize that smoking is a privilege, but I've also concluded that any man who smoked all the time would sooner or later decide that he preferred one particular brand. And if he did, he'd buy and smoke the same brand all the time. Is it because we're crazy that we get a different brand every week, or what?"

Ruben frowned quizzically, and looked at me for a long time. He is a good-looking young guy (in a rather coarse way), twenty-five or six, with strong white teeth, and friendly enough, but when he examines me for a long time that way without replying I have a premonition that he doesn't truly like me, and that he might possibly be a doctor's spy. But then Ruben grinned fraternally, and I knew that he was all right.

"Do you know something, Blake," he said with unfeigned sincerity, "you're the only nut in my whole ward who's got good sense."

This incongruous remark struck both of us as funny, and we had to laugh. "No, seriously," Ruben went on, "that comment was a sign of progress, Blake. Do you possibly remember, from before maybe, smoking one particular brand of cigarettes? Think hard."

"No," although I didn't even try to think, "but this talk about cigarettes makes me want one. How about a light?"

"Sure," as he flipped his lighter he said, "if you ever do feel a preference for any particular brand, let me know. Nobody's trying to deliberately deprive anyone of their favorite cigarettes. But I've been working here for two years now, and you're the first patient who's even mentioned the subject."

"Then maybe I'm not so crazy after all?" I smiled.

"Oh, you're crazy all right!" Ruben laughed. "Would you like some coffee? I'm going to make a fresh pot.". . .

III

I cannot always orientate the sequence of daily events. It's probably because of the sameness here. The only real difference between day and night is that it's quieter at night (except for Old Man Reddington in Number Four); and there is quite a bit of activity in the mornings. Breakfast, the cleaning up, the doctor making his rounds, and I have my chess problems to puzzle over every morning. I work out two or three problems every morning, although I'd never admit it to Dr. Adams.

"A man's mind is a tricky thing, Blake," Dr. Adams said, the day he brought me the board and chessmen. He made this statement as though I were unaware of this basic tenet. "But if you exercise your brain every day—and I think you'll enjoy working out these chess problems—it'll be excellent therapy for you. In fact, your memory will probably come back to you in its entirety—all at once." He snapped his soft, pudgy fingers. "But I don't want you to sit around trying to remember things. That's too hard. Do you understand?" And he handed me an elementary paperback book of chess problems to go with the chess set.

"Yes, I understand, Dr. Adams." I nodded solemnly. "I understand that you're a condescending sonofabitch."

"Of course I am, Blake," he agreed easily, humoring me, "but solving chess problems is merely an exercise to help you. For instance, a person with weak arches can strengthen them by picking up marbles with his toes, and—"

"I haven't lost my marbles," I broke in angrily. "They've only rolled to one side."

"Of course, of course," he said wearily, looking away from me. I've learned how to discomfit these expressionless psychiatrists every time. I stare straight into their moronic, unblinking eyes. "But you will try to work some of the problems, won't you, Blake?"

"I might." A noncommittal answer is the only kind a headshrinker understands.

So I've never given Adams the satisfaction of knowing that I work three or four problems every morning. When he asks me how I'm getting along I tell him I'm still on the first problem in the book, although I've been through the book four times already—or is it five? Ah! Here's Ruben with my coffee.

The coffee is strong, just the way I like it, with plenty of sugar and armored cow. And Ruben is relating the story again about why he elected to become a male nurse. He's told me all this before, but each time he tells it a little differently. His fresh details don't fool me, however. He actually took the two-year junior college nursing course to be the only male student in a class of thirty-eight girls. But talking to me at night—or should I say, at me?—is probably good "therapy" for Ruben.

"By the way, Blake, your wife's scheduled to visit you tomorrow. You asked me to remind you."

"Already?" I made a clucking sound in my throat. "My, my, how time flies. It seems like only yesterday, and yet thirty happy, carefree days have sped by." I shook my head with mock dismay.

"Not for me," he said grimly. "Let me have your cup," and he closed my door.

I'm beginning to get accustomed to my wife now, but it was difficult at first. The first time she visited me I didn't even know the woman. I still don't recall marrying her or living with her before assuming the bachelor residence of this cell. But I had uncommonly good taste. Maria is a real beauty, still well under thirty, and she's a movie actress (she keeps reminding me). The first time they took me to the visiting room to see her, I made the undiplomatic mistake of asking her what her name was—and she cried. I felt so sorry for her I've never made the same mistake again. Now, when I occasionally forget that her name is Maria I call her Honey or Sweetie-pants. She likes these pet names.

We usually spend our whole hour together talking about

the movies, about technical details mostly, and she often asks me intelligent questions about acting techniques. (The doctor probably briefed her to ask me such questions to help me regain my memory, but I enjoy giving Maria advice.) I'm an expert in the field of falsely induced emotions, and although I don't remember directing any of the plays or movies or TV shows she told me I directed, I am apparently well-acquainted with all of the terms and practically every aspect of the craft—or so it seems. Maria may be lying to me, of course. It's quite possible that this vast store of film intelligence I dredge up and dispense with so freely during our monthly visits was gained by reading books on the subject before I came here. . . .

IV

I drank slowly, steadily, spacing my drinks, enjoying the silent evening and the yellow sky about Glendale far below. Hours, or many minutes later, I was giggling, lurching through the empty house in search of a razor blade. A sixty-thousand-dollar home, mortgaged for seventy-five, a swimming pool, and no blades. How can a man slash his wrists with an electric razor? The phone kept ringing all the time. Needlers. Sympathizers. At last I found a blade, a used, rusty blade, in an old plaid train case that had belonged to my wife. The ancient blade had once nibbled persistent stubble from her long legs, in all probability. I giggled again as I eased the blade with concentrated caution into a fresh cake of soap. I didn't want to accidentally cut the fingers holding the blade—too painful—and yet I wanted to slice my wrists. Such paradoxical prudence was very amusing indeed.

The private hospital was a warm white womb.

There was a glass-enclosed porch parallel to the end of our ward, and the meals were served right on schedule in the dining room. I liked every one of my fellow eighteen patients—a charming, mixed-up group—and I would have been content to remain dormant in this friendly ward forever. My closest friend was Dave Tucker, an actor who had been possessed (literally) by the devil. He had played *The Devil and Daniel Webster* in summer stock a few months before, and while he was immersed in the role of Daniel, the devil had actually managed to get inside of his skin. Our unimaginative doctor, unfortunately, couldn't exorcize the devil from poor old Dave because the psychiatrist didn't believe that the devil was really under Dave's hide.

"The worst thing about Him, J.C.," Dave told me, scratching under his pajama jacket, "is the constant itching. He squirms around so much I itch all the time, and scratching can't get to Him."

Poor Dave. I believed him, of course. Why would any man lie about something like that? But I still couldn't resist giving Dave the business once in a while. "Your case is the inevitable result of method acting," I told him, "but it could've been worse."

"How's that?"

"You could've been playing *Jumbo*."

"Move," he said irritably, clawing his chest, "it's your move." And we continued our chess game on the sunny porch.

I see now that it was a mistake to become friendly with Dave Tucker, or for that matter, with anyone. It hurt me too much—it was only a few days later—when the devil finally got him. We were playing chess again, smoking, not saying much of anything when Dave urgently stage-whispered my name: "Jake! Get the doctor, somebody! He turned on the heat!"

I looked up from the chessboard, startled. Dave's handsome face was as fiery as a record jacket featuring exotic Hawaiian music. There was no perspiration; the devil had caught Dave in an unguarded moment, and he didn't even have time to perspire.

I rushed frantically into the ward, yelling my head off for the doctor. And I returned to the porch with Dr. Fellerman within a minute and a half—two minutes at most—but Dave was dead. The devil had boiled Dave's blood for him and fled. I was unreasonable then, more than a little hysterical, and I cursed Fellerman for all he was worth (which wasn't much), although it hadn't been entirely his fault. It was a matter of time; the devil would have taken Dave sooner or later anyway. But the swiftness of the attack unnerved me, and I had a long miserable crying spell.

After Dave, I dropped out of sight. No more friends for me. Not after Dave. I simply couldn't stand the emotional damage, and I was wise enough to see that much. . . .

V

Before retiring to my walled-in secret garden—before Dave—I'd been on the Camino Real, the road to recovery. All of the senseless oral and written psychological tests had been taken docilely; the tiny needles had been inserted into my scalp for the recording of the brain waves; and I had been a reluctant, but participating, member of Ward Fourteen's Group Therapy group. We met on Mondays, Wednesdays and Fridays at 11 A.M. in Ward Eleven, under the joint chairmanship of Doctors Fellerman and Mullinare.

There were four of us, not counting the two doctors (they merely observed and listened): Tommy Amato, a seventeen-year-old boy, the son of a well-known male movie star, and every night Tommy drowned his bed; Randolph Hicks, an ex-hotel manager who had deliberately crashed his car and now had a corrugated skull and a permanent eye-squinting headache; Marvin Morris, a pop songwriter, who, like me, had attempted suicide unsuccessfully—and there was me.

I never did understand fully what we were supposed to accomplish during these triweekly sessions. The doctors never uttered a sound; they sat impassively in their metal folding chairs looking us over like a pair of bespectacled owls caught out at high noon. We, the sick ones, were supposed to talk out our problems; I believe that was the general idea. But the atmosphere in the scaly, gray-walled ward was not conducive to talk of any kind; it was too depressing. The first five minutes of each meeting was always awkward, taut with the clearings of dry apprehensive throats.

Ward Eleven was an unused ward, pressed into service as a group therapy meeting place because of hospital space shortage, and we sat around in a rough semicircle, chain-smoking cigarettes. It was difficult to keep our eyes away from the six unoccupied mattresses—each covered with a soiled white sheet—on the floor near the doorway. The electroshock machine rested on a small gray table in one corner of the room, and there was a padded, rubber-sheeted treatment table beside it. When the shock treatments were given early in the morning, the unconscious bodies were deposited on the mattresses until they awakened, and then the dazed patients were led away to eat breakfast. No, this ward was not an inspiring meeting hall to discuss problems of the mind.

It's against federal law to photograph nuts in a Funny Factory, but these group therapy sessions were great human comedies that should have been captured on film. They were the kind of comedies that cause strong men to weep copious tears. Albert McCleery would have loved to film them on television's Cameo Theater, cutting back and forth from one place to the next.

After the nervous silence became almost unbearable, young Tommy was invariably first to break into the uneasiness.

"I wet my bed again last night." A simple statement of fact. Tommy was no longer embarrassed by his chronic enuresis, now that the doctors had convinced him that his was a psychosomatic condition, and he felt that we older men could help him. We were grateful to Tommy every time, of course, for breaking the sound barrier, and we wanted to help him.

"Ah, did you try elevating your feet?" Marvin would ask eagerly.

"Yes, I slept with three pillows under my feet last night, but they didn't do any good."

And then the group therapy session was underway. Once started, it was easier to talk than it was to just stare at each other. We discussed the movies, B.B., Russia, bridge, paperback novels, the quality of the hospital food, taxes, the L.A. traffic problem, the long distance dial system; everything; everything, in fact, except our individual and personal problems. Tommy, however, was always provided with fresh, thoughtful suggestions for his little problem—not that any of them ever worked. The two doctors never took notes, they never made any comments or suggestions, and they never attempted to steer our conversations. For their silence we were grateful, all of us, and I believe we did our best to entertain them so they wouldn't be too bored during their listening-in hour. But maybe the meetings did the doctors some good—I really don't know. After Dave, I refused flatly to attend the mental torture sessions anymore.

Ward Fourteen wasn't a locked ward, and within the hospital we had considerable freedom. There were movies at night (16 mm) in the patients' lounge. There was a library, a TV set on the porch, and there was a snack bar where the patients could sit around drinking coffee and eating sandwiches between meals. But I gave up these frivolous activities for the fulltime occupation of my uncomfortable bedside chair. I ate my three full meals every day, marching to the dining room with the others when it was our ward's turn to eat, but I returned immediately to my chair. After supper each night I went to bed, and slept dreamlessly until 6:30 A.M. I could've slept all the time, I think, but we weren't allowed on our beds during the day. Unable to drowse in my hard metal chair, I meditated and read, meditated and read again—and it was always the same book: *The Silent Life*, by Thomas Merton.

I was fascinated by these accounts of monastic life; the Carthusians, particularly, with their isolated hermitages, were brilliant men who had found the right answer to the complexities of life, and I was saddened by the knowledge that I could never be one of them. These holy monks had a curious mixture of humility and vanity I could never hope to achieve. They believed that if they were humble enough they would see God when they died—surely this was a naive vanity—so innocent and touching the tears welled from my eyes. But I knew that God would never look at a wretch like me. However, there was another path, and now that I had time to think—more time than I'd ever had in my life before—the tantalizing challenge appealed to me more and more. To reach the top wasn't really difficult; I'd been up there three times already—but the pyramid at the bottom was much broader.

How many American males had consciously directed every effort to achieving the absolute bottom of the pile, burrowing their way deliberately to the exact center of the bottom of humanity? If I could only get down there, really down, all the way down, without any outside help—ah!—here was a unique and terrible aspiration! How? How? An intelligent man could meditate for years on this fascinating challenge!

VI

My deliberations were interrupted one morning by Dr. Fellerman. He had approached my bed in a surreptitious manner and tapped me on the shoulder. He asked me if I would like to talk to him alone in his office twice a week.

"I've got an hour open on Thursday, Mr. Blake, and another on Monday. I'll squeeze you in."

"Squeeze in somebody else," I told him coldly. "I have nothing to say to you." Unbidden, uninvited, he had interrupted a very important train of thought, and I glared at him to express my annoyance. Fellerman was a tall, almost cadaverous man, with a concave chest. His face was lined, tired; an ostensibly overworked man. In his loose, knee-length white coat, with his humped shoulders, and with his narrow head cocked to one side, he always reminded me of an unskilled mechanic listening to an unidentifiable engine knock.

"And you won't return to our little group therapy sessions, either?"

"No. But if I come up with a valid suggestion for Tommy Amato's bed-wetting problem," I said sarcastically, "I'll write it down and give it to him in the dining room."

I arose from my chair, turned my back on the doctor,

and sat down again facing the wall, thereby terminating the unwelcome interview. This brief discussion took place on a Monday afternoon. On Wednesday morning, right after breakfast, the male nurse, Luchessi, told me that I had to visit Dr. Fellerman's office. Any mental patient has the privilege of arguing with his doctor, but only a crazy man will argue with a male nurse. Without protest, I accompanied Luchessi to Fellerman's private office.

"Mr. Blake," Fellerman said calmly, without preamble, "I've decided to give you a short series of nine electroshock treatments." The sentence was a nail on a slate.

The hand, my right, carrying the cigarette to my mouth, was arrested in midair. I was frightened, yes, but my astonishment was even greater. The hair at the nape of my neck bristled; goose bumps crawled on my arms. The six, white-sheeted mattresses on the floor in Ward Eleven appeared vividly, sickeningly, in my mind. And the small electroshock machine, which resembled a cheap portable phonograph when the lid was closed, became a leather-covered symbol of terror—sudden, terrible death!

"No!" I blurted, shaking my head. "You aren't serious!"

He shrugged. "I don't know what else to do with you, Mr. Blake. You won't help yourself, you won't attend the group therapy sessions, you've refused private conferences. Do you still believe that it was the devil, instead of apoplexy, that killed your actor friend, Mr. Tucker?"

I said nothing; he was trying to trap me.

"You aren't getting any better, and the shock treatments will help you."

"Depression is something I can learn to live with," I said bitterly, "but I can't live with death."

"Now you're being melodramatic."

"Am I? How many people survive electric shock treatments?"

"The fatality percentage is so small, it's practically unimportant."

"It's important to me! What is the percentage?"

"I don't know offhand; less than one fatality in every three or four thousand, if that high—"

"Nine treatments in a row drops those odds down to a damned dangerous level!"

"If we thought there was any real danger, Mr. Blake," he said quietly, "we wouldn't give you shock therapy. You're a strong healthy man, although you're a little overweight. To lessen the convulsion, we'll give you curare to relax you first."

"Poison? If the shock doesn't kill me, the curare will! Is that the idea?"

"I assure you, you have nothing to worry about. The treatments start tomorrow. Don't go to breakfast in the morning."

"And if I refuse?"

"Don't you want to get well?"

"Not if I have to take shock treatments, I don't!"

"There's no pain, none whatsoever."

"I don't care about pain, but I don't want to lose my memory. My memories may be bitter, but they're all I've got left and I want every single one of them."

"There's a slight loss of memory, but it's only a temporary condition—"

"Well, I refuse to take the treatments. And that's final!" The cigarette burned my fingers, and I dropped it into his desk ashtray—a white ceramic skull. The ashtray alone, if more evidence was needed, gave the key to the psychiatrist's sadistic nature.

"The choice isn't yours to make," he reminded me gently.

"You're frightening me now, Doctor—"

"You needn't be. Your wife has consented to the treatments, and—"

"I don't believe you!"

"It's true, nevertheless. Don't build these simple treatments up out of all proportion in your mind. If all goes well, as expected, you may not need all nine of them. Sometimes six are plenty, and you'll be going home before you know it."

"But I don't *want* to go home." I wailed unhappily. The tears I could no longer restrain washed my face. "All I want, all I ever wanted, is to be let alone . . ." Blubbering childishly into my sleeve I stumbled blindly out of the office and Luchessi took me back to the ward.

VII

Later, and considerably calmer, I realized upon reflection that most of my knowledge about electroshock therapy had been learned second-hand from a fellow patient, Nathan Wanless, during idle bull sessions on the porch. Unintentionally, Nate had implanted dread of the little machine in my head by innocently underplaying the description of his own course of treatments.

"I didn't mind too much, Mr. Blake," he told me quietly. His eyes already had a puzzled expression, and at the time he had only had three treatments. "On the first one I asked to go first, you see, because I was a little scared and wanted to get it over with. I climbed up on the table in Ward Eleven and four male nurses—Luchessi's one of them—grabbed me by the pajamas and bathrobe. One guy held both feet. When the old electricity shoots through your brain you get one hellova big convulsion, and if these guys didn't hold you in a tight brace you'd get your back broken. It'd snap like a match. Anyway, Dr. Fellerman slipped the little harness over my head and it's got a chromium electrode that clamps tight over each temple. Then they stick a curved piece of rubber hose in your mouth to bite down on and that's it."

"What do you mean, that's it?" I asked him tensely.

"Blooey, that's all."

"Blooey?"

"Blooey. I didn't feel anything. Next thing I know I'm awake and looking up at the ceiling, flat on my back on one of the mattresses in Ward Eleven. You know the—"

"I know, I know. But what did you feel? Did you have any screwy dreams while you were out, anything like that?"

"No, just blooey, that's all. One minute I was wide awake, a little scared, looking up at Dr. Fellerman, and then I was on the mattress looking at the ceiling instead.

A funny feeling. Soon's the nurse sees you're awake, he sends you across the hall, to the little kitchen in Ward Ten for scrambled eggs. Ward Ten's the locked ward, you know."

"I know. But there must be more to the treatments than that, Nate. You make the whole business sound too simple."

"It is simple, Mr. Blake. The second time I watched some of the other guys take theirs to see how it worked, and that was it. Soon's the electrodes are in place Dr. Fellerman turns on the two knobs on the machine. There can't be more'n one hundred and ten volts, because the cord's just plugged into the wall socket. All the same, I imagine Dr. Fellerman watches the needle pretty close."

"What needle?"

"There's a needle on the gauge. The machine might be pre-set, but I don't think there's any rheostat, so when the needle hits the right number on the gauge the doctor turns off the machine. And that's it."

"The patient on the table. What kind of convulsion does he have?"

"You can't really tell, not with all those guys holding him and all. All in all, I guess, it's a very humane machine. I imagine the electric chair works the same way when they execute somebody. They put the guy in the chair, flip the old switch, and blooey, that's all. Of course," Nate frowned thoughtfully, "they have to strap the guy into the electric chair because the electricity's so much more powerful." He giggled. "The guy's back must get broken anyway, but he's dead by that time so it doesn't make any difference."

"The analogy—electric chair and shock machine—doesn't seem quite humane to me, Nate." I shuddered.

"Why not? It doesn't hurt you none. Blooey, that's all, except that on shock treatments you wake up later. In the electric chair you don't—not in this lousy world anyway."

Nate Wanless was no longer with us. The course of shock treatments had helped him—perhaps they had eliminated his mental depression altogether—and he had been discharged from the hospital. But after a few treatments he'd developed a frowning, perplexed expression. He was unable to recall entering the hospital, or any of the events that had led up to his admission. I had talked to him several times before his release, and except for his memory block, which worried him very little, he was a rational, perfectly normal—nothing—that was it, nothing! He was neither excited nor depressed. He was stonily indifferent to his past and future, and he had believed Dr. Fellerman when he was told that his memory would return, all in good time. . . .

VIII

My palms were wet. My throat was dry. For the first time in my life I knew true fear! Ordinary fear was a familiar emotion I'd known intimately, many times—the fear of losing an arm or a leg in battle, when I had fought (for a blissfully short three months toward the very end) in Korea; the fear of being absolutely broke; the fear of success and the fear of failure; and certainly, the fear of death. And I had also known that secret, unvoiced fear, the kind no one ever admits to anyone, and only rarely to himself; the unknown terror of afterdeath. Is there an afterlife or is there not? And if there is, how will a man fare there? Will he be able to withstand the punishment meted out to him according to his earthly record?

But what were any of these childish, mundane fears in comparison with the worst fear on earth, the worst possible misfortune that could happen to mortal man? The fear of becoming a vegetable. Could any misfortune be worse?

His memories, his ability to laugh at his follies and stupidities—when the chips were finally down, these were the only things a man had left to him. Otherwise, a man is a pine tree, a turnip, a daisy, a weed, existing through the grace of the sun and photosynthesis during the day, and ridding himself of excess carbon dioxide during the long night. I was still a fairly young man; if the choice had been the simple one of life and death I could have accepted it, I believe, at any age. Perhaps I could have even feigned some kind of insouciant bravery if I had to choose death—I didn't really know.

But I had only to go to the glass windows on the porch and look out over the verdant hospital grounds. From the windows I could always see three or four hospitalized human vegetables sitting on their benches beneath the sun. Most of them were old men, white-thatched, harmless, of course, and when the weather was nice they were allowed to remain outside all day long. They never bothered anyone, they didn't think, they couldn't remember anything, not even their names, and their ability to laugh was completely gone. Plants. Vegetables.

Mental patients live for an uncommonly long time, and I was only thirty-two. I was also gifted with that accursed trait that every director or actor must have to achieve any measure of success in the world of make-believe: the ability to put myself in someone else's place. Empathy. I could project myself now into the future, near and far; Blake the Vegetable, sitting in the sunlight year after year until he was a feeble, drooling old man of eighty—no, ninety!—the damned busy-body medicos were learning more about geriatrics every day.

No longer was I J. C. Blake the Arrogant, the one man in Hollywood who had never taken anything from anybody. I was transformed instantaneously by my cool, logical imagination into Blake the Abject, Blake the Beggar, Blake the Craven. All right, then. If Dr. Fellerman wanted me to crawl I would crawl. If he wanted me humbled, if he wanted his feet washed, I would wash his feet and anoint them with scented oils. The gelid dread that twisted my entrails was panicky, and there was so little time! The clock above Luchessi's desk told me that it was 11:40. I had to see Fellerman now, before he left the hospital at noon. When tomorrow morning came it would be too late; they would inject their South American curare into my veins and then destroy my fine mind forever with their machine. Controlling my inner conflict as well as I could I approached Luchessi's desk.

"You should've reminded me," I said, smiling, "about the group therapy session in Ward Eleven."

"I thought you dropped out of group therapy?" But he wasn't suspicious; he was already filling in a hall pass for me.

"I did, Luchessi, but I was supposed to start back today. That's what the doctor wanted to see me about this morning."

"You're late, you know." Luchessi frowned as he handed me the pass. "But it isn't my fault."

"I know; it's mine, but I simply forgot about it. It's probably too late to go at all now, but if I didn't make the attempt Dr. Fellerman would say that I was being uncooperative. You know how he is."

"Sure. You'd better get a move on."

I had escaped legally from the ward, and if an official stopped me in the corridor on my way to Ward Eleven the pass would be a valid ticket. When I reached the ward the group therapy meeting was just breaking up. Tommy Amato was the first patient through the door. I nodded absently to him before he could start a conversation, brushed by the other three emerging patients and entered the ward. Dr. Fellerman and Dr. Mullinare were still seated in their metal chairs at the far end of the ward—holding a post-mortem on the session, I supposed. I hesitated, not allowing myself to look to the right, toward the shock machine and treatment table.

"Well, hello there, Blake!" Mullinare called out cheerily. "Long time no see." (This Mullinare character was a real cornball.)

"Good morning, Dr. Mullinare," I responded pleasantly. "Sorry to intrude on you gentlemen this way, but I wanted to talk for a few moments with Dr. Fellerman." I moved toward them, holding myself erect, my back stiff.

"That's quite all right, Blake," Fellerman said. "We're finished here." He winked at Mullinare. "Call me tonight, Kevin, and we'll see."

"Sure." Mullinare clasped my shoulder with a meaty,

sweaty hand. "We've missed you at our little sessions, Blake," he said lightly.

"I've missed them, too, Doctor," I lied. "Perhaps Dr. Fellerman will let me rejoin the group."

Mullinare didn't reply. He left the ward, closing the doors behind him. I wet my parched lips, wondering how to begin. The rehearsed, practiced silence peculiar to psychiatrists puts every patient on the defensive from the first moment on. These doctors rarely, if ever, ask questions, except perhaps with their incurious, unblinking eyes. But even their eyes are distorted unnaturally, as a rule, behind glasses. Fellerman, his skinny shoulders hunched, his narrow head cocked to the right as he looked up at me from his seated position, gave me no help. How could any man, a human being, approach such a machine?

"I've been hoping, sir," I began humbly—and I regretted the lack of a Balkan peasant cap that could have been snatched respectfully from my head as I began to address him—"that you might reconsider your idea of putting me on shock treatments. My attitude has been poor all along, sir, and I realize that now. And I apologize, most sincerely. If I am to help myself, I must cooperate fully with you and the other doctors. And I want you to know, Dr. Fellerman, I'm ready to turn over a new leaf. If you'll only allow me to do so, I'll return gladly to the group therapy sessions. And if you still have those two free hours open you mentioned I'd like to take advantage of them, too. Why," I smiled, "when I finally got it through this thick dumb head of mine, Doctor, that I was only hurting myself by my incorrigible attitude, I began to feel better right away. Yes, sir, and that's the truth! Why I'm not nearly so depressed as I was when I talked to you earlier this morning!"

I essayed a light laugh then, and it was indeed a pitiful, strangling sound. Is there anything more heartrending than the forced sound of false gaiety?

"And what's more, sir," I plodded on, "I think my change in attitude will be beneficial to my fellow patients too. I really do. Outside in the hall just now, when I bumped into Tommy Amato, my heart went out to that young boy.

I realized how selfish I've been all along, thinking only of myself instead of others. And as you remember, Doctor, I talked quite a bit at group therapy, just as much if not more than any of the other patients. I've got a good mind, Dr. Fellerman, and if I truly put all of my intelligence to work, I'll bet you any amount you care to wager that I can come up with a valid solution to Tommy's bed-wetting problem. Yes, sir! If you'll just cancel those shock treatments I'll get a notebook and pencil and I'll start working on young Tommy's problem right away. I know it sounds funny, now that I'm a mental patient, but when I was in college I got straight A's in Logic. And I'll just bet you, sir" (for a brief instant I considered injecting another forced, merry little laugh into my monologue, but I swiftly changed my mind, knowing I couldn't pull it off convincingly) "that once I solve Tommy's problem I'll also solve my own!

"From what little knowledge I have about Freud—of course, I don't pretend to know nearly as much as you do, what with your wonderful training and the brilliant record you've established, and all—but it's a sign of progress, isn't it? I mean, when a mental patient begins to think about the feelings of others instead of just himself, isn't that a sign of recovery? Well, maybe not. But what I want to get over to you is that I'm not in any badly depressed state any longer. Shock treatments are for people who really need them, and when we get into our private consultations—just the two of us—I don't like to confess to really personal experiences in a group therapy session, but when it's just you and me, I'll tell you everything!"

I lowered my voice confidentially, to an intimate level.

"Sex, for instance. I know how interested you psychiatrists are in sex, and you are aware, of course, that I'm married to Maria Chavez, the movie star. Well, when we were first married we were very much in love, you see. And we did all kinds of things together when we made love. I know you're anxious to go to lunch now, but when we meet alone I'll tell you every tiny detail. I'll make some notes, so I don't forget a single moment of it. With my screen experience I've learned how to tell a story well, and I'll tell you all about our love life together so you'll be able to get a real vicarious thrill out of it. I'll do anything, anything, only please, please, please—!"

I was unable to continue; my invention had flagged. Dr. Fellerman's expression hadn't changed once. Nothing I had said (or possibly could say) made any impression on the man. I dropped abjectly to my knees and kissed his shoes. He wore black, rather old-fashioned, high-topped shoes, and white socks. I was furious with myself because I couldn't cry. The needed tears refused to flow, and I had a desperate need for every crutch on the emotional scale to elicit sympathy from this stone, this dehumanized machine.

"Get up, Blake, get up from the floor," Fellerman ordered quietly.

"Yes, sir." I scrambled hurriedly to my feet. "You'll take me back into group therapy, sir? And you won't put me on shock treatments."

He got up, stretching his long skinny arms as he yawned, and yawn he did. "No, Blake, I'm convinced that electroshock treatments will do you a lot of good." Without a backward glance he started toward the exit doors.

Before he took three steps I caught up with him. My fingers dug into his neck before he could cry out. He struggled, but he didn't have a chance. I kicked his feet out from under him and followed him to the floor, still clutching his scrawny neck. I squeezed relentlessly until my fingers tingled with pain, but the moment I was positive his limpness was unfeigned I dragged his unconscious body to the treatment table in the corner. Using ripped strips of a sheet I took from one of the mattresses on the floor, I quickly tied his body to the table. As I began to stuff his slack mouth with wadded paper towels from the pile on the smaller table, Fellerman gagged slightly and opened his eyes. Without his thick glasses, which had been dislodged during our unrehearsed wrestling match, Dr. Fellerman's big brown eyes were very expressive indeed, particularly when my fumbling fingers adjusted the elastic harness over his head and I centered the shiny electrodes to his temples.

A simple, impersonal, uncomplicated machine. I plugged the long cord into the wall outlet, turned the two plastic knobs as far to the right as they would go and left them there. The sensitive needle on the gauge banged against the red plus-pole so hard it almost bent, jiggled slightly, and remained there without a quiver. The body convulsions were terrible to see, and I turned my head away. I couldn't bear the sight of this long skinny body buckling and jerking beneath the steady flow of electricity. I lit a cigarette and left the ward. As I hurried down the corridor (it was time to get into the lunch line for the march to the dining room) I considered the involved technical problems of capturing this unusual scene on film. Handled exactly right, the scene would scare the hell out of any average movie audience. Good background music was mandatory. When a man takes six or seven aspirin tablets his ears ring; this amplified ringing sound would be excellent on the sound track. But if the scene weren't done perfectly—only one little slipup, and a nervous audience would burst into a giggling, embarrassed type of laughter. A point of view would have to be decided upon—Fellerman's or mine? Here was a scene that couldn't be left to the discreet, unblinking eye of the camera—no.

IX

My transfer to the state hospital came through quickly, but I was never given electroshock treatments. They gave me insulin shock treatments instead. Every morning they awakened me at 3 A.M., dragging me down the corridor kicking and screaming to a dark little room where I was tied hands and feet to another bed and my veins were filled with insulin. And there they destroyed my mind, or so they thought. The dreams under insulin were too real to be dreams, but I finally had enough of the horrors to stop fighting them. And when I stopped fighting them, they stopped the treatments. My spirit isn't broken yet, but they don't know it, by God!

"Are you all right, Blake?" Ruben's voice is genuinely concerned. "What's the matter?"

"I'm all right, Ruben. Every once in a long while a peal of that screwy laughter gets away from me inadvertently. I'm sorry. But after all, if I weren't crazy I wouldn't be locked up permanently in the State Asylum for the Criminally Insane—or would I?"

"Take it easy, Blake. You don't want to get Old Man Reddington started, do you?" He closed the door; this time he locked it.

I like Ruben. He is a nice guy. But I'll have to watch myself more carefully, particularly that wild dramatic laughter. So long as I keep my big mouth shut and do everything they tell me to (within reason), I'll be able to stay here forever. I doubt if they would ever try me now for the murder of Fellerman, but if they found out that most of my memory has returned, they'd return me to the outside world again as soon as they could. After all, I still haven't reached rock bottom yet, and I must bear in mind that the competition for my hard-won private cell is getting keener all the time.

All the time. . . .

18

SANITY THROUGH SUFFOCATION*

From *Medical World News*

> The most recent fashions in "psychiatric treatment" might be dismissed as absurd or ridiculous were they not so real and terrifying. The following report shows that, by failing to prosecute its perpetrators as criminals, the medical and psychiatric professions, in capitalist and Communist countries alike, have become the sworn enemies of individual freedom and dignity. It remains only for the general public to more clearly support such quasi-medical methods of social control, and the Age of Madness will perhaps have reached its zenith.

Before psychiatrists and tranquilizers came on the scene, the violent inmate of an insane asylum was put in a padded cell or straitjacket. If that didn't make him behave, he was likely to be beaten or immersed in cold water—what might now be considered aversive therapy of an unacceptably brutal kind.

Two state institutions in California have recently experimented with succinylcholine—the "vanishing" muscle relaxant that anesthesiologist Carl F. Coppolino used to mur-

---

* From "Scaring the Devil Out: Two coast prisons have been using succinylcholine as an aversion tool to make incorrigibles think they're going to die," *Medical World News*, 11:29–30 (Oct. 9), 1970.

der his wife—as a modern aversive tool. The institutions have been using succinylcholine on criminally violent men who keep assaulting others or mutilating themselves—and on whom nothing else is said to have worked. More than 100 men at the Atascadero State Hospital for the criminal insane and at the California Medical Facility in Vacaville, a prison psychiatric institution, have received intravenous injections of 20 mg to 40 mg of succinylcholine. This dosage, about the same as an anesthesiologist would use in operative procedures, is sufficient to induce general paralysis and respiratory arrest lasting up to two minutes.

At Vacaville, most of the prisoners signed consent forms. But in five cases, the hospital's special treatment board authorized the treatments even though the inmates declined to give their consent. And at Atascadero, consent was neither requested nor obtained.

The treatment is, frankly, fear-producing. The subject remains fully conscious as he goes through a sensation of suffocation akin to drowning. While the psychiatrist intones reminders that the man's acting-out behavior has brought him to this pass, the therapist assures the subject that he will be able to breathe again and suggests group psychotherapy or other ways to amend the behavior. When the apnea passes, the psychiatrist stops talking, and the man is soon returned to his ward.

Both California institutions report that this therapy has worked. That is, the prisoners haven't committed as many disciplinary infractions afterwards. And the psychiatrists say there have been no complications, either. But both institutions have nonetheless halted the treatments. Atascadero State Hospital, which originated the aversion therapy and gave it to 90 inmates, was ordered last December 24 to stop it unless and until the therapists could come up with a research protocol that could win the approval of the Department of Mental Hygiene's research advisory council.

Explains the department's deputy director, Dr. Elmer F. Galioni: "The preliminary report I saw didn't answer enough questions and didn't show that succinylcholine could do an awful lot more than other forms of operant conditioning or, say, suggestion under sodium amytal. A clinical impression that the treatment is useful doesn't justify its ongoing use."

Thus rebuked, Dr. Sterling W. Morgan, the hospital superintendent, Dr. Martin J. Reimringer, psychiatrist and assistant medical director, and Dr. Paul F. Bramwell, a clinical psychologist, have no plans to resurrect the treatment, though in a published paper they call for "carefully controlled studies." The researchers reported that their patients, including the "overtly psychotic, mentally retarded, and sociopathic," were selected on the basis of "frequent fights, verbal threatening, deviant sexual behavior, and stealing" plus unresponsiveness to the hospital's group therapy programs. The team went on to say that the standard ways of handling such behavior—medication, transfer to the disturbed ward, or temporary restraints— are "both time-consuming and costly in terms of benefit to the patient."

Succinylcholine was chosen, the authors say, because in the conscious patient it "produces a decidedly unpleasant and fearful sensation during which the sensorium is intact and the patient rendered susceptible to suggestion." Yet the drug is hydrolized so quickly by the body's cholinesterase that complete recovery from the single dose usually takes place within five minutes. Oxygen and positive-pressure breathing equipment were kept on hand, since the drug can cause bradycardia. . . .

Taking his cue from Atascadero, Dr. David Owens, then chief medical officer at the Vacaville prison hospital, launched a similar treatment program several years ago. "I had a desperate problem with a man who had had about 15 laparotomies for removal of sharpened bed springs he had swallowed," recalls the psychiatrist. "We tried group psychotherapy, individual therapy, tranquilizers, antidepressants, and shock, to no avail. Finally, we tried succinylcholine, and we stopped his self-mutilative behavior." . . .

With the succinylcholine therapy, says Dr. Owens, overburdened prison psychiatrists can cope with acting-out behavior and prisoners can get out of "stir" sooner.

The 15 succinylcholine-treated men at Vacaville, who were followed up, subsequently accumulated 29.5% fewer disciplinary reports than they had in the same period of time prior to treatment. For a control group of 18 prisoners, who signed consent forms but were not treated, the decrease was 22.9%.

Despite the equivocal results, Vacaville psychologist Arthur Mattocks believes succinylcholine is useful. He feels the non-treatment group may have been deterred by the prospect of treatment. Indeed, Dr. Arthur G. Nugent, chief psychiatrist at Vacaville, says the main reason succinylcholine has not been used for the past 18 months is that nobody wants to consent to it. "The prison grapevine worked fast," he says, "and even the toughest have come to fear and hate the drug. I don't blame them—I wouldn't have the treatment myself for the world."

EPILOGUE

From the dawn of civilization to our day, the chronicles of man's inhumanity to man play a large and characteristic role. Every age and civilization has its own typical modes of interpersonal and social control which determine the ways in which human beings "use" themselves and each other. Recent political barbarities notwithstanding, modern man prides himself—with some justification—on having overcome and abolished time-honored patterns of organized inhumanities, such as cannibalism and slavery.

The taming of man's inhumanity to man, however, is a slow and uncertain process. No age in recorded history, including our own, has cause for self-congratulation. Indeed, as the accounts of involuntary mental hospitalization and treatment assembled in this volume show, modern man, with the aid of science and medicine, has developed an especially abhorrent method of controlling his fellow man.

As physicians came to share in the power of the modern state, they, too, succumbed to its corrupting influence. It is difficult to see how they could have escaped this fate any more than any other group of men could. The only protection from this corroding effect of power, as all history teaches us, is limits on power. To the extent that constraints on psychiatric power have been insufficient or lacking, the psychiatrist became his patient's political superior and hence often his personal oppressor.

Man's struggle against the inhumanity of his fellow man is as eternal, and as finite, as human life itself. One thing is clear: the individual cannot delegate the task of defending his basic human rights—to dignity, liberty, and responsibility—to any group of protectors, be they priests, politicians, or psychiatrists. For if the protectors are successful, they inevitably become oppressors; or as Bertrand Russell put it, "It is the fate of rebels to found new orthodoxies."[1] Hence, protection of the weak from the strong must forever rest on the precise recognition of the danger that threatens the former from the latter: this is the first, and most important, defense against it. The pieces assembled in this collection are offered in the hope that they might be of value in recognizing the nature and extent of the threat which institutional psychiatry poses to modern man.

What can the individual do to resist this or any other kind of threat to his independence? For an adequate answer, the reader must search the classic works of men of letters, and, above all, the stirrings of his own soul. I shall conclude by citing some comments on this timeless human problem by one of the greatest literary figures of our day, Albert Camus. In *The Plague* Camus presents a moving parable on the individual's adaptation to coercion, specifically, to totalitarian power: he shows how some men accept evil, how others co-operate with it, and how still others resist it, however feeble and unavailing their efforts might be. At the end of the story, Camus has this to say about his protagonist, Dr. Rieux:

". . . Dr. Rieux resolved to compile this chronicle, so that he should not be one of those who hold their peace but should bear witness in favor of those plague-stricken people; so that some memorial of the injustice and outrage done them might endure; and to state quite simply what we learn in a time of pestilence: that there are more things to admire in men than to despise.

"None the less, he knew that the tale he had to tell

---

[1] Bertrand Russell, "The Psychoanalyst's Nightmare," in *Nightmares of Eminent Persons* (London: Bodley Head, 1954), p. 21.

could not be one of final victory. It could only be the record of what had to be done, and what assuredly would have to be done again in the never ending fight against terror and its relentless onslaughts, despite their personal afflictions, by all who, while unable to be saints but refusing to bow down to pestilence, strive their utmost to be healers."[2]

[2] Albert Camus, *The Plague* (1947), trans. by Stuart Gilbert (New York: The Modern Library, 1948), p. 278.

INDEX

INDEX

Act for Regulating Madhouses (1774), 7
Age of Faith, 1–4
Age of Reason, 2–4
Agrippa, quoted, 28
America. *See* United States
American Journal of Insanity, 77 n; on democracy as mental disease, 47; on madness and blackness, 43–46
American Psychiatric Association, 23; position statement on medical treatment of the mentally ill, 231–41
Animal Farm (Orwell), xi
Atascadero hospital, 357, 358
Athenaeum, 47
Atlantic Monthly, The, 300 n
Augusta Triumphans (Defoe), 7–9
Austria, Kraus on madness and morality in, 127–41

Bachrach (government councilor), 137
Bateson, Gregory, 29–30
Bavaria, Ludwig II of, 82–83
Beedy, William, 59, 60
Benedikt, and Coburg case, 128–29
Berkley, Dr., Benjamin Rush on, 27
Betegek és Bolondok (Karinthy), 161–70
Bicêtre, 22
Bickford, J. A. R., 193–97
Blacks and blackness (Negroes): first patient admitted to Dorothy Dix Hospital, 48–49; madness and, *American Journal of Insanity* on, 43–46
Blakeburn, Ralph, 200
Bluebottle, The (Tarsis), 177
Bonfield, Thomas P., 62
"Boodle gang," the, 84–88
Bowman, Karl, 234–35
Boyd, B. A., 226 ff.
Boyle, Earl and Beverly, 225
Braceland, Francis J., 231
Bradley, John, 201–2
Bramwell, Paul F., 358

Brisslington, Fox's asylum at, 29 ff.
Britain. *See* England
Brown, J. W., 64–67
Bruton, Peter, 217
Burke, on belief, 27

California, use of suffocating drug in, 356–59
Camus, Albert, 361–62
Canada, Fawcett case in, 217–30
Carlyle, Thomas, 273
Census, and madness and blackness, 43–46
Cerletti, Ugo, 153–56
Chekhov, Anton Pavlovich, 89–126
Chicago, 88
Chicago Inter Ocean, 88
Childbed fever, xii
Christianity, 1–4. *See also* Religion
City Psychiatric (Leonard), 318–32
Civil rights, 237–38
Clevenger, Shobal Vail, 84–88
Coburg, Louise von, 127–37
Colchester, England, 197
Connecticut, madness and blackness in, 44
Conolly, John, 10–11
Constitutional Rights of the Mentally Ill, 231 n
Contractual vs. institutional psychiatry, xii n–xiii n
Cook County Asylum, 88
Coppolino, Carl F., 356–57
Crankshaw, Edward, 171
Currell, Harvey, 217 ff.

Deaths (murders), 88, 246 ff.
Deception and terror as cures, Benjamin Rush on, 23–28
Defoe, Daniel, 7–9
De La Pole Hospital, 193, 196
Delaware, madness and blackness in, 44
Democracy as mental disease, 47
Dependency and institutionalization, 267–77
Deutsch, Albert, 53–54
Dewsbury, England, 200
Dix, Dorothy, Hospital, 48–49
Döer, Conrad I., petition of, 15–17
Dogs, and electroshock, 154
Dole, Abijah, 68–71
Doncaster, England, 200, 201
Don Quixote of Psychiatry, The (Robinson), 85 n
Draft Act Governing Hospitalization of the Mentally Ill, 238–39
Drinking, 25, 26–27
Dymond, Matthew, 228

Eberhart, Richard, 285
Electric shock: development of, 153–56; Frame's *Faces in the Water* on, 203–16; Seymour Krim and, 285; Willeford's "Machine in Ward Eleven" on, 333–55
Emergency commitments, 236

England (Britain), 239; conviction of Dr. Fellows, 9–10; Defoe on conditions, 7–9; illegitimacy and insanity in, 198–202; patient labour in, 193–97; Perceval's description of treatment in, 29–42
Ethics of Psychoanalysis, The (Szasz), xiii n
Euphrasia Township (Ontario), Fawcett case, 217–30
Europe (*see also* specific countries): Age of Faith in, 1–2
Ewalt, Jack R., 231
Expert testimony, Ordronaux on, 77–81

Faces in the Water (Frame), 203–16
Fackel, Die, 127–41
Fawcett, Fred, 217–30
Fawcett, Reta (sister of Fred), 223, 225
Fellows, Dr., conviction of, 9–10
Florida, and Draft Act, 238
Fortesque-Aland, Sir John, 9 n
Fox, Dr., Perceval on, 29, 35, 36, 38, 40, 41
Frame, Janet, 203–16
France, Pinel on asylums in, 18–22
Friern Hospital (London), 201–2
Fugger, Marie, 134

Galioni, Elmer F., 357–58
Georgia, madness and blackness in, 44
Ginsberg, Allen, 289
Goffman, Erving, 251–66
Grashey, Professor, and Ludwig II, 83
Great Physiodynamic Therapies in Psychiatry, The, 153 n
Greenwich Village, 287 ff.
Groddeck, M., on Democracy as madness, 47
Group therapy, 265
Guardian, The, on illegitimacy and insanity, 198–202
Gudden, Bernhard von, 82, 83

Hagen, Dr., and Ludwig II, 83
Hanford, Zalmon, 59, 60
Haslet, William, 59, 60
Hinterstoisser, and Coburg case, 128, 134
History of the Pennsylvania Hospital (Morton), 12 n
Hogs, and development of electroshock, 153–54
Holland, 239
Howey, Stuart R., 218–19
How I Came to Perform Prefrontal Leucotomy (Moniz), 157 n
"Howl" (Ginsberg), 289
Hubrich, Dr., and Ludwig II, 83
Huddersfield, England, patients from, 197

Hungary, Karinthy story from, 161–70
Hunter, Richard, excerpts from *Three Hundred Years of Psychiatry*, 7–11

Idaho, and Draft Act, 238
Idiocy, and blacks, 44, 45
Illegitimacy and insanity in Britain, 198–202
Illinois: "boodle gang" at county asylum, 84–88; Packard case, 53–76
Inquiry Concerning the Indications of Insanity (Conolly), 10 n
"Insanity Bit, The" (Krim), 280–99
Institutionalization, 267–77
Institutional vs. contractual psychiatry, xii n–xiii n
Insulin shock, Krim and, 282
Iron Heel, The (London), 142–50
Italy, development of electroshock therapy in, 153–56

Jacksonville, Illinois, Packard case in, 53–76
Jauregg, Wagner von, 129, 132, 133
"Johnny Panic and the Bible of Dreams" (Plath, 300–17
Jones, S. S., 55
Journal of the American Medical Association, 84 n, 85 n
Journey Round My Skull, A (Karinthy), 161 n

Kankakee City, Illinois, Packard case, 56–74
Kankakee *Gazette*, 72–74
Karinthy, Frigyes, 161–70
Katz, Sidney, 217, 225 n, 226 n, 229
Kentucky, madness and blackness in, 44, 45
Kleeborn (prosecutor), 137
Knott, Christopher W., 62–64
Koshchenko Hospital, 172
Kott, Bernard, 227
Krafft-Ebing, Richard von, 130 ff.
Kraus, Karl, 127–41
Krim, Herbert J., 281
Krim, Seymour, 280–99

Labour by patients in British mental hospitals, 193–97
Lake, C. A., 62
Lancet, The, 193 n
Law, Liberty, and Psychiatry (Szasz), 82 n
Leeds, England, hospitals in, 197
Lenin, V. I., 89
Leonard, Frank, 318–32
Lima, Almeida, 159
Lobotomy, discovery of, 157–60
London, Jack, 142–50
London (England), Friern Hospital in, 201–2
Loomis, Mason B., 60, 62
Loring, H., 59
Louisiana, madness and blackness in, 44, 45–46
Ludwig II, King, 82–83

Lying, 25–26

MacAlpine, Ida, excerpts from *Three Hundred Years of Psychiatry*, 7–11
McFarland, Andrew, 56, 62, 74–75
"Machine in Ward Eleven, The" (Willeford), 333–55
Mad Monarch, The (Richter), 82 n
Maine, madness and blackness in, 44, 45
Manufacture of Madness, The (Szasz), xiii n, 3
Marriage: Coburg case, 127–37; Packard case, 53–76
Marti-Ibañez, F., 153 n
Maryland, madness and blackness in, 44
Massachusetts, madness and blackness in, 44
Mattassich, Lt., 130 ff.
Mattocks, Arthur, 359
Medical Inquiries and Observations Upon the Diseases of the Mind (Rush), 23–28
Mental Deficiency Act (Britain–1913), 200, 201
Mental Health Act (Britain–1959), 199, 201
Mental Hygiene, 267
Mentally Ill in America, The (Deutsch), 53 n
Middle Ages, 1–2
Missouri, and Draft Act, 238
Modern Persecution or Insane Asylums Unveiled (Packard), 54 n
Modern Persecution or Married Woman's Liabilities (Packard), 56 n
Moniz, Antonio Caetano Abreum Freire Egas, 157–60
Moore, Stephen R., 56 n, 59
"Moral career" of patient, 251–66
"Moral treatment," Rush on, 23–28
Morgan, Sterling W., 358
Morton, Thomas G., 12–17
Murders. *See* Deaths

Narrative of the Treatment Experienced by a Gentleman, during a State of Mental Derangement (Perceval), 29–42
National Advisory Mental Health Council, 238
National Association for Mental Health (Britain), 199
National Association for Mental Health (U.S.): position statement on medical treatment for the mentally ill, 231–41
National Mental Health Foundation, 242
Negroes. *See* Blacks and blackness
New Hampshire, madness and blackness in, 44
Newington, Charles, 29, 37 ff.
New Jersey, madness and blackness in, 44

New Mexico, and Draft Act, 238
New York, 88; expert testimony in, 78–79; Leonard's *City Psychiatric* based on hospitals in, 318–32; madness and blackness in, 44, 45; Seymour Krim's experiences, 283 ff.
New Yorker, The, 278
New York Hospital, 12
New York *Observer*, 43–46
New Zealand, Janet Frame's story from, 203–16
Next-of-relation, and "moral career" of patient, 254–55 ff.
Nightmares of Eminent Persons, 361 n
North Carolina: Dorothy Dix Hospital in, 48–49; madness and blackness in, 44
Nugent, Arthur G., 359

Observer, The, 171
Ohio, madness and blackness in, 44, 45
Ontario, Canada, Fawcett case in, 218–30
Ordronaux, John, 77–81
Orr, J. W., 59
Orwell, George, xi
Out of Sight, Out of Mind, 242–50
Owens, David, 358–59

Packard, E. P. W., 53–76

Pamphlete, Parodien, Postscripta (Torberg), 127 n
Penetanguishene Mental Hospital, 222, 225 ff.
Pennsylvania, blackness and madness in, 44
Pennsylvania, University of, 25
Pennsylvania Hospital, 12–17
Perceval, John Thomas, 29–42
Perceval's Narrative (Bateson), 30 n
Pinel, Philippe, 18–22, 24
Pipe (psychologist), 284
Plague, The (Camus), 361–62
Plath, Sylvia, 300–17
Pregnancy and childbirth: illegitimacy and insanity in Britain, 198–202; and infection, xii
Psychiatric Justice (Szasz), 217 n
Psychiatry, 251 n
Psychotherapy, 153 n
Puerperal fever, xii
Purdy, Maitland, 225

Raleigh, North Carolina, Dorothy Dix Hospital at, 48–49
Rawcliffe, England, 200
Ray, Isaac, 234
Reimringer, Martin J., 358
Religion, 1–4; in Packard case, 56–58, 63 ff.
Report of Select Cases in all the Courts of Westminster Hall, 9 n
Rhode Island, madness and blackness in, 44

Richter, Werner, 82–83
Robarts, John, 225 ff.
Robinson, Victor, 85
Rollins, Robert, 48 n
Rome, development of electro-shock in, 153–56
Runwell Hospital (England), 197
Rush, Benjamin, 23–28
Russell, Bertrand, 361
Russia: Chekhov's "Ward No. 6," 89–126; lobotomy illegal in U.S.S.R., 157; Tarsis' *Ward 7*, 171–92

Sachs, Maria, 127
Sackler, A. M., 153 n
Sackler, M. D., 153 n
Sackler, R. R., 153 n
Saghalien Island (Chekhov), 89
St. Catherine's Hospital (Doncaster), 200, 201
Science, and the Age of Reason, 2 ff.
Science Fiction Quarterly, 333
Seabrook, Henry G., 218
Semmelweis, Ignaz Philipp, xii
Semmelweis, His Life and Doctrine (Sinclair), xii n
Seven Short Stories by Chekhov, 89 n
Severalls Hospital (Colchester), 197
Short Novels of the Master, 90 n
Sick and the Mad, The (Karinthy), 161–70
Sinclair, William J., xii n

Sittlichkeit und Kriminalität (Kraus), 127 n, 137 n
Slaves, and madness, 45
South Carolina: and Draft Act, 238; madness and blackness in, 44
Spence (Ontario judge), 224–25
Starr, Charles R., 56 ff., 72
Struve, Gleb, 89 n
Succinylcholine, 356–59
Suffocation, treatment by, 356–59
Suicide. *See* specific persons
Swadron, Barry B., 226
Szasz, George, 127
Szasz, Thomas, works by. *See* specific titles

Tarsis, Valeriy, 171–92
Terror and deception as cures, Benjamin Rush on, 23–28
Three Hundred Years of Psychiatry (Hunter and MacAlpine), 7–11
Thurber, James, 278–79
Thurber Carnival, The, 278 n
Ticehurst, Newington's asylum at, 29
Torberg, Friedrich, 127 n
Toronto *Daily Star*, 217, 225 ff.
Toronto *Telegram*, 217
Treatise on Insanity, A (Pinel), 18–22

"Unicorn in the Garden, The" (Thurber), 278–79
United States (*see also* specific authors): adjustment

United States (cont'd)
  to total institution in, 267–77; "boodle gang" at Illinois hospital, 84–88; deception and terror as cures in, Rush discusses, 23–28; expert testimony in, Ordronaux discusses, 77–81; first Negro admitted to Dorothy Dix Hospital, 48–49; madness and blackness in, 43–46; "moral career" of patients, 251–66; Packard case, 53–76; Pennsylvania Hospital, 12–17; position statement by American Psychiatric Association and National Association for Mental Health, 231–41; report of National Mental Health Foundation, 242–50; treatment by suffocating drugs, 356–59
U. S. Public Health Service, 238
U.S.S.R. *See* Russia
Utah, and Draft Act, 238
Utazás a Koponyám Körül (Karinthy), 161

Vacaville, California, 357, 358–59
Vatican, and Lobotomy, 157
Vermont, madness and blackness in, 44
Victoria, Queen, 219, 220
Views of a Nearsighted Cannoneer (Krim), 280 n
Virginia, madness and blackness in, 44
Vogl, Dean, 132

Wakefield, England, patients from, 197
Wales, Byron G., 267–77
War of the Classes, The (London), 142
Warble Fly Act, 221–22
"Ward system," 262–63
"Ward No. 6" (Chekhov), 89–126
Ward 7 (Tarsis), 171–92
Wasserman, Mike, 86
Way, Joseph H., 67–68
Welsh, Emerson, 225
Willard, Julia, 88
Willeford, Charles, 333–55
Willerby, England, De La Pole Hospital in, 193, 196
Willis, Dr., Pinel on, 21
Wishart, Arthur, 225
Wright, Frank L., Jr., 242–50

Yorkshire, sane women in mental hospital in, 198–99
Younglove, J., 59, 60

ANCHOR BOOKS

PSYCHOLOGY

ASYLUMS: Essays on the Social Situation of Mental Patients and Other Inmates—Erving Goffman, A277

THE BROKEN IMAGE: Man, Science and Society—Floyd W. Matson, A506

THE CHALLENGE OF YOUTH—Erik Erikson, ed., originally published as Youth: Change and Challenge, A438

CONFLICT AND RECOLLECTION: A Study in Human Relations and Schizophrenia—Helm Stierlin, A614

THE DEVELOPMENT OF POLITICAL ATTITUDES IN CHILDREN—Robert D. Hess and Judith V. Torney, A640

THE DOGMA OF CHRIST and OTHER ESSAYS ON RELIGION, PSYCHOLOGY AND CULTURE—Erich Fromm, A500

THE DYING SELF—Charles M. Fair, A760

DRUGS ON THE COLLEGE CAMPUS—Helen H. Nowlis, intro. by Kenneth Keniston, A670

AN ELEMENTARY TEXTBOOK OF PSYCHOANALYSIS—Charles Brenner, M.D., A102

THE EMOTIONALLY DISTURBED CHILD: An Inquiry into Family Patterns—J. Louis Despert, A720

EMOTIONAL PROBLEMS OF THE STUDENT—Graham B. Blaine, Jr. and Charles C. McArthur, eds., intro. by Erik Erikson, A527

ESSAYS IN PHILOSOPHICAL PSYCHOLOGY—Donald F. Gustafson, ed., A417

FREUD: The Mind of the Moralist—Philip Rieff, A278

THE FUTURE OF AN ILLUSION—Sigmund Freud; W. D. Robson-Scott, trans., revised by James Strachey, A381

A GENERAL SELECTION FROM THE WORKS OF SIGMUND FREUD—John Rickman, M.D. ed., appendix by Charles Brenner, M.D., A115

GUILT: Man and Society—Roger W. Smith, ed., A768

HAMLET AND OEDIPUS—Ernest Jones, A31

THE HIDDEN DIMENSION—Edward T. Hall, A609

IDEOLOGY AND INSANITY: Essays on the Psychiatric Dehumanization of Man—Thomas S. Szasz, A704

INTERACTION RITUAL: Essays on Face-to-Face Behavior—Erving Goffman, A596

LAW AND PSYCHOLOGY IN CONFLICT—James Marshall, A654

LIFE AND WORK OF SIGMUND FREUD—Ernest Jones; Lionel Trilling and Steven Marcus, eds., abridged, A340

MAY MAN PREVAIL?—Erich Fromm, A275

THE NATURE OF PREJUDICE—Gordon W. Allport, abridged, A149

NOBODY WANTED WAR: Misperception in Vietnam and Other Wars—Ralph K. White, A612

OF TIME, WORK AND LEISURE: A Twentieth-Century Fund Study—Sebastian de Grazia, A380

ORIGIN AND FUNCTION OF CULTURE—Géza Róheim, A748

PSYCHOLOGY (cont'd)

PAUL AND MARY: Two Case Histories from "Truants from Life"—Bruno Bettelheim, A237

THE PRESENTATION OF SELF IN EVERYDAY LIFE—Erving Goffman, A174

PRISON WITHIN SOCIETY: A Reader in Penology—Lawrence Hazelrigg, ed., A620

PSYCHE AND SYMBOL: A Selection from the Writings of C. G. Jung—Violet de Laszlo, ed., A136

PSYCHEDELICS: The Uses and Implications of Hallucinogenic Drugs—Bernard Aaronson and Humphry Osmond, A736

THE SCIENCE OF LIVING—Alfred Adler, intro. by Heinz Ansbacher, A667

SELF-CONSISTENCY: A Theory of Personality—Prescott Lecky, A622

WHITE MAN, LISTEN!—Richard Wright, A414

THE WORLD OF THE CHILD—Toby Talbot, ed., A634

ANCHOR BOOKS

SOCIOLOGY

THE ACADEMIC MARKETPLACE: An Anatomy of the Academic Profession—Theodore Caplow and Reece J. McGee, A440

AGAINST THE WORLD: Attitudes of White South Africa—Douglas Brown, A671

AGRARIAN PROBLEMS AND PEASANT MOVEMENTS IN LATIN AMERICA—Rodolfo Stavenhagen, ed., A718

AMERICAN RACE RELATIONS TODAY—Earl Raab, ed., A318

AMERICAN SOCIAL PATTERNS—William Petersen, ed., A86

ANATOMY OF A METROPOLIS—Edgar M. Hoover and Raymond Vernon, A298

AND WE ARE NOT SAVED: A History of the Movement as People—Debbie Louis, A755

THE ARAB WORLD TODAY—Morroe Berger, A406

ASYLUMS: Essays on the Social Situation of Mental Patients and Other Inmates—Erving Goffman, A277

BEHIND THE SHIELD: The Police in Urban Society—Arthur Niederhoffer, A653

THE BERKELEY STUDENT REVOLT: Facts and Interpretations—Seymour Martin Lipset and Sheldon S. Wolin, eds., A486

THE BROKEN IMAGE: Man, Science and Society—Floyd Matson, A506

CASTE AND CLASS IN A SOUTHERN TOWN—John Dollard, A95

THE CHALLENGE OF YOUTH—Erik H. Erikson, ed., originally published as Youth: Change and Challenge, A438

COMMUNITIES IN DISASTER: A Sociological Analysis of Collective Stress Situations—Allen H. Barton, Foreword by Robert K. Merton, A721

COMMUNITY AND PRIVACY: Toward a New Architecture of Humanism—Serge Chermayeff and Christopher Alexander, A474

THE DEATH PENALTY IN AMERICA—Hugo Adam Dedau, ed., A387

DEMOCRACY IN AMERICA—Alexis de Tocqueville; J. P. Mayer, ed.; George Lawrence, trans., AO5

DRUGS ON THE COLLEGE CAMPUS—Helen H. Nowlis, intro. by Kenneth Keniston, A670

THE DYING SELF—Charles M. Fair, A760

THE EMOTIONALLY DISTURBED CHILD: An Inquiry into Family Patterns—J. Louise Despert, A720

THE END OF THE JEWISH PEOPLE?—Georges Friedmann; Eric Mosbacher, trans., A626

EQUALITY BY STATUTE: The Revolution in Civil Rights—Morroe Berger, A591

THE ETHICAL IMPERATIVE: The Crisis in American Values—Richard L. Means, A735

THE EXPLODING METROPOLIS—Editors of *Fortune*, A146

THE FIRST NEW NATION: The United States in Historical and Comparative Perspective—Seymour Martin Lipset, A597

SOCIOLOGY (cont'd)

FREUD: The Mind of the Moralist—Philip Rieff, A278

FROM RACE RIOT TO SIT-IN: 1919 and the 1960s—Arthur I. Waskow, A557

THE GATHERING STORM IN THE CHURCHES: A Sociologist's View of the Widening Gap Between Clergy and Laymen—Jeffrey K. Hadden, A712

THE GUARANTEED INCOME—Robert Theobald, A519

GUILT: Man and Society—Roger W. Smith, ed., A768

THE HIDDEN DIMENSION—Edward T. Hall, A609

HITLER'S SOCIAL REVOLUTION: Class and Status in Nazi Germany 1933–1939—David Schoenbaum, A590

HUSTLERS, BEATS, AND OTHERS—Ned Polsky, A656

IDEOLOGY AND INSANITY: Essays on the Psychiatric Dehumanization of Man—Thomas S. Szasz, A618

INTERACTION RITUAL: Essays on Face-to-Face Behavior—Erving Goffman, A596

INVITATION TO SOCIOLOGY: A Humanistic Perspective—Peter L. Berger, A346

JACOB RIIS REVISITED: Poverty and the Slum in Another Era—Francesco Cordasco, ed., A646

KILLERS OF THE DREAM: An Analysis and Evaluation of the South—Lillian Smith, A339

THE LAST LANDSCAPE—William H. Whyte, A717

LAW AND PSYCHOLOGY IN CONFLICT—James Marshall, A654

LET THEM EAT PROMISES: The Politics of Hunger in America—Nick Kotz, A788

THE LIFE AND WORK OF SIGMUND FREUD—Ernest Jones; Lionel Trilling and Steven Marcus, eds., abridged, A340

MAIN CURRENTS IN SOCIOLOGICAL THOUGHT, Volume I: Montesquieu, Comte, Marx, Tocqueville, the Sociologists and the Revolution of 1848—Raymond Aron; Richard Howard and Helen Weaver, trans., A600a

MAIN CURRENTS IN SOCIOLOGICAL THOUGHT, Volume II: Durkheim, Pareto, Weber—Raymond Aron, A600b

THE MAKING OF A COUNTER CULTURE—Theodore Roszak, A697

MAN INCORPORATE: The Individual and His Work in an Organized Society—Carl B. Kaufman, revised edition, A672

MAN IN THE MODERN AGE—Karl Jaspers, A101

THE MAN WHO PLAYS ALONE—Danilo Dolci, A740

MARX IN THE MID-TWENTIETH CENTURY: A Yugoslav Philosopher Reconsiders Karl Marx's Writings—Gajo Petrović, A584

MAX WEBER: An Intellectual Portrait—Reinhard Bendix, A281

MOVEMENT AND REVOLUTION—Peter L. Berger and Richard J. Neuhaus, A726

MY PEOPLE IS THE ENEMY—William Stringfellow, A489

NATION BUILDING AND CITIZENSHIP: Studies of our Changing Social Order—Reinhard Bendix, A679

THE NATURE OF PREJUDICE—Gordon W. Allport, A149

SOCIOLOGY (cont'd)

THE NAVAHO—Clyde Kluckhohn and Dorothea Leighton; revised by Richard Kluckhohn and Lucy Wales, N28

THE NEGRO AND THE AMERICAN LABOR MOVEMENT—Julius Jacobson, ed., A495

THE NEWCOMERS—Oscar Handlin, A283

THE NEW MEDIA AND EDUCATION: Their Impact on Society—Peter H. Rossi and Bruce J. Biddle, eds., A604

OF TIME, WORK AND LEISURE: A Twentieth-Century Fund Study—Sebastian de Grazia, A380

ON INTELLECTUALS—Philip Rieff, ed., A733

THE ORGANIZATION MAN—William H. Whyte, Jr., A117

POLITICAL MAN: The Social Bases of Politics—Seymour Martin Lipset, A330

POPULATION: The Vital Revolution—Ronald Freedman, ed., A423

THE PRESENTATION OF SELF IN EVERYDAY LIFE—Erving Goffman, A174

PRISON WITHIN SOCIETY: A Reader in Penology—Lawrence Hazelrigg, ed., A620

PROTESTANT-CATHOLIC-JEW: An Essay in American Religious Sociology—Will Herberg, revised edition, A195

PSYCHEDELICS: The Uses and Implications of Hallucinogenic Drugs—Bernard Aaronson and Humphry Osmond, A736

RACE AND NATIONALITY IN AMERICAN LIFE—Oscar Handlin, A110

THE RADICAL RIGHT—Daniel Bell, ed., A376

REALITIES OF THE URBAN CLASSROOM: Observations in Elementary Schools—G. Alexander Moore, Jr., A568

THE REFORMING OF GENERAL EDUCATION: The Columbia College Experience in Its National Setting—Daniel Bell, A616

THE RELIGIOUS FACTOR—Gerhard Lenski, A337

REVOLUTION AND COUNTERREVOLUTION: Change and Persistence in Social Structures—Seymour Martin Lipset, A764

A RUMOR OF ANGELS: Modern Society and the Rediscovery of the Supernatural—Peter L. Berger, A715

THE SACRED CANOPY: Elements of a Sociological Theory of Religion—Peter L. Berger, A658

SOCIAL AND POLITICAL PHILOSOPHY: Readings from Plato to Gandhi—John Somerville and Ronald Santoni, eds., A370

THE SOCIAL CONSTRUCTION OF REALITY: A Treatise in the Sociology of Knowledge—Peter L. Berger and Thomas Luckmass, A589

SOCIALIST HUMANISM: An International Symposium—Erich Fromm, ed., A529

SOCIETY AND DEMOCRACY IN GERMANY—Ralf Dahrendorf, A684

SOCIOLOGISTS AT WORK: The Craft of Social Research—Phillip E. Hamond, ed., A598

STRUCTURAL ANTHROPOLOGY—Claude Lévi-Strauss, A599

STUDIES OF LATIN AMERICAN SOCIETIES—T. Lynn Smith, A702

TAMING MEGALOPOLIS, Volume I: What Is and What Could Be, 16Cb

SOCIOLOGY (cont'd)

Volume II: How to Manage an Urbanized World—H. Wentworth Eldredge, ed., A593a, b

THE TOOLS OF SOCIAL SCIENCE—John Madge, A437

UNION DEMOCRACY—Seymour Martin Lipset, Martin A. Trow, and James S. Coleman, Foreword by Clark Kerr, A296

THE URBAN COMPLEX—Robert C. Weaver, A505

URBAN RENEWAL: People, Politics, and Planning—Jewel Bellush and Murray Hausknecht, eds., A569

VILLAGE OF VIRIATINO: An Ethnographic Study of a Russian Village from Before the Revolution to the Present—Sula Benet, trans. and ed., A758

WALK THE WHITE LINE: A Profile of Urban Education—Elizabeth M. Eddy, Ph.D., A570

WHITE MAN, LISTEN!—Richard Wright, A414

WHO DESIGNS AMERICA?—Laurence B. Holland, ed., A523

WHO NEEDS THE NEGRO?—Sidney Willhelm, A789

ANCHOR BOOKS

FICTION

ARROW OF GOD—Chinua Achebe, intro. by K. W. J. Post, A698
THE COUNTRY OF THE POINTED FIRS AND OTHER STORIES—Sarah Orne Jewett, A26
A DIFFERENT DRUMMER—William Melvin Kelley, A678
DOWN SECOND AVENUE—Ezekiel Mphahlele, A792
DREAM OF THE RED CHAMBER—Tsao Hsueh-Chin; Chi-Chen Wang, trans., A159
ENVY AND OTHER WORKS—Yuri Olesha; Andrew R. MacAndrew, trans., A571
GOD'S BITS OF WOOD—Ousmane Sembene, A729
HALF-WAY TO THE MOON: New Writing From Russia—Patricia Blake and Max Hayward, eds., A483
A HERO OF OUR TIME—Mihail Lermontov; Vladimir Nabokov and Dmitri Nabokov, trans., A133
INFERNO, ALONE AND OTHER WRITINGS—August Strindberg; in new translations, Evert Sprinchorn, ed., A492c
A MAN OF THE PEOPLE—Chinua Achebe, A594
MOTHER EARTH AND OTHER STORIES—Boris Pilnyak; Vera T. Reck and Michael Green, trans. and eds., A625
19 NECROMANCERS FROM NOW: An Anthology of Original American Writing for the 70s—Ishmael Reed, A743
POCHO—José Antonio Villarreal, intro. by Dr. Ramon Ruiz, A744
POOR PEOPLE and A LITTLE HERO—Fyodor Dostoevsky; David Magarshack, trans., A619
REDBURN—Herman Melville, A118
RETURN TO LAUGHTER—Elenore Smith Bowen, Foreword by David Riesman, N36
THE SCARLET LETTER and YOUNG GOODMAN BROWN—Nathaniel Hawthorne, Alfred Kazin, ed., A732
THE SECRET AGENT—Joseph Conrad, A8
THE SHADOW-LINE AND TWO OTHER TALES—Joseph Conrad, intro. by Morton Dauwen Zabel, A178
SISSIE—John A. Williams, A710
THE TALE OF GENJI, I—Lady Murasaki; Arthur Waley, trans., A55
TEN GERMAN NOVELLAS—Harry Steinhauer, ed. and trans., A707
THREE SHORT NOVELS OF DOSTOEVSKY—Constance Garnett, trans.; Avraim Yarmolinsky, ed. and revised, A193
UNDER WESTERN EYES—Joseph Conrad, intro. by Morton Dauwen Zabel, A323
VICTORY—Joseph Conrad, A106
THE WANDERER (LE GRAND MEAULNES)—Henri Alain-Fournier; Françoise Delisle, trans., A14
WHAT MAISIE KNEW—Henry James, A43